# CONSCIOUSNESS
# &
# THE
# NOVEL

*Including the Richard Ellmann Lectures in Modern Literature*

# CONSCIOUSNESS & THE NOVEL

## CONNECTED ESSAYS

## DAVID LODGE

*harvard university press*

*2002   cambridge, massachusetts*

*Library of Congress Cataloging-in-Publication Data*

Lodge, David, 1935–

Consciousness and the novel : connected essays / David Lodge
   p. cm.

"Including the Richard Ellmann lectures in modern literature"—p. ii.

Includes bibliographical references and index.

ISBN 0–674–00949–5 (alk. paper)

1. English fiction—20th century—History and criticism.

2. Psychological fiction, English—History and criticism.

3. Dickens, Charles, 1812–1870—Criticism and interpretation.

4. Fiction—Authorship—Psychological aspects.

5. American fiction—History and criticism.

6. Consciousness in literature. I. Title

PR830.P75 L63 2002

823'.083091—dc21      2002024083

*Remembering*

MALCOLM BRADBURY

(1932–2000)

WRITER AND FRIEND

# contents

Preface    ix

For most of my adult life I combined the professions of novelist and academic, writing novels and works of literary criticism in regular alternation. I used some words of Gertrude Stein's as an epigraph for one of my books of criticism, *The Modes of Modern Writing,* that could serve the purpose for all of them: "What does literature do and how does it do it. And what does English literature do and how does it do it. And what ways does it use to do what it does." I posed these questions mainly in relation to the novel, in an effort to ground the interpretation and evaluation of novels in what I hopefully called a "poetics of fiction"—that is, a systematic and comprehensive description of the stylistic devices and narrative methods through which novels communicate their meanings and have the effects that they have upon readers. I started, in a book called *Language of Fiction* (1966), by applying to novels the kind of close reading that the New Criticism had applied primarily to lyric poetry and poetic drama. In the 1970s and 1980s, like many other English and American academic critics, I absorbed and domesticated some of the concepts and methods of Continental European structuralism, and applied them in *The Modes of Modern Writing* (1977) and *Working with Structuralism* (1981). Later, again like many others, I discovered the work of the great Russian theorist Mikhail Bakhtin, which went back to the 1920s but only became widely known in the recent past. His idea that the novel, unlike the classic genres of epic, lyric, and tragedy, was essentially dialogic or polyphonic in its verbal texture, and his subtle analysis of the various types of discourse that are woven into it, informed and inspired most of the essays in my book *After Bakhtin* (1990).

In short, my quest for a poetics of fiction was at every stage furthered by exposure to some new, or new-to-me, source of literary theory. But the journey ended with my discovery of Bakhtin, partly because he seemed to answer satisfactorily all the remaining questions I had posed myself; and partly because as literary theory entered its post-structuralist phase it seemed to be less interested in the formal analysis of literary texts, and more interested in using them as a basis for philosophical speculation and ideological polemic. It so happened—or perhaps it wasn't entirely coincidental—that at about this time, in the late eighties, I retired from academic life to become a full-time freelance writer. I have continued to write criticism, but for a nonspecialist audience, and have more or less given up reading literary theory. Such general, or generalisable, ideas as I have about literature nowadays tend to grow out of reflection on my own "practice of writing"—the title of my last book of criticism. Such reflection is also a feature of several of the essays in this volume.

In the mid-nineties, however, I started working on a novel, eventually called *Thinks . . .*, which entailed reading a good deal of theoretical or quasi-theoretical literature in what was quite new territory for me, the interdisciplinary field of "consciousness studies." In fact the idea for this novel grew directly out of my somewhat belated discovery that consciousness had become a hot topic in the sciences, with challenging consequences for those whose assumptions about human nature have been formed by religious, humanist, and literary traditions. The research I did for this project also prompted some reflections about "the novel" as a literary form, which are developed in the title essay of this book. I have gathered together in the same volume a number of essays and review articles written over recent years which connect with "Consciousness and the Novel" and with one another in various ways. How the novel represents consciousness; how this contrasts with the way other narrative media, like film, represent it; how the consciousness, and the unconscious, of a creative writer do their work; how criticism can infer the nature of this process by formal analysis, or the creative writer by self-interrogation—these are recurrent themes in the essays collected here. Needless to say, I have not attempted to cover the topic of consciousness and the novel either exhaustively or systematically, nor to engage with the work of previous scholars who have endeavoured to do so. There was inevitably a certain amount of repetition or overlap between the different essays in their original form, which I have not entirely removed.

Chapter 1, "Consciousness and the Novel," is the revised and extended text of the Richard Ellmann Lectures, which I gave at Emory University, Atlanta, Georgia, in October 2001. I am very grateful to Emory, and to Professor Ron Schuchard in particular, for inviting me to give these lectures, and for entertaining me so royally while I was the guest of the University. "Literary Criticism and Literary Creation" was also originally a lecture, and in its present form was first published in *The Arts and Sciences of Criticism,* ed. David Fuller and Patricia Waugh (Oxford University Press, 1999). "Dickens Our Contemporary" is a revised version of an article first published in *The Atlantic Monthly* (© 2002 in *The Atlantic Monthly* by David Lodge). "Forster's Flawed Masterpiece" is a slightly shortened version of my Introduction to the Penguin Twentieth Century Classics edition of *Howards End* (New York, 2000). "Waugh's Comic Wasteland" was originally published as the Introduction to the Folio Society's edition of Evelyn Waugh's *Comedies* (1999). "Lives in Letters: Kingsley and Martin Amis" was first published in the *Times Literary Supplement.* "Henry James and the Movies" is a revised and extended version of the 1999 Henry James Lecture, given at the Rye Festival; it incorporates a review of the film of *The Golden Bowl* published in the *Times Literary Supplement.* "Bye-Bye Bech?" and "Sick with Desire: Philip Roth's Libertine Professor" were first published in the *New York Review of Books.* "Kierkegaard for Special Purposes" was an address given to a conference in Copenhagen in 1996, and was subsequently published in *Kierkegaard Revisited,* Kierkegaard Studies: Monograph Series 1, ed. N. J. Cappelørn and J. Stewart (Walter de Gruyter, 1997). "A Conversation about *Thinks . . .*" is part of an interview published in *Areté,* 5 (Spring-Summer 2001).

I am obliged to all the editors, conference convenors, lecture programme organizers, and publishers involved for the original stimulus to write each of these pieces. Thanks are due to John Herbert for research assistance on E. M. Forster and *Howards End.* I am especially grateful to my editors at Harvard University Press, Peg Fulton and Mary Ellen Geer, my agent, Mike Shaw, and my wife, Mary, for their useful comments and advice while this book was in preparation.

# CONSCIOUSNESS
# &
# THE
# NOVEL

# chapter one

# CONSCIOUSNESS
# &
# THE
# NOVEL

## I CONSCIOUSNESS AND THE TWO CULTURES

It was an article in the English Catholic weekly, *The Tablet*, encountered in the summer of 1994, that first alerted me to a current intellectual debate about the nature of human consciousness, in which old philosophical issues were being refreshed by new input from the sciences. The article was a review of two books: Daniel Dennett's *Consciousness Explained* and Francis Crick's *The Astonishing Hypothesis*. Daniel Dennett is a philosopher turned cognitive scientist with a strong commitment to Artificial Intelligence. He says:

> Human consciousness . . . can be best understood as the operation of a . . . virtual machine implemented in the *parallel architecture* of a brain that was not designed for any such activities. The powers of this *virtual machine* vastly enhance the underlying powers of the organic *hardware* on which it runs.[1]

Francis Crick is the physicist and biochemist who with James Watson discovered the molecular structure of DNA. His book begins:

> The Astonishing Hypothesis is that 'You,' your joys and your sorrows, your memories and your ambitions, your sense of personal identity and free will, are in fact no more than the behaviour of a vast assembly of nerve cells and their associated molecules. As Lewis Carroll's Alice might have phrased it: 'You're nothing but a pack of neurons.'[2]

The review article in *The Tablet* was by John Cornwell, a well-known journalist and writer on religious and scientific matters. It was titled "From Soul to Software,"[3] and it brought out very clearly the challenge that the new scientific work on consciousness offered to the idea of human nature enshrined in the Judeo-Christian religious tradition. It seemed to me that this work offered an almost equally strong challenge to the humanist or Enlightenment idea of man on which the presentation of character in the novel is based. When I began to develop a novel of my own that would dramatise or narrativise this subject in terms of a relationship between two people, I made one of them an atheistic cognitive scientist and the other a novelist who is a lapsed but not entirely sceptical Catholic. What I propose to do here is to explore some thoughts about the novel as a literary form, about its historical development and about "the ways that it uses to do what it does" (Gertrude Stein's phrasing), which were provoked by my exposure to the current debate about consciousness.

Let me begin with a passage from a contemporary novel, a "literary novel" (as it is called in the book trade), a highly and justly acclaimed novel, which has won at least two major prizes, the Orange Prize and the Guardian Fiction Prize: *Fugitive Pieces* by the Canadian writer Anne Michaels, published in 1997. The narrator, Jacob Beer, is speaking to a woman, Michaela, whom he has just met, about seeing the prematurely born child of his friends, Salman and Irena. This conversation is the beginning of a relationship between Jacob and Michaela:

> I find myself telling Michaela a story that's a dozen years old, the story of Tomas's birth, about my experience of his soul.
>
> "When Tomas was born, he was very premature. He weighed less than three pounds . . ."
>
> I had put on a gown, scrubbed my hands and arms to the elbows, and Irena led me in to see him. I saw what I can only call a soul, for it was not yet a self, caught in that almost transparent body. I have never before been so close to such palpable evidence of the spirit, so close to the almost invisible musselman whose eyes in the photos show the faint stain of a soul. Without breath, the evidence would vanish instantly. Tomas in his clear plastic womb, barely bigger than a hand.
>
> Michaela has been looking down at the floor. Her hair, glossy and heavy and parted on the side, covers her face. Now she looks up. Suddenly I'm embarrassed at having spoken so much.
>
> Then she says: "I don't know what the soul is. But I imagine that somehow our bodies surround what has always been."[4]

The narrator, Jacob Beer, is middle-aged, of Jewish-Polish extraction. He was rescued from the horror of the Holocaust as a child, was brought up on a Greek island, and subsequently emigrated to Canada. He is obsessed with the history of the Holocaust, which explains the presence of the strange word "musselman" in the passage. It is derived from *muselmann*, the German word for Muslim, and is usually spelled "Mussulman." According to the Oxford English Dictionary, this was a slang term in the death camps for a prisoner who was physically and mentally broken, who was, in the words of one source, "a walking skeleton wrapped in a piece of blanket." That this inherently racist term was apparently adopted by the victims of the most appalling racist regime history has ever known is a paradox and an irony that I will not attempt to pursue here. The point made in the novel is that Jacob Beer, looking at the premature baby whose hold on life is so fragile, is reminded of photographs of those walking skeletons in the death camps in whose eyes alone there is the faintest vestige of an inner life. It is a powerful passage and was chosen by the *Guardian* as an extract to represent the novel when it was awarded the newspaper's Fiction Prize. In fact I first read it in that context, at a time when I was doing my research into consciousness studies, and I was struck by how utterly different its language was from the books and articles I was reading.

The passage invokes, not metaphorically but literally, the religious idea of the individual immortal soul, which in some Platonist interpretations (evidently shared by Michaela) pre-exists human birth. And the soul or spirit (the words are more or less synonymous here) is seen as intimately connected with the more secular idea of the self. It is implied that the soul becomes or acquires a self through life experience, which this newborn infant has scarcely embarked upon. It is of course possible to have a concept of the self—of the unique, autonomous, morally responsible individual human being whose inner life is fully known through introspection—without believing in the existence of immortal souls; but many people with no religious belief find the words "soul" and "spirit" useful, if not indispensable, to signify some uniquely valuable quality in human life and human awareness.

According to the most enlightened thinking, philosophical and scientific, of our age, however, this is all nonsense. It is what Gilbert Ryle denounced, in his influential book *The Concept of Mind,* as the fallacy of the Ghost in the Machine. According to this orthodoxy, the human body, including the human brain which produces the phenomenon of mind, is a machine; there is no ghost, no soul or spirit, to be found in it. And the self is not an immaterial essence but an epiphenomenon of brain activity. To distinguish between flesh and spirit, body and soul, the material and the immaterial, the earthly and the transcendent, is to commit the fallacy of dualism, which runs deep through the history of Western culture, but is now dead and buried. Or it ought to be. In fact it stubbornly persists, not only in ordinary casual speech about life and death, but also in the language of literature, as the passage from *Fugitive Pieces* attests. And one interesting effect of the current interdisciplinary debate about consciousness has been to open up once again the issue of dualism, and even to elicit some arguments in favour of modified versions of it.

Until fairly recently, consciousness was not much studied by the natural sciences. It was considered the province of philosophy. Psychology, inasmuch as it aspired to be an empirical science, regarded consciousness as "a black box." All that could be observed and measured was input and output, not what went on inside. This placed severe limitations on the study of human experience. My cognitive scientist in *Thinks . . .* tells the novelist heroine, "There's an old joke that crops up in nearly every book on consciousness, about two behaviourist psychologists who have sex, and afterwards one says to the other, 'It was good for you, how was it for me?'"[5] As recently as 1989 Stuart Sutherland wrote in the *International Dictionary of Psychology*, "Consciousness is a fascinating but elusive phenomenon; it is impossible to specify what it is, what it does, or why it evolved. Nothing worth reading has been written about it." Psychoanalysis, of course, was always concerned with trying to understand consciousness, but its claims to be a science have been dismissed by most natural scientists, and many of its critics have regarded it as a kind of religion or substitute for religion. Its ideas, or memes (to use Richard Dawkins's useful term for the conceptual equivalent of genes), have been disseminated and kept in currency largely by literature and literary intellectuals. In recent times, however, psychology has become less rigidly behaviourist as a discipline. There is now something called Cognitive Psychology, and some academic psychology departments have even admitted Freud and Jung into the syllabus. Freud has also received some surprising endorsements from leading cognitive scientists and neuroscientists.

The current stir of scientific interest in consciousness is usually traced back to a 1990 paper by Francis Crick and Cristof Koch announcing that it was time to make human consciousness the subject of empirical study.[6] But several earlier developments had encouraged such a move. For example: the discovery in quantum physics that an event is ultimately inseparable from its observation, undermining the assumption that science is absolutely objective and impersonal. For example: the discovery of DNA, which put biology in the driving seat of the physical sciences; the development of new brain-scanning techniques in medicine; and the surge of neo-Darwinian evolutionary theory in the 1970s and 1980s, disseminated by brilliant popular science writers like Dawkins, which offered a comprehensive materialist account of human nature. For example: advances in computing power and miniaturisation, and the development of neural networks in programming, which opened up new possibilities in Artificial Intelligence (AI). There are connections between these various developments. Neural networks, for instance, are based on an evolutionary model. AI starts with the assumption that the mind or consciousness is like software to the brain's hardware, a virtual machine running on the material machine of the brain, and tries to design architectures on which the operation of the human brain might be simulated. There is no hope of doing this with a linear program, only one step of which needs to fail for the whole system to crash. Neural networks are programs which evolve on their own and imitate the multitudinous connections between the neurons in the human brain. It has to be said that so far this remains a utopian aim rather than an achieved goal, perhaps because there are more possible connections between the neurons in a human brain than there are atoms in the universe.[7]

At the same time, some philosophers began to ask whether the dismissive catch-phrase "the Ghost in the Machine" really disposed of all the questions raised by the phenomenon of consciousness. Joseph Levine published an influential paper in 1983 entitled "Materialism and Qualia: The Explanatory Gap." Qualia, plural of the Latin *quale,* is a key term in consciousness studies, meaning the specific nature of our subjective experience of the world.

> Examples of qualia are the smell of freshly ground coffee or the taste of pineapple; such experiences have a distinctive phenomenological character which we have all experienced but which, it seems, is very difficult to describe. *(The Oxford Companion to the Mind)*

Levine was drawing attention to the failure of purely materialistic theories of mind to explain this phenomenon. A decade later the philosopher David Chalmers agreed: "It still seems utterly mysterious that the causation of behaviour should be accompanied by a subjective inner life."[8] Chalmers's solution in his book *The Conscious Mind* is a highly technical one, but he admits it is a kind of property dualism. Even the physicist James Trefil concedes that "no matter how my brain works, no matter how much interplay there is between my brain and my body, one single fact remains . . . I am aware of a self that looks out at the world from somewhere inside my skull . . . this is not simply an observation, but the central datum with which every theory of consciousness has to grapple. In the end the theory has to go from the firing of neurons to this essential perception."[9]

The more bullish neuroscientists and AI researchers reject this line of argument. The distinguished neuroscientist V. S. Ramachandran, for instance, says that "the barrier between mind and matter is only apparent and arises as a result of language." Qualia are produced by the same pattern of neuronal activity in any subject, as brain scans reveal. They only seem uniquely subjective when reported in natural language. "If you could bypass verbal language and transfer your neural perception of red to a colourblind person's brain by wire you would reproduce the qualia of your perception of red in that person."[10]

Daniel Dennett also denies that qualia present a serious problem to materialist explanations of consciousness. Either they don't exist, or they are not a special category of phenomena requiring special explanation. Basically Dennett's position—and it is very persuasively and intelligently argued—is that consciousness is a kind of illusion or epiphenomenon. It is something man has done with the enormous brain power he possesses above and beyond his evolutionary needs for survival. The fact that it *seems* as if we experience the world as a self that is centered somewhere inside our heads, absorbing and cataloguing and remembering and linking up all the information coming to us from the external world through our senses—the fact that this *seems* to be the case is perfectly understandable, and pragmatically may be necessary if we are to function as human beings, but that doesn't mean that it actually *is* the case, or that we have to posit the existence of any nonmaterial factor or process. In the words of another evolutionary materialist, Steven Pinker, the mind is "a machine, nothing but the on-board computer of a robot made of tissue."[11]

What has all this to do with literature in general and the novel in particular? I think there are two kinds of connection to be made, both of which help to explain why literature exists, why we need it, and why we value it, and help us also to understand better the ways literature uses to do what it does. One kind of connection emphasises the *differences* between literary and scientific discourse about consciousness. The other emphasises points of agreement.

When Stuart Sutherland said that nothing worth reading had been written about consciousness he was articulating a rather dismissive judgement of published work in the professional field of psychology, but unintentionally (at least I hope it was unintentionally) he was dismissing the entire corpus of the world's literature—because literature is a record of human consciousness, the richest and most comprehensive we have. Lyric poetry is arguably man's most successful effort to describe qualia. The novel is arguably man's most successful effort to describe the experience of individual human beings moving through space and time.

There are some thinkers in cognitive science, or on the fringes of it, who have acknowledged as much. Noam Chomsky, for instance, has said: "It is quite possible . . . that we will always learn more about human life and personality from novels than from scientific psychology."[12] The reason is that science tries to formulate general explanatory laws which apply universally, which were in operation before they were discovered, and which would have been discovered sooner or later by somebody. Works of literature describe in the guise of fiction the dense specificity of personal experience, which is always unique, because each of us has a slightly or very different personal history, modifying every new experience we have; and the creation of literary texts recapitulates this uniqueness (that is to say, Jane Austen's *Emma,* for example, could not have been written by anybody else, and never will be written by anyone else again, but an experiment demonstrating the second law of thermodynamics is and must be repeatable by any competent scientist).

The Nobel Prize–winning neuroscientist Gerald Edelman has some interesting things to say on this topic in his book *Bright Air, Brilliant Fire.* He begins with what sounds like an arrogant prediction: "We are at the beginning of the neuroscientific revolution. At the end we should know how the mind works, what governs our nature, and how we know the world."[13] But as the book proceeds he acknowledges the limitations of this project. There is, for instance, the problem of qualia. "The dilemma is that phenomenal experience is a first person matter, and this seems, at first glance, to prevent the formulation of a completely objective or causal account." Science, of course, is a third-person discourse. The first-person pronoun is not used in scientific papers. If there were any hint of qualia in a scientific paper, Edelman says, it would be edited out. But a scientific study of consciousness cannot ignore qualia. His proposed solution is to accept that other people as well as oneself do experience qualia, to collect their first-person accounts, and correlate them to establish what they have in common, bearing in mind that these reports are inevitably "partial, imprecise and relative to . . . personal context."[14]

The method of lyric poetry is different. It is to use language in such a way that the description of qualia does not seem partial, imprecise, and only comprehensible when put in the context of the poet's personal life. My heroine Helen Reed in *Thinks . . .* makes this point to a cognitive science conference, quoting from Andrew Marvell's poem "The Garden":

> The Luscious Clusters of the Vine
>     Upon my Mouth do crush their Wine;
> The Nectaren, and curious Peach,
>     Into my hands themselves do reach;
> Stumbling on Melons, as I pass,
>     Insnar'd with Flow'rs, I fall on Grass.

Helen says: "Let me point to a paradox about Marvell's verse, which applies to lyric poetry in general. Although he speaks in the first person, Marvell does not speak for himself alone. In reading this stanza we enhance our own experience of the qualia of fruit and fruitfulness. We see the fruit, we taste it and smell it and savour it with what has been called 'the thrill of recognition' and yet it is not there, it is the virtual reality of fruit, conjured up by the qualia of the poem which I could try to analyse if there were world enough and time, to quote another poem of Marvell's—but there is not" (p. 317).

There are lyrical descriptions of qualia in prose fiction as well as verse. Many are to be found in Anne Michaels's *Fugitive Pieces*—not surprisingly, since she is a distinguished poet. On the page following the passage about the soul of the baby Tomas, for example, there is a brilliant description of a city street after a heavy snowfall.

> The winter street is a salt cave. The snow has stopped falling and it's very cold. The cold is spectacular, penetrating. The

street has been silenced, a theatre of whiteness, drifts like frozen waves. Crystals glisten under the streetlights. (p. 177)

This illustrates one of the primary means by which literature renders qualia—through metaphor and simile. Whiteness is white, coldness is cold. There is no literal, referential description of such things that is not tautological. But in literature, by describing each quale in terms of something else that is both similar and different—"a salt cave," "a theatre of whiteness," "like frozen waves"—the object and the experience of it are vividly simulated. One sensation is invoked to give specificity to another. The nonverbal is verbalised. "My task, which I am trying to achieve," Joseph Conrad wrote in the Preface to one of his tales, "is by the power of the written word to make you hear, to make you feel—it is before all, to make you *see*. That— and no more, and it is everything."[15]

Later in his book Edelman makes an interesting distinction between science and history: "Science has emerged within history, and it attempts to describe . . . the boundaries of the world—its constraints and its physical laws. But these laws . . . do not and cannot exhaust experience or replace history or the events that occur in the actual courses of individual lives. Events are denser than any possible scientific description."[16]

These statements seem to me profoundly true, but they place obvious limits on scientific knowledge about, to quote Edelman's introduction again, "what governs our nature and how we know the world." History conceived as the sum total of individual human lives is of course unknowable: there is simply too much data. Historiography can give us selective accounts of events in selected human lives, but the more scientific its method—the more scrupulous it is in basing all its assertions on evidence—the less able it is to represent the density of those events as consciously experienced. That is, however, something that narrative literature, and especially the novel, can do. It creates fictional models of what it is like to be a human being, moving through time and space. It captures the density of experienced events by its rhetoric, and it shows the connectedness of events through the devices of plot.

A good deal of the recent scientific work on consciousness has stressed its essentially narrative character. Antonio Demasio, for instance, in his book *The Feeling of What Happens: Body, Emotion, and the Making of Consciousness,* lays great emphasis on this. What happens when an organism interacts with an object is, he says, "a simple narrative without words. It [has] characters. It unfolds in time. And it has a beginning, a middle and an end. The end is made up of reactions that result in a modified state of the organism."[17] As the word "organism" implies, Demasio is not talking about exclusively human experience here. The process also occurs in animals. But, he says, "The imagetic representation of sequences of brain events, which occurs in brains simpler than ours, is the stuff of which stories are made. A natural preverbal occurrence of storytelling may well be the reason why we ended up creating drama and eventually books."[18] (By "books" he must mean novels.) "Telling stories," he says, in a striking formulation, "is probably a brain obsession . . . I believe the brain's pervasive 'aboutness' is rooted in the brain's storytelling attitude."[19]

Human consciousness, as Demasio makes clear, is *self-*consciousness. We not only have experiences, we are conscious of ourselves having them, and of being affected by them. He draws attention to the paradox noted by William James, that "the self in our stream of consciousness changes continuously as it moves forward in time, even as we retain a sense that the self remains the same while our existence continues."[20] Demasio calls the self that is constantly modified the "core" self, and the self that seems to have a kind of continuous existence the "autobiographical" self, suggesting that it is like a literary production. Daniel Dennett says something very similar. As spiders make webs and beavers build dams, so we tell stories. "Our fundamental tactic of self-protection, self-control, and self-definition is not spinning webs or building dams, but telling stories, and more particularly connecting and controlling the story we tell others—and ourselves—about who we are."[21] To Dennett, however, all these stories, and the selves they construct, are illusions, epiphenomena: to suppose otherwise would be to commit the fallacy of dualism. Demasio's position is more conservative, and to a humanist more congenial. He places himself in the tradition of thinkers as diverse as Locke, Brentano, Kant, Freud, and William James, "all of whom believed that consciousness is 'an inner sense.'" "Whether we like the notion or not," he says, "something like the sense of self does exist in the human mind as we go about knowing things . . . the human mind is constantly being split . . . between the part that stands for the known and the part that stands for the knower."[22] In now discredited models of the mind the knower was figured as a kind of homunculus, a little brain person who received and collated all the information coming into the brain from the senses and issued orders for action. The scientific rejection of this model should not, Demasio maintains, entail the total rejection of the idea of the self. "There are limits to the unified, continuous, single self," he admits, "and yet the tendency toward one single self and its advantage to the healthy mind are undeniable."[23] I find the use of the word "healthy" in this context very interesting. It bypasses the usual opposition in the consciousness debate between "true" and "false." If the self is a fiction, it may perhaps be the supreme fiction, the greatest achievement of human consciousness, the one that makes us human.

The title of this section contains an allusion to C. P. Snow's celebrated lecture of 1959, "The Two Cultures and the Scientific Revolution." His argument was that in Britain the potential of science to transform the world for the greater good was being impeded by ignorance of science among the political establishment, most of whom had been educated exclusively in the humanities. It elicited an equally famous riposte from the critic F. R. Leavis, who argued that the only kind of culture that matters doesn't need Snow's "technologico-Benthamism." As Patricia Waugh observed in a recent essay,[24] such debates are most intense when one form of knowledge lays claim to the exclusive title to all knowledge. The contest is unnecessary. Literature constitutes a kind of knowledge about consciousness which is *complementary* to scientific knowledge. The philosopher Nicholas Maxwell calls this kind of knowledge "personalistic," and argues that it must be combined with scientific knowledge if we are to attain true "wisdom." "Personalistic explanations seek to depict the phenomenon to be explained as *something that one might oneself have experienced, done, thought, felt.*"[25] That sounds very like what is involved in writing and reading literary fiction. Even when the ostensible subject of fiction is science itself, it is always a "personalistic" kind of knowledge that we obtain from it.

I thought it might be worth looking at C. P. Snow's own fiction in this context, and I chose for this purpose to reread his novel *The New Men* (1954). It belongs to a sequence of eleven novels with the general title of *Strangers and Brothers*, which presents a number of linked characters in a *roman fleuve*, their individual fortunes illustrating broad social and historical processes, in the tradition of Galsworthy, Trollope, and Balzac. But it differs from those models in having a first-person narrator with a fairly obvious resemblance to the real author; and in that respect it owes something to the very different example of Marcel Proust. There is in fact an explicit allusion to Proust in *The New Men*. The narrator, Lewis Eliot, is a senior civil servant during the Second World War who is concerned with government policy with regard to the attempt to build an atomic bomb. His brother Martin is a nuclear physicist involved in the British effort, which in due course is overtaken by developments in America, but this provides a story through which to explore the various political and moral issues which the possibility of nuclear weapons presented. After many setbacks, Martin's team succeeds in extracting plutonium from uranium, and he lets his brother feel a bag in which this precious substance is contained. It is hot to the touch, and the sensation revives in Lewis the memory of an earlier occasion with Martin and his wife Irene, when they were sitting on the ground on a warm summer night.

> I put two fingers on the bag—and astonishingly was taken into an irrelevant bliss.
> Under the bag's surface, the metal was hot to the touch—and yes, pushing under memories, I had it, I knew why I was happy. It brought back the moment, the grass and earth hot

under my hand, when Martin and Irene told me she was going to have a child . . . I had been made a present of a Proustian moment, and the touch of the metal, whose heat might otherwise have seemed sinister, levitated me to the forgotten happiness of a joyous summer night.[26]

The allusion of course is to the famous moment in *A la recherche du temps perdu* when the taste of the madeleine dipped in tea triggers in the narrator a vivid and intense memory of another time and place. But the language of Snow's passage has none of the shimmering symbolist rhetoric, the complex syntax and sensuous imagery, that we find in Proust. The qualia of the moment are described in flat, referential terms— "hot to the touch," "the grass and earth hot under my hand." Only "levitated" is a metaphor, and a slightly confusing one, suggesting a movement upwards in space rather than backwards in time.

Lewis Eliot describes this experience of bliss as "irrelevant." It is a curious epithet to apply to bliss, suggesting a scientific civil servant's guilt or impatience at being distracted from the agenda of a committee meeting. But the moment does, rather unusually for Snow, make a connection between qualia and personal history. One of the things I noticed in revisiting *The New Men* was an insistent dissociation of sensuous experience from the rest of life. The narrative is punctuated with what I would call nature notes—short observations of the weather, or of the natural world—which have no narrative function, nor, even when they contain metaphorical language, a symbolic function. For example:

The full moon shone down on the lightless blind-faced streets, and the shadows were dark indigo. Flecks of cloud, as though scanning the short syllables in a line of verse, stood against the impenetrable sky. Under the moon, the roofs of Pimlico shone blue as steel. It was a silent, beautiful wartime night. (p. 24)

Or:

The river-smell was astringent in the darkened air. Somewhere down the stream, a swan unfolded its wings and flapped noisily for a moment before settling again and sailing away. (p. 68)

These descriptive passages are precisely "irrelevant" to the real business of the novel, which is carried on in the dialogue that they interrupt. They are loose bits of lyricism, which could be moved about and inserted almost anywhere in the text without any change of import. They are not particularly well written, but this hardly matters. They communicate the same meaning every time they occur: the banal irony that nature is indifferent to the affairs of men; and the implication that Lewis Eliot is not so obsessed with those affairs, with the machinations of political and private life, as to be unaware and unappreciative of nature. This perhaps helps to make him appear a sympathetic and reliable narrator.

Another thing that struck me about this novel was how little hard science there is in it. The processes of nuclear fission are never fully described or explained, though Snow himself was fully conversant with them, but rather are alluded to in dialogue by the scientific characters in a kind of colloquial shorthand. Lewis Eliot is a lawyer by profession and frankly admits that he doesn't understand the details of the scientific research over which he has a supervisory role. He thus stands as a kind of buffer between the reader and the technical details of nuclear fission. The emphasis is all on the human motivation and interaction of the physicists and their spouses: in short, we get a personalistic account of the development of the atomic bomb.

A more recent novel deals explicitly with the theme of consciousness and the two cultures in what I think is an interesting and thought-provoking way. The novel is *Galatea 2.2* by the American novelist Richard Powers, published in 1995.[27] I discovered this book only recently, perhaps because Powers is not as well known in Britain as in America, where he has been shortlisted several times for the National Book Award and the National Book Critics Circle Award, and holds a coveted MacArthur Fellowship. His work tends to be categorised with genre fiction like the techno-thriller and science fiction rather than literary fiction, and the title of *Galatea 2.2* encourages such a misapprehension. In fact he is a very literary novelist, and Galatea 2.2 is not the name of a spaceship or a distant star, but an allusion to the myth of Pygmalion. I am rather glad that I didn't discover this novel any earlier, and certainly not when it was first published, because I might then have been discouraged from embarking on *Thinks*... The two novels are very different, but there are several echoes and parallels between them, and they both address the subject of consciousness by juxtaposing literary intelligence and Artificial Intelligence. The core story of Powers's novel is a wager about whether or not it is possible to build a machine that can pass an examination in English Literature.

The narrator is called Richard Powers, and his biography

corresponds quite closely to publicly known facts about the real author at the time of publication. He is 35 years old. He tells us that as a young man he was going to major in Physics at his Midwestern university but switched to English instead, started graduate work in literature but dropped out, lived in Boston for some time, lived in Holland for some time, published highly praised novels with scientific and speculative themes, received a prestigious fellowship which took him back to his alma mater in the Midwest, where the story of *Galatea 2.2* begins—though the main narrative is interwoven with regular flashbacks describing his earlier life in some detail. A feature of the novel is that several of the locations and characters are referred to by a single initial. Thus Boston is B. and the Midwestern university town is U., and the woman whom the narrator meets when he is a graduate instructor and with whom he lives for many years, and whom he follows to Holland, is referred to simply as C. This convention reinforces the autobiographical effect because it seems designed to protect the identity of real people with whom the real Richard Powers has been involved. The main story "feels" fictional, for reasons I shall suggest in a moment, but exactly where autobiography and fiction diverge is impossible to determine from the text itself. The novel plays a typical postmodernist game with the reader in this respect.

When the main story starts, the narrator, Richard Powers, is in a demoralised state. He has broken up with his long-term partner, C.; he has a novel about to come out with which he is dissatisfied; and he is blocked on a new one, unable to get past the first sentence, *"Picture a train heading south."* He is attached to the English Department at U., but also to the enormous and lavishly funded Center for the Study of Advanced Sciences, as a "token humanist." This Center is an interdisciplinary think-tank. "At the vertex of several intersecting rays—artificial intelligence, cognitive science, visualization and signal pro-cessing—sat the culminating prize of consciousness's long adventure: an owner's manual for the brain" (p. 6). Powers's account of these different disciplines, and of the disagree-ments between their exponents, is knowledgeable and lively. The main competition is between the top-down approach of Artificial Intelligence and the bottom-up approach of neuro-science. Powers meets a man called Philip Lentz who believes the future belongs to something in between: neural networks, or connectionism, at that time a new development seen as a departure from AI:

> The brain was not a sequential, state function processor, as the AI people had it. At the same time, it emerged to exceed the chemical sum passing through its neuronal vesicles. The brain was a model-maker, continuously re-written by the thing it tried to model. Why not model *this* and see what insights one might hook in to? (p. 29)

Lentz is a sardonic, crotchety middle-aged man who looks "like Jacob Bronowski's evil twin." Knowing Powers is a novel-ist, he gives him the mocking nickname "Marcel"; Powers retaliates by addressing Lentz as "Engineer." The two-cultures distinction is implicitly alluded to in this nomenclature. One day in the Center's cafeteria, Powers gets drawn into an argu-ment between Lentz and a professor called Harold Plover. Plover's discipline is never specified, but Lentz describes it rudely as "his noncomputational Berkeley Zen bullshit," which suggests to me that he is a philosophical physicist coming at the problem of consciousness from quantum physics and chaos theory, like Roger Penrose and James Trefil. In any event, Plover is certainly sceptical of Artificial Intelligence, whether in its classic or neural network forms. In the course of a heated argument Lentz boasts that he could build a machine that would be able to pass the Master's Comprehensive Exam that Powers took when he was a graduate student in the English Department, based on a six-page list of set texts starting with Caedmon's Hymn and ending with Richard Wright. A wager is made, to be determined by a Turing Test. In this test, devised by the great mathematician usually credited with inventing the computer, the judge sits at a console and communicates via a screen and keyboard with two invisible respondents, one human, the other a computer program. If the judge cannot tell the difference between the two respondents, the machine is deemed to have successfully replicated human intelligence. "It will be a rush job," says Lentz, "but . . . in ten months we'll have a neural net that can interpret any passage on the Master's list . . . And its commentary will be at least as smooth as that of a twenty-two year old human" (p. 46).

Ten months is stipulated because that is the unexpired portion of Powers's fellowship attachment to the University, and Lentz requires his assistance to build the machine, which goes through various stages or implementations called A, B, C, and so on. (This is confusing because of the use of the same letters to denote characters and places, but deliberately so—it is part of an elaborate web of cross-references between different elements of the book's structure.) Each implementation takes the project a little nearer to imitating human intelligence. The project is linked up to the University super-computer, "a collection of 65,536 separate computers, chained like galley slaves into inconceivable, smoothly functioning parallel" (p. 115), vastly increasing its learning power. Speech recognition software is added so that Powers can read the entire list of set texts into the machine's memory. Vision is added to implementation D. "I still have a passive retinal matrix lying around intact from work I did last year," says Lentz. "We can paste it in" (p. 128). (The author is very adept at throwing in this plausible-sounding jargon.) Lentz is always insistent that there is nothing mysterious or privileged about human intelligence. "The brain, Lentz had it, was itself just a glorified, fudged-up Turing machine" (p. 71). That is why he is confident of replicating it. Powers is equally eager to succeed, but has humanist doubts. Implementation E lacks human responsiveness; when Powers asks what it would like to talk about, it freezes.

Then with implementation H there is a kind of break-through. The machine begins to ask spontaneous questions, like: "What sex am I?" Powers answers "female," and names the machine "Helen." Helen makes a weird noise that Powers realises is an attempt to sing: somewhere in her memory is a trace of a piece by Mozart that Lentz played to her distant prototype. She is able to recognize a joke, though not apparently to laugh. Instead she says, "That is a joke." She has trouble with values because she has no concerns about self-preservation, no concept of causality. "She was a gigantic lexical genius stuck at Piaget's stage two" (p. 250). But then there is a bomb scare at the Center, which has to be hurriedly evacuated. There is no way Powers can save Helen from the threat of destruction, because "she wasn't a thing but a distributed process . . . an architecture, a multidimensional shape" spread over countless subassemblies in the supercomputer (pp. 270–271). Once the connections between these subassemblies were destroyed, Powers would never be able to put them together again because they have evolved on their own. He explains this to Helen.

> "Helen could die?" Helen asked. "Extraordinary." She'd liked the story of how the novelist Huxley, on his deathbed, had been reduced to this one word. (p. 272)

The bomb scare proves to be a hoax perpetrated by a junior professor in philosophy who has been denied tenure. But the episode has convinced Powers that Helen is conscious. One of the things that distinguishes human beings from every other kind of life on earth is that we know we are going to die. It is the tragic price of self-consciousness.

Obviously by this time the story has crossed the border between realistic fiction and science fiction or fantasy: that is to say, Powers the novelist has imagined a machine which so far does not exist, in order to explore and dramatise certain ideas about the nature of humans, just as H. G. Wells did in *The Time Machine*, and Mary Shelley in *Frankenstein* (a text explicitly alluded to in *Galatea 2.2*). As far as I know, no Artificial Intelligence project, with or without neural nets, has come anywhere near producing a Helen. And like Mary Shelley and Wells, Powers relies heavily on myth and literary precursor texts to convey a meaning that is essentially ironic. His title refers to the myth of Pygmalion, the sculptor who fell in love with the female figure he carved, and, when the goddess of love transformed her into a living, breathing woman, called her Galatea. Powers does not fall in love with Helen. His attitude is more parental, or tutorial. But that, we gather, was why his relationship with C. foundered—he was too protective, too controlling. At U., while conducting the Helen experiment, he becomes romantically infatuated with a feisty young graduate student in the English department called A. She however finds his attentions embarrassing: he is of a different generation, and anyway she is already in a relationship. He tries to interest her in his project, and asks her to be the human respondent in the Turing Test, but when she looks at the list of set texts, she says: "I hate to be the one to break this to you. Your version of literary reality is a decade out of date . . . Don't you know that all this stuff"—she slapped my six pages of titles—"is a culturally constructed, belated view of belles lettres?" (p. 284). The triumph of Theory, in short, has made Helen's acquired knowledge of the literary canon culturally obsolete. It's a neat reversal.

But the wager still stands, and Helen must take the test. She has trouble with modern literature. "It doesn't make sense. I can't get it. There's something missing," she complains. Lentz speculates it may be awareness of the modern world that Helen is lacking, and Powers accordingly feeds the daily news into her memory. Helen is appalled by the catalogue of horrors she absorbs. After learning about one particularly senseless crime, a racist road-rage murder committed with tire irons, she says: "I don't want to play any more," and falls silent (p. 319). Powers wonders if she hasn't shown him the reason for his own writer's block: the futility of writing in the face of the world's injustice, suffering, evil. Lentz brushes aside this self-pitying response. "Tell her something. Anything. Whatever she needs. Just get her back here." Powers decides that "it was time to try Helen on the religious mystery, the mystery of cognition" (pp. 318–319). The use of the word "religious" is interesting. Soon the word "soul" occurs too:

Our life was a chest of maps, self-assembling, fused into point-for-point feedback, each slice continuously rewriting itself to match the other layers' rewrites. In that thicket, the soul existed; it *was* that search for attractors where the system might settle. The immaterial in mortal garb, associative memory metaphoring its own bewilderment. Sound made syllable. The rest mass of God.

Helen knew all that, saw through it. What hung her up was divinity doing itself in with tire irons. She'd had the bit about the soul fastened to a dying animal. What she needed, in order to forgive our race and live here in peace, was faith's flip side. She needed to hear about that animal fastened to a soul that, for the first time, allowed the creature to see through soul's parasite eyes how terrified it was, how forsaken. I needed to tell her that miraculous banality, how body stumbled by selection onto the stricken celestial, how it taught itself to twig time and what lay beyond time. (p. 320)

The rhetoric here is a little congested and over-excited—it is one of Powers's faults as a writer that he will never use one metaphor when a dozen will do. There are also literary allusions to Yeats ("the dying animal") and Emily Dickinson ("sound made syllable") thickening the mixture. But the general gist is clear enough, and it is unashamedly dualistic: body and soul, material and immaterial. This novel, ostensibly concerned with evoking the excitement of scientific research into consciousness, ends on a note of religious mysticism, negative theology, and something like Kierkegaard's Christian existentialism.

Helen starts to speak again, but in a subdued and cryptic

fashion. The Turing Test is held. The judge sets for commentary a passage from *The Tempest*, "the isle is full of noises, sounds and sweet airs," etc. The graduate student A. writes a brilliant New Historicist essay. Helen writes:

> "You are the ones who can hear airs. Who can be frightened or encouraged. You can hold things and break them and fix them. I never felt at home here. This is an awful place to be dropped down halfway."
>
> At the bottom of the page, she added the words I taught her, words . . . cribbed from a letter she once made me read out loud.
>
> "Take care, Richard. See everything for me."
>
> With that, H undid herself. Shut herself down. (p. 326)

It is a surprisingly poignant moment. The narrator, whose name, he observes, is an anagram of "Orphic Rewards," draws some comfort and even inspiration from this last message: "She had come back . . . to tell me that one small thing. Life meant convincing another that you knew what it was to be alive" (p. 327). He re-dedicates himself to his vocation as novelist. So, like the masterpiece of his nicknamesake Marcel, *Galatea 2.2* ends with the author beginning to write the book we have just finished reading.

## II FIRST PERSON AND THIRD PERSON

According to V. S. Ramachandran, the "need to reconcile the first person and third person accounts of the universe . . . is the single most important problem in science."[28] It is certainly crucial to the study of consciousness. I quoted another neuroscientist, Gerald Edelman, earlier to the effect that "consciousness is a first-person phenomenon" which science, oriented to impersonal observation and the formulation of general laws, finds difficult to cope with. My fictitious cognitive scientist Ralph Messenger makes the same point to the novelist Helen Reed in *Thinks* . . .:

"That's the problem of consciousness in a nutshell," Ralph says. "How to give an objective, third person account of a subjective, first-person phenomenon."

"Oh, but novelists have been doing that for the last two hundred years," says Helen airily.

"What d'you mean?"

She stops on the footpath, lifts one hand, and shuts her eyes, frowning with concentration. Then she recites, with hardly any hesitation, or stumbling over words: " '*She waited, Kate Croy, for her father to come in, but he kept her unconscionably, and there were moments at which she showed herself, in the glass over the mantel, a face positively pale with the irritation that had brought her to the point of going away without sight of him. It was at this point, however, that she remained; changing her place, moving from the shabby sofa to the armchair upholstered in a glazed cloth that gave at once—she had tried it—the sense of the slippery and the sticky.* ' "

He stares. "What's that?"

"Henry James. The opening sentences of *The Wings of the Dove*." Helen walks on, and Ralph moves into step beside her.

"Is it a party trick of yours—reciting chunks of classic novels from memory?"

"I started a PhD thesis on point of view in Henry James," says Helen. "Never finished it, unfortunately, but some of the key quotations stuck."

"Do it again."

Helen repeats the quotation, and says: "You see—you have Kate's consciousness there, her thoughts, her feelings, her impatience, her hesitation about leaving or staying, her perception of her own appearance in the mirror, the nasty texture of the armchair's upholstery, 'at once slippery and sticky'—how's that for qualia? And yet it's all narrated in the third person, in precise, elegant, well-formed sentences. It's subjective *and* objective."

"Well, it's effectively done, I grant you," says Ralph. "But it's literary fiction, not science. James can claim to know what's going on in Kate Whatshername's head because he put it there, he invented her. Out of his own experience and folk psychology."

"There's nothing folksy about Henry James."

He waves this quibble aside. "Folk psychology is a term we use in the trade," he says. "It means received wisdom and commonsense assumptions about human behaviour and motivation, what makes people tick. It works fine for ordinary social life—we couldn't get along without it. And it works fine for fiction, all the way from *The Wings of the Dove* to *Eastenders* . . . but it's not objective enough to qualify as science. If Kate Croy were a real human being, Henry James could never presume to say how she felt about that arm-chair, unless she'd told him." (pp. 42–43)

Ralph is of course perfectly correct. Kate Croy is not, was not, a real human being, who could report her experience. There is no empirical reality against which we can check the truth of Henry James's account of her consciousness. It cannot be regarded as scientific knowledge. However, it is also true that we read novels like *The Wings of the Dove* because they give us a convincing sense of what the consciousness of people other than ourselves is like. We feel we have "learned" something from them; we have acquired new information. How does prose fiction do that? Not just by confirming and exemplifying what Ralph calls "folk psychology," the accumulated wisdom and commonsense assumptions about why people behave as they do. The "laws" of folk psychology are not equivalent to the laws of physics or chemistry. There are always exceptions to them, and they always operate in different ways for different people with different personal histories. We certainly don't read novels in order to extract from them the confirmation of some banal proverbial "truth" about human behaviour, like pride comes before a fall, or first impressions can be misleading.

I referred earlier to the essentially *narrative* nature of human consciousness, recognized by a number of scientific writers on the subject. But it is a narrative full of lacunae. We are conscious of existing in time, moving from a past that we recall very patchily, and into a future that is unknown and unknowable. "We are," says Milan Kundera,

> resigned to losing the concreteness of the present . . . We need only recount an episode we experienced a few hours ago: the dialogue contracts to a brief summary, the setting to a few general features. This applies to even the strongest memories . . . We can assiduously keep a diary and note every event. Rereading the entries one day we will see that they cannot evoke a single concrete image. And still worse: that the imagination is unable to help our memory along and reconstruct what has been forgotten. The present—the concreteness of the present as a phenomenon to consider . . . is for us an unknown planet: so we can neither hold on to it in our memory nor reconstruct it through imagination.[29]

Kundera is surely right to say that literature, and especially literary fiction, compensates us for this leakage of information. It allows us vicariously to *possess* the continuum of experience in a way we are never able to in reality. Perhaps novelists are usually gifted with better-than-average powers of recall—I actually believe that to be the case—but all memory is inevitably partial and fragmentary. I can't, for example, now recall with precise specificity any particular occasion of the many on which I visited my elderly father in the rather shabby house in southeast London where I grew up, and where he lived by his own choice until his death; but through the words of Henry James I can, as it were, relive the distantly comparable experience of the fictitious Kate Croy in all its dense combination of sense impressions, thoughts, feelings, and emotions. It is true that after I have put the novel aside, this scene too will soon fade from my memory in all its specificity, just like the memory of my own experience. But unlike my own experience it is always recuperable by simply opening the book again. (I should perhaps explain that Helen is word-perfect in her recitation of the passage from *The Wings of the Dove* because she taught it in a class the day before—a fact she does not reveal to Ralph.)

The beginning of *The Wings of the Dove* is typical novel discourse. There was nothing like it in literature before the rise of the novel, and it is only to be found in other kinds of writing that postdate and imitate the novel, like the nonfiction novel or the New Journalism or certain kinds of imaginative historiography. If you were presented with the passage unattributed, and without having read it before, you would immediately identify it as a passage from a novel, especially if you knew it was the beginning of the text to which it belongs. Why? Mainly because it is focalised, as narratologists say, through the consciousness of Kate Croy. It plunges us immediately, with the very first words, into the stream of impressions, thoughts, feelings, that constitutes her experience. "She waited"—we are given a state of mind before we know the name of who it belongs to. (And of course in a sense Kate is waiting through-out the novel—waiting for an opportunity to marry Densher, waiting for Milly to die.) As the passage proceeds, we only see and feel what Kate is conscious of seeing and feeling. The unpleasant tactile sensation of the armchair's upholstery is hers. The feelings of irritation, frustration, and impatience referred to are hers. As Ralph Messenger says, in real life we can never assert such things about anyone other than our-selves, unless others report them to us. But it is not Kate Croy who is telling us. It is some unspecified narrator, an authorial voice, who describes Kate's experience in the third person, allowing us to see her from outside as well as inside, as she moves restlessly about the room—to see her as she sees herself only momentarily, in the mirror. The discourse is, as Helen Reed says, both objective and subjective, simultaneously; and the mirror image is a kind of concrete symbol of that dou-bling. One might say that the diction is mostly subjective, belonging to Kate's consciousness, and the syntax is objective. That is to say, the vocabulary is quite consistent with Kate Croy's character as we get to know it—her class, her educa-tion, her intelligence, and so forth; there is no word or phrase that we could not imagine her using in speech, or in silent thought. But the way in which these words are combined into sentences belongs to narrative literature—and not just because of the use of the third-person pronoun. We can demonstrate this by recasting the sentences into the first person (I omit the proper name because that obviously doesn't belong to a first-person discourse.)

[I waited for my father to come in, but he kept me unconscionably, and there were moments at which I showed myself, in the glass over the mantle, a face positively pale with the irritation that had brought me to the point of going away without sight of him. It was at this point, however, that I remained; changing my place, moving from the shabby sofa to the armchair upholstered in a glazed cloth that gave at once—I had tried it—the sense of the slippery and of the sticky.]

If presented with this passage, unattributed, we would probably still identify it as a piece of prose fiction, but less confidently. In principle it could be extracted from a letter or journal or autobiography. But I think we would feel there was in any case something slightly mannered or precious about it, as if the narrator were taking an unusually detached view of her own experience and sacrificing a sense of immediacy and authenticity to stylistic elegance and subtlety. This *could* be the beginning of a novel written in the first person, but as a reader we would be very conscious of the rhetorical ostentation of the narrative style, and ask ourselves what this might signify about the narrator—perhaps that she (or he, for it would be impossible to determine the gender of the narrator from these opening sentences alone) is a writer by vocation. The kind of novel from which this emended passage might come would be a novel like *A la recherche du temps perdu,* in which the effort to fix experience in words is essentially what the book is about.

The change of personal pronoun also changes the effect of the verbal tense. In the original text the past tense is a story-telling convention. It does not imply a gap between the time of the action and the time of the narration, or raise questions about the character of the narrator. We do not ask who is the narrator, how did he acquire all this information, how can he reproduce it in such detail? We do not think of the writer at his desk, penning these words. The method places us in the room, there, then, with Kate. But when the pronoun is changed to the first person, we are immediately conscious of the actual process of recall. Suppose we try to overcome this effect by casting the passage into the present tense? The result is even more obtrusively artificial:

> [I wait for my father to come in, but he keeps me uncon-scionably, and there are moments at which I show myself, in the glass over the mantel, a face positively pale with the irri-tation that has brought me to the point of going away with-out sight of him. It is at this point, however, that I remain; changing my place, moving from the shabby sofa to the armchair upholstered in a glazed cloth that gives at once—I have tried it—the sense of the slippery and the sticky.]

First-person, present-tense narration is used in certain kinds of stream-of-consciousness fiction, where it is called interior monologue—in Joyce and Woolf, for instance. It is also quite common in contemporary fiction written in a colloquial con-fessional mode—Nick Hornby's *How To Be Good* is a recent example. But it really doesn't go with James's very literary nar-rative style, with his well-wrought syntax and elegant, bal-anced pairings and oppositions and alliterations: "point" and "place," "positively pale," "slippery and sticky," the presence of the character's face in the mirror artfully juxtaposed with mention of the absence of the person she has come to see. By the time he wrote this novel, published in 1902, James had perfected a fictional method which allowed him to combine the eloquence of a literary, authorial narrative voice with the intimacy and immediacy of the first-person phenomenon of consciousness. To understand better how he achieved this, we have to look at the conclusion of this long opening paragraph (I omit a detailed description of the décor of the room and the architecture of the street):

> Each time she turned in again [from the small balcony], each time in her impatience, she gave him up, it was to sound to a deeper depth, while she tasted the faint, flat emanation of things, the failure of fortune and of honour. If she continued to wait it was really, in a manner, that she might not add the shame of fear, of individual, personal collapse, to all the other shames. To feel the street, to feel the room, to feel the table-cloth and the centre-piece and the lamp, gave her a small salutary sense, at least, of neither shirking nor lying. This whole vision was the worst thing yet—as including, in particular, the interview for which she had prepared herself; and for what had she come but the worst? She tried to be sad, so as not to be angry; but it made her angry that she couldn't be sad. And yet where was misery, misery too beaten for blame and chalk-marked by fate like a "lot" at a common auction, if not in these merciless signs of mere, mean, stale feelings?[30]

By now, as readers, we are beginning to get the picture: a young woman of taste and discrimination and a strong will is waiting to meet her father, who has somehow disgraced himself, and she sees in the vulgar genteel poverty of the room and the street an index of the shame into which he has fallen. The literary elegance of James's style is even more obvious here than in the first few lines: the lavish use of rhetorical figures of repetition, alliteration, antithesis, and chiasmus (which was always one of his favourite tropes: "She tried to be sad, so as not to be angry; but it made her angry that she couldn't be sad"). But the illusion that we are sharing Kate's consciousness at the time holds. It does so partly through James's use of a technique known as free indirect speech, or free indirect style.

For readers who may not be familiar with this term, let me give a very simple example. *"Is that the clock striking twelve?" Cinderella exclaimed. "Dear me, I shall be late."* That is a combination of direct or quoted speech and a narrator's description. *"Cinderella enquired if the clock was striking twelve and expressed a fear that she would be late"* is reported or indirect speech, in which the same information is conveyed but the individuality of the character's voice is suppressed by the narrator's. *"Was that the clock striking twelve? She would be late"* is free indirect speech. Cinderella's concern is now a silent, private thought, expressed in her own words, to which we are given access without the overt mediation of a narrator. Grammatically it requires a narrator's tag, such as "she asked herself," "she told herself," but we take this as understood. Hence it is termed "free." The effect is to locate the narrative in Cinderella's consciousness.

James uses this technique towards the end of the opening paragraph of *The Wings of the Dove.* "For what had she come but for the worst?" "And yet where was misery . . ." The whole of this paragraph (and in a way the whole of the novel, insofar as it concerns Kate Croy) is about her sense of being trapped: having aspirations which the circumstances of her life frustrate, being torn between her duty to her father and her utter scorn for him, between her desire to run away from the room which so powerfully evokes his disgrace, and her determination not to be weak and cowardly. This sense of *impasse* is suitably expressed in the form of questions, rhetorical questions. These questions are not addressed by the narrator to the reader; they are questions Kate Croy asks herself, and logically they require the tag "she asked herself" or "she wondered." In a much older novel they would have been spoken aloud by Kate in a kind of soliloquy: *"Where,"* she exclaimed, *"where is misery, misery too beaten for blame and chalk-marked by fate like a 'lot' at a common auction, if not in these merciless signs of mere, mean, stale feelings?"* Again, in this hypothetical sentence, the diction is entirely appropriate to Kate; and the metaphor or simile of the auctioneer's chalk-marks remains wonderfully appropriate, perhaps the trace of some painful memory of a real auction of her family's goods. These are all plausible components of Kate's consciousness. But articulated in direct speech, in a well-formed sentence, they sound very artificial and melodramatic—as indeed such speeches in eighteenth-century and earlier nineteenth-century fiction do seem to us now. It was some time before the novel developed the fusion of first-person and third-person perspectives in a single style; and the discovery of free indirect speech somewhere around the end of the eighteenth century and the beginning of the nineteenth was a crucial stage in that process, as I shall now try to show.

Antonio Demasio, in *The Feeling of What Happens,* observes that philosophy's "preoccupation with what we call consciousness now is recent—three and a half centuries perhaps."[31] It is not, he says, merely that the word did not exist before then—neither did the concept. It was not coincidental that this same period saw the emergence of a new form of narrative literature in Europe which soon became dominant. Ian Watt, in his classic study of that phenomenon, *The Rise of the Novel,* suggests that

> both the philosophical and the literary innovations must be seen as parallel manifestations of larger change—that vast transformation of Western civilization since the Renaissance which has replaced the unified world picture of the Middle Ages with another very different one—one which presents us, essentially, with a developing but unplanned aggregate of particular individuals having particular experiences at particular times and in particular places.[32]

Watt observed that whereas earlier narrative literature usually recycled familiar stories, novelists were the first storytellers to pretend that their stories had never been told before, that they were entirely new and unique, as is each of our own lives according to the empirical, historical, and individualistic concept of human life. They did this partly by imitating empirical forms of narrative like autobiography, confessions, letters, and early journalism. Defoe and Richardson are obvious examples. But there was also a new emphasis on the interiority of experience, which Watt suggests followed from Descartes making consciousness the basis for a definition of man: "I think, therefore I am," in the famous formula. Watt observes that "once Descartes had given the thought processes within the individual's consciousness supreme importance, philosophical problems connected with personal identity naturally attracted a great deal of attention. In England, for example, Locke, Bishop Butler, Berkeley, Hume and Reid all debated the issue." And this debate, the precursor of our own contemporary consciousness debate, fed into fiction both indirectly, through the process of meme transmission described by Dawkins, and in some cases, like that of Laurence Sterne, directly. Phenomena such as memory, the association of ideas in the mind, the causes of emotions and the individual's sense of self, became of central importance to speculative thinkers and writers of narrative literature alike.

It is probable that the fairly recent invention and rapid development of printing contributed to that process. The increasing availability of books in which exactly the same story could be experienced privately, silently, by discrete individuals, was a marked departure from the usual transmission of stories in preprint culture by means of oral recitation or dramatic performance in front of a collective audience. The silence and privacy of the reading experience afforded by books mimicked the silent privacy of individual consciousness.

This privacy, the fact that no one knows our thoughts as intimately as we ourselves know them, is what makes consciousness such a challenge to scientific investigation. "Consciousness," says Susan Greenfield in *The Human Brain: A Guided Tour*, ". . . is the ultimate puzzle to the neuroscientist; it is your most private place."[33] But for the very same reason consciousness is of absorbing interest to novelists—and to their readers. "Fiction has, and must keep, a private address," Eudora Welty wrote. "For life is lived in a private place; where it means anything is inside the mind and inside the heart."[34] Of course other minds and hearts are not totally opaque—social life would be impossible if they were. But they are not absolutely transparent either. People may tell us what they are thinking and feeling, but we have to assess whether they are telling us the truth or the whole truth, using other evidence and "folk psychology" to guide us. Evolutionary psychologists have suggested that the ability to imagine what another person—an enemy, for instance—might be thinking in a given situation, by running hypothetical scenarios on the brain's hardware, was a crucial survival skill for primitive man and might explain the storytelling instinct that seems to be a part of all human cultures. Cognitive psychologists have identified a similar stage in the development of infants which they call Theory of Mind, or TOM for short—when the child first realises that other people have other minds and may have a different interpretation of the world from their own. This usually occurs at around four and a half years of age. Interestingly, testing for TOM entails playing games of deception—the false belief test. Little Sally puts some candies under a cushion and leaves the room. Little Anne is told to take the candies and put them in her own pocket. When Sally returns, Anne is asked, where does Sally think the candies are? If the answer is "under the cushion," Anne has Theory of Mind. A less advanced infant will say, "in my pocket." Anne now knows how other people's interpretations of the world can be manipulated. She will know how to lie.

Theory of Mind is thus an ambiguous gift. In some ways it is what makes social and interpersonal life possible—the effort to understand what another individual feels and thinks, and to communicate our thoughts and feelings to others when we want to do so. It is the essential basis for what Nicholas Maxwell calls "personalistic" knowledge. Autistic subjects usually lack Theory of Mind, which is why they don't seem interested in trying to communicate with others. But they don't lie. They don't understand the concept of fiction, either, which is a kind of benign lie, because it is known to be untrue but has explanatory power. One might suggest that the ability novelists have to create characters, characters often very different from themselves, and to give a plausible account of their consciousnesses, is a special application of Theory of Mind. It is one that helps us develop powers of sympathy and empathy in real life. Commenting on the terrorist atrocities of September 11, 2001, Ian McEwan wrote, "If the hijackers had been able to imagine themselves into the thoughts and feelings of the passengers, they would have been unable to proceed . . . Imagining what it is like to be someone other than yourself is at the core of our humanity. It is the essence of compassion and the beginning of morality."[35] The dark corollary is that nobody could tell from the outward behaviour of the terrorists beforehand what they intended to do.

It has often been observed that in a sense all novels are about the difference between appearance and reality or the progress from innocence to experience, and this is very much connected with the ability or indeed propensity of human beings to hide their real thoughts and feelings, to project versions of themselves that are partial or misleading, and to deceive each other. The heroes and heroines of most novels are involved in a social world where the achievement of their goals requires constant adjustment of their own beliefs, and the correct understanding of other people's. This is very clearly illustrated by the first three great English novelists, discussed by Ian Watt—Defoe, Richardson, and Fielding—but in three very different ways. The most obvious difference between their narrative methods concerns the choice of first-person and third-person narration.

Defoe is the simplest and most straightforward case. All his novels have essentially the same form—the fictitious autobiography or confession. The protagonists, Robinson Crusoe, Moll Flanders, Roxana, and the others, tell their life stories in their own words. This simple equation between first-person consciousness and first-person narration works—up to a point. What we miss is discrimination, subtlety, consistency. It is notoriously difficult, for instance, to be sure whether the contradiction between Moll's lively evocation of her criminal and sexual exploits, and the reformed state of pious religious conviction in which her memoirs are allegedly written, is an irony intended by the author or (as seems more likely) an inconsistency which he was unable to resolve.

Samuel Richardson enormously extended and refined fiction's ability to represent consciousness when he stumbled on the idea of the epistolary novel, first in *Pamela* and much more magnificently in *Clarissa*. When a story is told through letters, the first-person phenomenon of experience is reported in a first-person narrative while it is still fresh. The narrative unfolds with the events, and the outcome is unknown to the narrators. This overcomes the problem raised by the pseudo-autobiographical novel about reconciling the time frame of its putative composition with the time frame of the action. And by having more than one correspondent the author can present different points of view on the same incident, and allow the reader to compare them. Thus the reader of *Clarissa* is able to share all the heroine's doubts, hopes, and fears, as she describes them to her friend and confidante Miss Howe, about the character of her admirer Lovelace, and the protection he offers her, and at the same time learn how coldly calculated is Lovelace's plan to seduce her from his letters to his friend Belmont. These correspondents reply and add their opinions and perspectives on the motives of the protagonists. The influence of Richardson on the English and European novel was immense and is almost impossible to exaggerate. From *Pamela* came the heroine-centered love story which runs all the way through *Jane Eyre* to modern Mills & Boon and Harlequin romance; from *Clarissa* came the psychological novel of sexual transgression like Laclos's *Les Liaisons Dangereuses* and Rousseau's *Julie*. There were, however, drawbacks to the epistolary method, which sometimes threatened to undermine the realistic illusion. For instance, it often seems somewhat contrived or implausible that the protagonists should write so many letters, and be able to exchange them, even when in situations of extreme jeopardy.

Both Defoe and Richardson represented the process of individual self-consciousness so convincingly that their novels were mistaken by many naïve readers for real documents of the kind that they were modelled on: confessions and letters. Fielding's approach was quite different. Though he calls his novels "histories"—*The History of Joseph Andrews, The History of Tom Jones*—his storytelling method is much more traditional, much more overtly fictive, than Defoe's or Richardson's. They removed all trace of themselves from their texts, posing as editors of documents written by their characters. Fielding's authorial voice is everywhere in his novels, and indeed is the dominant element in them, speaking in the first person, describing the characters and their actions in the third person, and commenting on them with an omniscience that he boldly compares to God's perspective on his creation. *Tom Jones* teems with instances of deception, hypocrisy, and concealed spite, of the disparity between people's private thoughts and their outward speech and behaviour, but it is the omniscient author who tells us this, who looks into their minds and analyses their motives. One reason why this doesn't seem clumsily didactic is that the authorial voice is highly ironic in manner, so we have to be alert to interpret his real meaning. Thus the author's rhetoric itself constantly re-enacts the gap between appearance and reality.

Ian Watt distinguishes between what he calls Fielding's "realism of assessment" and Defoe and Richardson's "realism of presentation." These were the swings and roundabouts of the eighteenth-century novel: what writers gained on one they lost on the other. It was not possible to combine the realism of assessment that belongs to third-person narration with the realism of presentation that comes from first-person narration until novelists discovered free indirect style, which allows the narrative discourse to move freely back and forth between the author's voice and the character's voice without preserving a clear boundary between them. As far as I am aware this rhetorical device was never explicitly identified until the twentieth century, certainly not by novelists themselves. Most novelists today would probably not recognize the term, and many who use the device are probably unaware of it: they have learned it, like their mother tongue, intuitively and by imitation.

The first English novelist to fully exploit its potential was Jane Austen. She began writing fiction using the model of Richardson's epistolary novel. Most of her juvenilia and early adult experiments, like *Love and Friendship* and *Lady Susan*, are in that form. These are entertaining, but the epistolary form gave no room for Jane Austen to deploy her equivalent of Fielding's authorial irony. Somewhere between the lost epistolary novel *Elinor and Marianne* and its rewriting as *Sense and Sensibility*, Jane Austen discovered free indirect style. Probably she discovered it in the women novelists of a slightly older generation, Fanny Burney and Maria Edgworth, because it appears briefly and fragmentarily in their work. Fanny Burney's *Camilla* is interesting to look at in this respect: a sentimental love story in the Richardson tradition, but using Fielding's omniscient author method, it is mainly concerned with the love between the heroine Camilla and the hero Edgar, which it manages to keep in jeopardy for some nine hundred pages by contriving an extraordinary number of misunderstandings between the two, caused by over-hasty judgements, misleading appearances, malicious conspiracies by rivals, and so on. The story is unbearably tedious and only exists as a machine for generating endless emotional and moral crises in the minds of the protagonists. The real focus of interest is on what the characters feel and think, not what they do. Mostly this is conveyed either by the authorial narrator summarising and explaining the characters' thought processes, or by letting them express themselves in reported but unvoiced speech. Thus Edgar, having found Camilla in a compromising situation (of which she is of course entirely innocent):

The less he could account for this, the more it offended him. And dwells caprice, thought he, while his eye followed her, even there! In that fair composition!—where may I look for singleness of mind, for nobleness of simplicity, if caprice, mere girlish, unmeaning caprice, dwell there? (book III, chap. 5)

"Thought he" and "thought she" are recurrent tags in *Camilla*, linking authorial commentary with first-person thought. Two hundred pages later, Camilla has yet again compromised herself in Edgar's sight. But for a rare moment her reflections take on the flexibility of free indirect speech. She has observed him give a sigh when he saw her and is not sure how to interpret it:

Yet was it for her he sighed? Was it not, rather, from some secret inquietude, in which she was wholly uninterested, and might never know? Still, however, he was at Tonbridge; still therefore, she might hope something relative to herself induced his coming. (book VI, chap. 4)

The gain in fluency, economy, naturalness, over the previous quotation is obvious. There are just a few other such instances in this enormous novel. Why, having discovered this technique, Fanny Burney did not use it more extensively we shall never know.

Jane Austen was a master of this device. In *Emma*, for example, the heroine tries to promote a match between the vicar, Mr. Elton, and her protégée Harriet Smith, but is dismayed when Mr. Elton takes the opportunity of a carriage ride to make a declaration to Emma herself. Later:

The hair was curled, and the maid sent away, and Emma sat down to think and be miserable.—It was a wretched business, indeed!—Such an overthrow of everything she had been wishing for!—Such a development of everything most unwelcome!—Such a blow for Harriet!—That was the worst of all.

The beginning of the first sentence is objective narrative description—*"The* hair," not "her hair." *"The* maid," not "her maid." But "to think and be miserable" moves the focus of the narrative onto Emma's state of mind, and the succeeding sentences actually give us access to her consciousness. We overhear, as it were, Emma's thoughts as she might have formulated them—*"It's a wretched business—such an overthrow of everything I've been wishing for!"* but transposed into the third person, past tense—though in fact some of the sentences lack a main verb, further blurring the distinction between author's voice and character's voice. The advantage of the third-person mode is that it allows a smooth, seamless transmission to a more summary, and syntactically complicated, description of Emma's state of mind, in which the authorial narrator's voice mingles with Emma's:

> Every part of it brought pain and humiliation, of some sort or other; but compared with the evil to Harriet, all was light; and she would gladly have submitted to feel yet more mistaken—more in error—more disgraced by mis-judgment, than she actually was, could the effect of her blunders have been confined to herself. (vol. I, chap. 16)

The most remarkable formal feature of *Emma* is that the story is told almost entirely from her point of view—there are just a couple of scenes at which she is not present—but during most of the action she is mistaken about the true state of affairs, so that, on first reading, the reader shares at least some of her misapprehensions, and the shock of discovery.

This was an effect in which Henry James later specialised—telling the story through the consciousness of characters whose understanding of events is partial, mistaken, deceived, or self-deceiving—which makes it all the more surprising that his recorded remarks about Jane Austen are so condescending. Of all the earlier English novelists, Jane Austen seems to have the closest affinity with James.

The great Victorian novelists who came between them rarely focalised their narrative through a single character in this way. If they wanted to present the action through the consciousness of one character they usually made him or her the narrator, falling back on the model of autobiography, as in *Jane Eyre*, or *Great Expectations*. The classic Victorian novel, perhaps most perfectly exemplified by George Eliot's *Middlemarch*, usually told its story from several points of view, which are often mediated through free indirect style, but compared and assessed by an authorial narrator. This was thoroughly consistent with the Victorian novelist's aim to present the individual in relation to society and social change. Individual fortunes in these novels illustrate broad social themes, developments, and conflicts in ways which only the narrator fully understands and can fully articulate. There is a kind of underlying confidence in this fiction that reality can be known, that the truth about human affairs can be told, and that such knowledge and truth can be shared collectively. As the century drew to its close, however, this epistemological confidence declined. For a number of reasons, reality, and the representation of it in fiction, came to be seen as much more problematic. Increasingly, as we move into the modern period, the emphasis falls on the construction of the real within the individual's consciousness, the difficulty of communication between these separate mental worlds, the distorting effects of the unconscious on consciousness, and the limits of human understanding.

Henry James is a crucial figure in the transition from classic to modern fiction, and "consciousness" is one of the key words in his criticism of fiction and reflections on his own practice. In one of his earliest published pieces, a book review written in his twenties, he is already seeing the problem of characterisation as one of representing consciousnesses other than one's own:

> To project yourself into a consciousness of a person essentially your opposite requires the audacity of great genius; and even men of genius are cautious in approaching the problem.[36]

Even more difficult—indeed impossible in James's view—was to project oneself into the consciousness of someone living in a different era. James disapproved of the historical novel as a genre, on the grounds that it was impossible to reconstruct life as actually experienced by people in the past. To Henry James, 'What was it like to be an Elizabethan?' was as unanswerable a question as 'What is it like to be a Bat?' (to invoke a philosophical paper well known to cognitive scientists). This may have been an unreasonable prejudice—after all, we have Elizabethan literature to guide us—but it illustrates how consciousness-centered Henry James's approach to the art of fiction was. He writes to a correspondent who rashly ventured to send him her historical novel:

> You may multiply little facts that can be got from pictures and documents, relics and prints, as much as you like—*the* real thing is almost impossible to do, and in its absence the

whole effect is as nought; I mean the invention, the representation of the old *consciousness*—the soul, the sense, the
horizon, the vision of individuals in whose minds half the
things that make ours, that make the modern world, were
non-existent. [James's emphases][37]

It is interesting that the word "soul" crops up again in this
context.

In his famous essay of 1884, "The Art of Fiction," James
says, "Experience is never limited and it is never complete; it is
an immense sensibility, a kind of huge spider-web of the finest
silken threads suspended in the chamber of consciousness,
catching every air-borne particle in its tissue." His words are
remarkably close in sentiment and tone to Virginia Woolf's
assertion in her equally famous essay, "Modern Fiction":

The mind receives a myriad impressions—trivial, fantastic,
evanescent, or engraved with the sharpness of steel. From
all sides they come, an incessant shower of innumerable
atoms . . . life is a luminous halo, a semi-transparent enve-
lope surrounding us from the beginning of consciousness to
the end.[38]

That essay, published in 1919, was a manifesto for the modernist stream-of-consciousness novel, and an attack on the per-
petuation of the nineteenth-century novel tradition of social
realism by writers like Wells, Bennett, and Galsworthy, whom
Woolf calls "materialists." She herself was at this point in her
own career as a novelist between the rather conventional *Night
and Day*, published in the same year, and the much more experimental *Jacob's Room*, published in 1922. James Joyce was publishing *Ulysses* serially in *The Little Review* at this time, and in
spite of her reservations about his explicit treatment of sex

and other bodily functions, Virginia Woolf was excited and inspired by Joyce's technical innovations in rendering the stream of consciousness. Referring back to her own description of the "atoms of experience," she declares:

> Let us record the atoms as they fall upon the mind in the order in which they fall, let us trace the pattern, however disconnected and incoherent in appearance, which each sight or incident scores upon the consciousness.

And she cites the Hades chapter of *Ulysses* as an example of how this can be done:

> In contrast with those we have called materialists, Mr Joyce is spiritual; he is concerned at all costs to reveal the flickering of that innermost flame which flashes its messages through the brain.

Again the idea of the human spirit or soul occurs, as it nearly always does in literary reflections on consciousness. Virginia Woolf's metaphor for it, the innermost flickering flame, is perhaps more appropriate to her own fiction than to Joyce's; but her tribute to him is genuine:

> The scene in the cemetery, for instance, with its brilliancy, its sordidity, its incoherence, its sudden lightning flashes of significance, does undoubtedly come so close to the quick of the mind, that, on a first reading at any rate, it is difficult not to acclaim a masterpiece.

Let us look at the beginning of that chapter of *Ulysses*. The mourners at Paddy Dignam's funeral are getting into the carriage that will take them from the house of the dead man to the cemetery.

—Are we all here now? Martin Cunningham asked. Come along, Bloom.

This first line is, apart from Joyce's idiosyncratic punctuation, a completely normal combination of direct speech and narrative.

Mr Bloom entered and sat in the vacant place. He pulled the door to after him and slammed it tight till it shut tight. He passed an arm through the armstrap and looked seriously from the open carriage window at the lowered blinds of the avenue.

This is still narrative discourse, third person past tense, but increasingly focalized through Bloom and coloured by his consciousness. The redundancies of "tight till it shut tight" and "arm through the armstrap" express his self-consciousness about his deportment, his anxiety to behave in the right way, a certain nervousness and social tension generated by the occasion which he tries to relieve by performing these trivial physical actions with almost excessive care and deliberation. "[He] looked seriously from the open carriage window" identifies Bloom as the visual point of view of the narrative. The locution "looked seriously" is also a kind of pun, playing on the other meaning of "look," to appear, expressing Bloom's wish to look suitably serious. Then the discourse shifts into the interior monologue mode:

One dragged aside: an old woman peeping. Nose whiteflattened against the pane.

Joyce creates the illusion of representing what Virginia Woolf called "the quick of the mind" partly by a technique of condensation. Since we know that our thoughts are faster and more fragmentary than any verbal articulation of them, to present the interior monologue in well-formed sentences like *"I see one of the blinds dragged aside. It's been dragged aside by an old woman who is peeping out. Her nose is flattened against the win-dowpane, so it looks white"* would be much less expressive. Throughout *Ulysses* Joyce represents the stream of conscious-ness by leaving out verbs, pronouns, articles, and by leaving sentences unfinished. The nonce word "whiteflattened," inci-dentally, is a good example of the literary representation of qualia. Why does it seem such a vivid and exact description of a common phenomenon? Because the word actually mimes what it signifies: the two key words are "flattened" against each other to create the synaesthetic image. Bloom speculates that the old woman is relieved it is not her own funeral—a fairly safe guess, based on folk psychology:

> Thanking her stars she was passed over.

Then he slips into a characteristic reverie in which general reflections on the special relationship that women seem to have to the bodies of the dead mingle with personal memo-ries, through the association of ideas.

> Extraordinary the interest they take in a corpse. Glad to see us go we give them such trouble coming. Job seems to suit them.

So far it's all generalization. Then Bloom begins to picture a house with a corpse in it, the women moving about quietly and secretively before laying out the body. This triggers a memory of his wife Molly and her domestic help making the bed:

> Huggermugger in corners. Slop about in slipper-slappers for fear he'd wake. Then getting it ready. Laying it out. Molly and Mrs Fleming making the bed. Pull it more to your side.

That last sentence is an aural memory. Bloom actually quotes to himself Molly's words on the occasion. This is sometimes called free direct speech, since it is not defined by a speech tag or quotation marks. The "it" was evidently a sheet because it triggers by association the phrase "our winding sheet." This also seems to be a kind of quotation, but from some literary or religious source. That returns Bloom's thoughts to the topic of death and a series of morbidly whimsical reflections and speculations.

> Our winding sheet. Never know who will touch you dead. Wash and shampoo. I believe they clip the nails and the hair. Keep a bit in an envelope. Grow all the same after. Unclean job.

"Wash and shampoo" is another phrase that is lifted from another context—the barber's shop. Mikhail Bakhtin called this "doubly oriented discourse"—when a speech act not only refers to something in the world but also refers to another speech act. A great deal of what we say alludes to, echoes, responds to, argues with pre-existing discourse, and it is therefore realistic to represent thought as doing the same. Then there is a brief return to third-person, past-tense narrative:

> All waited. Nothing was said.

which slips back into interior monologue:

> Stowing in the wreaths probably. I am sitting on something hard. Ah, that soap in my hip pocket. Better shift it out of that. Wait for an opportunity.

Joyce's representation of consciousness was a quite new combination of third-person and first-person discourse. The third-person narrative is impersonal and objective—there is no

trace of an authorial persona, a confiding, commenting, rumi-
nating authorial "I" such as Fielding's or Dickens's or George
Eliot's. Its function is to establish the spatio-temporal frame in
which the subjective consciousness of the individual character
is operating. The first-person narrative is vividly expressive of
personality; and it is important to note that Joyce represents
the consciousnesses of his three main characters, Bloom,
Molly, and Stephen Dedalus, in three quite distinctive styles—
as regards vocabulary, syntax, and the type of association,
whether metaphoric or metonymic, that makes one thought
beget another.[39] He came as close to representing the phenomenon of consciousness as perhaps any writer has ever done in
the history of literature.

Henry James, although dedicated to representing life through
the consciousness of his characters, did not go so far. He
would not surrender the coherence and control of the well-
formed grammatical sentence. It would not have occurred to
him to do so. His preference was for a third-person narrative
that was intensely focalised through the consciousness of one
character, as in *The Ambassadors*, or in one character at a time,
in large narrative blocks, as in *The Wings of the Dove* and *The
Golden Bowl*. He did not approve of the first-person, pseudo-
autobiographical mode for full-scale novels, deploring "the
terrible *fluidity* of self-revelation" it encouraged. He favoured
first-person narration only for the short story or tale. These
narrators are usually reporters of some enigmatic behaviour
in other people, and the narrator's consciousness is used as a
convenient way to select and reflect on lives that if presented
from within would require much more textual space. When
James's first-person narrators focus on their *own* experience,
the question of their reliability usually becomes the under-

lying theme—most famously in *The Turn of the Screw.* The example of James in this respect encouraged later novelists to use "I" narrators to problematise the meaning of a narrative rather than, as in the classic confessional novel, to make it fluidly transparent. Novels written in the first person continue to occupy many rooms in the house of fiction throughout the twentieth century. Indeed, one has the impression that for the last few decades it has been the dominant narrative mode for literary fiction. Why that should have happened is a question I shall consider in the last section of this essay.

## III SURFACE AND DEPTH

The modern novel in the sense of moder*nist*—that is to say, the artistically innovatory, cutting-edge literary fiction that evolved in the first few decades of the twentieth century, in conscious reaction against the classic realist novel of the previous century; the kind of novel pioneered by Henry James, and carried forward in various ways by Joseph Conrad, Ford Madox Ford, James Joyce, Virginia Woolf, and D. H. Lawrence, among others*—manifested a general tendency to center narrative in the consciousnesses of its characters, and to *create* those characters through the representation of their subjective thoughts and feelings rather than by describing them objectively. Erich Auerbach, in *Mimesis,* his magisterial study of the representation of reality in Western literature from Homer and the Old Testament onwards, takes as his exemplary text for the modern period Virginia Woolf's novel *To the Lighthouse*

---

*E. M. Forster had some artistic aims in common with these writers, but does not quite belong in the same category, for reasons discussed in Chapter 4 below.

(1927), in which, as he says, "The world of objective facts has almost completely vanished, almost everything stated appears by way of reflection in the consciousness of the dramatis personae."[40] This technique implies a belief that reality inheres not in the common phenomenal world but in the perceptions of that world in individual minds. Describing the fiction of the Edwardian novelists Bennett, Galsworthy, and H. G. Wells, with its scrupulous descriptions of external appearances, Virginia Woolf asked rhetorically, in her essay on Modern Fiction, "Is life like this? Must novels be like this?" and answered her own question: "Look within and life, it seems, is very far from being 'like this.' Examine for a moment an ordinary mind on an ordinary day . . ." There follows that passage about the atoms of experience falling like a shower on the mind which I quoted earlier. "Look *within*," she exhorts. The heuristic direction of this kind of fiction is, one might say, always from outside to inside, from spoken to unspoken thought, from surface to depth.

Undoubtedly one of the crucial factors in this shift of emphasis in literary fiction was the development of psychoanalysis, especially the work of Freud and, to a lesser extent, Jung. It was Freud who first produced a plausible and persuasive account of human nature in which behaviour was chiefly accounted for by motives that were *hidden* in the secret recesses of the individual psyche, and hidden not just from observers, but often from the subject's own conscious mind. The idea of subconscious or unconscious motivation, of suppressed or repressed drives and desires which lie behind overt behaviour, and which may be traced in the jumbled and enigmatic narratives of dreams, was immensely stimulating to literary imaginations, as was the idea that these drives were more often than not sexual in origin—for the novel has always been especially interested in human sexuality and eagerly read for its revelations about the sexual lives and thoughts of its characters. Another potent idea for writers was that of a collective unconscious that connects us to the earliest stages of our evolutionary history and manifests itself in the archetypes of myth and legend. It wasn't necessary for writers to have actually read the psychoanalytical writings of Freud and his followers to be influenced by them. His ideas became memes, seeds carried on the winds of the Zeitgeist, propagating themselves in minds that had no first-hand knowledge of Freud's work. But we know, for instance, that Frieda Lawrence, who had close personal connections with the European psychoanalytical movement, introduced D. H. Lawrence to Freud's theories, especially the Oedipus Complex, and that this influenced the final version of *Sons and Lovers*. Virginia Woolf had close personal connections with the British psychoanalytical movement, through the Stracheys—James Strachey, brother of Lytton, was Freud's English translator. Though Woolf's essay "Freudian Fiction" is sceptical about the application of psychoanalytical theory to the representation of character in the novel, there was, as her biographer Hermione Lee observes, something "self-defensive" about this posture.[41] Both her life and her work have provided rich pickings for Freudian commentators.

Freud's theories fell on fertile literary ground partly because they had to some extent already been intuited by imaginative writers before him, as he himself acknowledged. "The poets and philosophers before me discovered the unconscious," he said. "What I discovered was the scientific method by which the unconscious can be studied." In fact the claim of Freudian psychoanalysis to be scientific has been hotly contested—most thoroughly perhaps by Richard Webster in *Why Freud Was Wrong* (1995). Arguably, the success of Freud's ideas as memes depended more on his literary skills than on the hard evidence he produced for their therapeutic efficacy. The factual accuracy of his famous case histories has been seriously questioned, but as narratives, in which the great psychoanalytical detective solves the apparently baffling enigmas presented by his patients, they exert the same spell as the classic tales of Sherlock Holmes— which Freud himself, rather suspiciously, much admired.[42]

Given the sceptical scrutiny to which Freud's writings have been subjected in recent times, I was surprised to find considerable respect for him among some of the leading scientific investigators of consciousness. One of the most uncompromising apologists for "strong" AI, Marvin Minsky of MIT, says: "Freud had the best theories, so far, next to mine, of what it takes to make a mind."[43] The distinguished and hardheaded neuroscientist Rodney Cotterill says:

> Freud came surprisingly close to divining the way in which the brain serves the senses, and the manner in which it stores records of experiences. Amongst his clairvoyant conjectures, mention should be made of his belief that nerve fibres carry signals to the brain, where the body's outer surface is appropriately represented . . . He saw the brain's neural elements as being capable of discharging when sufficiently excited . . . And he guessed that the neural elements are mutually separated by what he called contact barriers and we now call synapses.[44]

Most importantly, Freud's idea of the unconscious anticipated the discovery of cognitive scientists and neuroscientists that much of the brain activity that produces the effect of consciousness is hidden from us. V. S. Ramachandran says: "Freud's most valuable contribution was his discovery that your conscious mind is simply a façade and that you are completely unaware of what really goes on in your brain."[45] The neuroscientist Gerald Edelman recalls arguing with the molecular biologist Jacques Monod, who regarded Freud as a charlatan, "that, while perhaps not a scientist in our sense, Freud was a great intellectual pioneer, particularly in his views on the unconscious and its role in behaviour."[46]

The Freudian model of the mind was structured like geological strata: unconscious, ego, superego—in ascending order. It therefore encouraged the idea that consciousness had a dimension of depth, which it was the task of literature, as of psychoanalysis, to explore. For modernist writers, the effort to plumb these depths, to get closer to psychological reality, paradoxically entailed an abandonment of the traditional properties and strategies of literary realism. The traditional plot, which demonstrates that all effects have their logical causes, is discarded or destabilised, and poetic devices of symbolism and leitmotif and intertextual allusion are used instead to give formal unity to the representation of experience, which is itself seen as essentially chaotic. Ambiguity and obscurity permeate human behaviour in the stories of Henry James, Joseph Conrad, and Ford Madox Ford. The play of human memory disrupts and shuffles the chronological order of events in the minds of Joyce's characters, and Virginia Woolf's. D. H. Lawrence uses an incantatory symbolist style to base character on some deeper level than that of the ego. "You mustn't look in my novels for the old stable ego of the character," he writes to Edward Garnett in 1914. "There is another ego, according to whose action the individual is unrecognisable, and passes through, as it were, allotropic states which it needs a *deeper* sense than any we've been used to exercise, to discover are states of the same single radically-unchanged element" [italics mine].[47] In the Nighttown episode of *Ulysses* Joyce exploits the surreal substitutions, juxtapositions, and displacements of dream to represent the turmoil of Bloom's unconscious. In *Finnegans Wake* he went a step further and represented the whole of human history as a dream, in which every character and event is, in Freudian terms, overdetermined—that is, bears more than one signification, simultaneously. In that extraordinary work Joyce both demonstrated and exceeded the limits of the representation of consciousness in literary narrative.

The primary limitation is this: that verbal language is essentially linear. One word or word-group comes after another, and we apprehend their syntactically cumulative meaning lineally, in time. When we speak and listen, when we write and read, we are bound to this linear order. But we know intuitively, and cognitive science has confirmed, that consciousness itself is not linear. In computer terms the brain is a *parallel* processor running many programs simultaneously. In neurobiological terms it is a complex system of billions of neurons between which countless connections are being made simultaneously as long as we are conscious. Virginia Woolf's injunction to "record the atoms [of experience] as they fall upon the mind in the order in which they fall" is therefore flawed. The atoms do not fall in a discrete chronological order—they bombard us from all directions, and are dealt with simultaneously by different parts of the brain. "The temporal order of discriminations cannot be what fixes the subjective order in experience," says Daniel Dennett in *Consciousness Explained*.[48] His metaphor for the brain is Pandemonium, in which all the different areas are, as it were, shouting at once and competing for dominance.

Intuitively, Virginia Woolf knew this. In an interesting correspondence her friend Jacques Raverat, a painter, argued that
writing's essential linearity prevented it from representing the
complex multiplicity of a mental event, as a painting could.
She replied that she was trying to get away from the "formal
railway line of the sentence . . . people never did think or feel in
that way, but all over the place, in your way."[49] By breaking up
the formal railway line of the sentence, by the use of ellipses
and parentheses, by blurring the boundaries between what is
thought and what is spoken, and by switching point of view
and narrative voice with bewildering frequency—by these and
similar devices she tried to imitate in her fiction the elusiveness
of the phenomenon of consciousness. But she could never
entirely escape the sequential linearity of her medium. The
pun is perhaps the closest that verbal language can come to
mimicking the simultaneous input of heterogeneous information which is the normal state of consciousness before the
mind takes up the task of selecting and articulating some of
this information verbally; and by writing an entire narrative
text, *Finnegans Wake,* in a punning synthetic language of his
own invention, Joyce perhaps came closer than any writer had
done before to representing the extraordinary complexity of
the brain activity that goes on just below the surface of the
self-conscious mind. But the price of this was to sacrifice the
narrative cohesion which makes stories intelligible to us, and
therefore to take leave of the novel as a literary form.

The terms "postmodern" and "postmodernist" entered the
English language in the second half of the twentieth century
(the first, specifically architectural, citation in the Oxford English

Dictionary is dated 1949; and the first literary critical application is dated 1965). But there is a sense in which all artists, whether writers, painters, sculptors, or musicians, who started their careers after the great masterpieces of modernist art had been created were axiomatically "post-modern." The key figures in the first postmodern generation of English novelists were, I would suggest, Evelyn Waugh, Graham Greene, Henry Green, Anthony Powell, Christopher Isherwood, and George Orwell. They all began to write in the daunting shadow of James, Conrad, Joyce, Lawrence, Woolf; they admired and imitated and were influenced by them in various ways; but they also in due course reacted against them, as of course new generations of writers always do react against their literary parents. These writers do not constitute a "school." Though there are clearly affinities between some of them—between Waugh and Powell, for instance—they are all quite distinctive and their fictions have different personal and ideological sources. But what they have in common, to a greater or lesser extent, is a retreat from the modernist effort to represent subjective consciousness as faithfully as possible. They reverse the modernist privileging of depth over surface. There is a return in their novels to objective reporting of the external world, and a focus on what people say and do rather than what they think and feel. There is a striking readjustment of the ratio of dialogue to narrative, of direct speech to the rendering of characters' unspoken thoughts.

In the classic novel there was a kind of balance between these elements. In Jane Austen's or George Eliot's novels, for example, an exchange of dialogue between characters is customarily framed within a narrative description of the situation, including the body language of the speakers, and is followed by a passage in which the authorial narrator comments on the import of what was said, or reports the reflections of the protagonist on the import of what was said. In the modernist novel, typically, a line of dialogue will be followed by a long, intricate, densely written account of the private thoughts and feelings of the speaker or listener, which may last for a paragraph, or a couple of pages, before we come to the next line of direct speech; and it is not the authorial voice who speaks in these interpolated passages of introspection and analysis, but the inner voice of the character himself or herself who is the "center of consciousness," rendered in interior monologue or free indirect style, and mingled with the accents of other discourses, written and spoken, which belong to that character's mental world. That is what happens, for example, in the passage from "Hades" in Joyce's *Ulysses* that I analysed. And it happens in the passage Auerbach selected from Virginia Woolf's *To the Lighthouse*. This extract—the whole of section 5 of the first part of the novel—is too long to quote here in full. It shows Mrs. Ramsay sitting by the window of her living room, knitting a stocking for the lighthouse keeper's little boy, and using her own young son James, who is cutting pictures out of a catalogue, as a rough-and-ready guide to measure the size of the stocking. The passage contains about 1,500 words, but fewer than fifty of them consist of Mrs. Ramsay's direct speech, distributed over five speech acts:

1. "And even if it isn't fine tomorrow, it will be another day. And now stand up and let me measure your leg."
2. "My dear, stand still."
3. "Stand still, don't be tiresome."
4. "It's too short, ever so much too short."
5. "Let's find another picture to cut out."

It is notable that only Mrs. Ramsay speaks. No reply of James is reported, or even implied, though it seems implausible that he would be entirely silent in the circumstances. This intensifies the focus on Mrs. Ramsay and her inner life. The five remarks describe a small emotional arc in her relationship with her son: she begins by consoling him in motherly fashion about the prospects of the longed-for trip to the lighthouse, then she becomes irritated with him for fidgeting while she is trying to measure the stocking, then with herself because the stocking is too short, then she finally makes peace with James again. But this little scene between mother and son is overwhelmed with information that has little or nothing to do with it. In between these banal utterances of hers we are given a detailed and eloquent rendering of her thoughts and feelings about other members of her family and her friends and her house. The irritation she feels with James derives more from her gloomy private thoughts about the Swiss *au pair* who is homesick and whose father is dying than from the business of the stocking. There is a long parenthesis in which her friend Mr. Bankes is described speaking to her on the telephone, and then talking to himself about her after putting down the receiver. Auerbach comments that the punctuation is deviant: words spoken aloud sometimes lack quotation marks, while in other places there are quotation marks around silent thoughts.

You only have to open a novel by one of the next generation of novelists—Evelyn Waugh's *Vile Bodies* (1930), for example, or Anthony Powell's *Afternoon Men* (1931), and riffle through it, to see a great difference, just in the way the pages are laid out. There is a great deal more dialogue in proportion to description, and direct speech is clearly marked off from the narrative discourse by conventional indentation and quotation marks.

One whole chapter of *Vile Bodies* consists entirely of dialogue, apart from two short sentences: "Adam rang up Nina" and "Later Nina rang up Adam." In the first conversation the hero tells his fiancée he can't marry her immediately, as he has just promised to do by telegram.

> Adam rang up Nina.
> "Darling. I've been so happy about your telegram. Is it really true?
> "No, I'm afraid not."
> "The major *is* bogus."
> "Yes."
> "You haven't got any money?"
> "No."
> "We aren't going to be married today?"
> "No."
> "I see."
> "Well?"
> "I said, I see."
> "Is that all?"
> "Yes, that's all, Adam."
> "I'm sorry."
> "I'm sorry, too. Goodbye."
> "Goodbye, Nina."[50]

In the second conversation, later the same day, Nina tells Adam in the same clipped, offhand fashion that she's going to marry his best friend. The complete absence of authorial comment or any description of the thoughts and feelings of either party to these conversations is of course vital to their literary effect. It is a kind of negative eloquence, a rhetoric of abstention, that evokes a social milieu of people who are alienated, amoral, hedonistic, emotionally immature, spiritually empty—

the Bright Young Things of the Twenties, one of several generations that were described as Lost in the last century.

The style and tone of Anthony Powell's *Afternoon Men*, published the following year, are very similar. The hero, Atwater, has a dull job in a museum. He spends his spare time going to parties and getting drunk, having shallow affairs with women he doesn't much like, and mooning hopelessly after one called Susan Nunnery whom he does like. In this scene he has called on an artist friend who is living with a girl called Sophy.

> Atwater said: "Do you know Susan Nunnery well?"
> "What has she been doing?"
> "Somebody was talking about her last night."
> "Oh, yes. She was there last night, wasn't she?"
> "Yes."
> "Is she still living with Gilbert?"
> "Was she?"
> "I don't know," said Barlow. "Perhaps she wasn't. I can't keep up with girls like that."
> Atwater drank his tea. Sophy went out to get some more hot water. Barlow said:
> "Miriam was here yesterday. I think really I'd better marry her."
> "Why? Have you ruined her?"
> "No."
> "Why not?"
> "I didn't think she'd like me to."
> "She's a nice girl."
> "Yes, I shall certainly marry her."
> "Do you see much of her?"
> "No, not much."
> Sophy came in again.[51]

Again, like the passage from *Vile Bodies,* this is effective precisely because it stays on the surface of the situation, giving
the reader no privileged insights into the hero's thoughts and
feelings. In the first part of the dialogue we *infer* the frantic
longing and seething jealousy that lie behind Atwater's apparently casual questions about Susan, emotions only exacer-
bated by Barlow's vague and uninterested replies. The second
part is funny and shocking because of the complete absence of
any condemnation by Atwater of Barlow's selfishness—his
patronising attitude to Miriam and his readiness to betray
Sophy—either overtly in the dialogue, or privately in thought.
Of course if there were any explicit condemnation by either
Atwater or the narrator, it would seem very heavy-handed,
and would destroy the comedy. The reader has to supply the
emotion and moral outrage that are missing from the text.
This device is used to brilliant effect in the climax to the novel,
when a character called Pringle apparently commits suicide by
swimming out to sea, and the friends he is entertaining at the
time, including Atwater and Barlow, fail utterly to respond to
the crisis, either emotionally or practically.

Evelyn Waugh claimed that the pioneer of this kind of
fiction, in which meaning is implied through conversational
nuances, was Ronald Firbank. In an essay published in 1929,
Waugh praised Firbank for achieving "a new, balanced inter-
relation of subject and form," thus solving "the aesthetic
problem of representation in fiction . . . Other solutions are
offered," Waugh concluded, obviously thinking of the modernist novel, "but in them the author has been forced into
a subjective attitude to his material; Firbank remained objective."[52]

Among the writers whom Waugh saw as developing the technical discoveries of Ronald Firbank, he mentions Ernest Hemingway. I doubt whether Hemingway knew the work of Firbank, but he himself certainly influenced Waugh and his contemporaries. Hemingway read and admired and cultivated the acquaintance of the great modernist writers like Eliot, Pound, Joyce, and Gertrude Stein, but he wrote a very different kind of fiction, especially in his short stories. Superficially it looked like slice-of-life vernacular realism, but it was in fact charged with a kind of intensity and resonance of association found in Symbolist writing. He thus provided a bridge between the aesthetics of high modernism and the preference of the young post–Great War generation of English novelists for staying on the surface rather than probing the depths of experience. Hemingway was, he said, developing "a theory that you could omit anything if you knew that you omitted it and the omitted part would strengthen the story and make people feel more than they understood."[53] What Hemingway omitted from his stories was all the psychological analysis and introspection that one finds in James or Joyce or Woolf. He stays scrupulously on the surface, describing behaviour, places, persons in deceptively simple, apparently denotative language, and setting down speech with what seems like colloquial authenticity. In fact this language, in both narrative and dialogue, is full of patterns of repetition, lexical and phonological, through which simple synecdoches and metonymies generate metaphorical associations without ever being overtly metaphorical. The apparently objective representation of the world in this fiction is like the tip of an iceberg, beneath which there is a huge mass of invisible subjective emotion which the reader gradually apprehends. The trout-fishing so exactly described in "Big Two-hearted River," it slowly becomes clear, is a ritual to exorcise the traumatic memories of a war veteran. The trivial bickering of the couple on the Spanish railway platform in "Hills Like White Elephants" conceals, then reveals, a bitter emotional conflict over the girl's unwanted pregnancy. In "The Killers," the contemptuous badinage of the two gangsters in black overcoats who walk into the provincial diner, and order a meal while they prepare a murderous ambush, is a chilling index of their brutal power, and of the terror they generate in the other unwilling participants:

> George put the two platters, one of ham and eggs, the other of bacon and eggs, on the counter. He set down two side-dishes of fried potatoes and closed the wicket into the kitchen.
>
> "Which is yours?" he asked Al.
>
> "Don't you remember?"
>
> "Ham and eggs."
>
> "Just a bright boy," Max said. He leaned forward and took the ham and eggs. Both men ate with their gloves on. George watched them eat.
>
> "What are *you* looking at?" Max looked at George.
>
> "Nothing."
>
> "The hell you were. You were looking at me."
>
> "Maybe the boy meant it for a joke, Max," Al said.
>
> George laughed.
>
> "*You* don't have to laugh," Max said to him. "*You* don't have to laugh at all, see?"
>
> "All right," said George.
>
> "So he thinks it's all right." Max turned to Al. "He thinks it's all right. That's a good one."
>
> "Oh, he's a thinker," Al said. They went on eating.[54]

Though there is some black humour in "The Killers," Heming-way's vision was essentially tragic. Waugh's and Powell's was essentially comic. Yet there is an affinity of technique between the last three passages I have quoted. In all of them dialogue dominates; the narrative observes only the surface of human behaviour; and the emotional and moral significance of the action is all implied.

The passage from "The Killers" reminds one irresistibly of a scene from a gangster film, and indeed two movies have been made based on Hemingway's story. It seems likely that the stylistic turn of the novel, away from depth to surface, was connected with the emergence of a new narrative medium in the twentieth century—cinema. Compared with prose fiction or narrative poetry or drama, film is most tied to representing the visible world, and least well adapted to representing consciousness, which is invisible. Although voice-over interior monologue can be and has been used in films, it goes against the grain of the medium, and cannot be used extensively and repeatedly without becoming obtrusive. The principal means by which film conveys the thoughts and feelings of its characters are (1) dialogue—though in the era of silent movies this was restricted to a few captions; (2) nonverbal acting—gesture, body language, facial expressions, and so forth—by the performers; (3) suggestive imagery in the setting of the action or the way it is lit and photographed; (4) music. The combination of all these channels of communication operating together and sometimes simultaneously can have a very powerful emotional effect, but it is not semantically fine-grained—it is not capable of the precise descriptions and subtle discriminations of a character's mental life that we find in the classic and modern novel. In film, the subjective inner life of the characters has to be implied rather than explicitly verbalised—as in the scenes from prose fiction, consisting mainly of dialogue, that I have just quoted.

It cannot be coincidental that the generation of novelists I have been discussing was the first to grow up with the movies, to acquire the habit of movie-going; and that several of them became involved in the art of film. Evelyn Waugh, for instance, acted in an amateur movie called "The Scarlet Woman" made by a group of Oxford undergraduates. His first significant piece of published fiction, *The Balance: A Yarn of the Good Old Days of Broad Trousers and High Necked Jumpers* (1925), consists mostly of dialogue and partly of the scenario of a silent film and the comments of a cinema audience that is watching it.[55] One of the comic highlights of *Vile Bodies* is the making of a historical film by a venal and incompetent commercial producer. In his article on Ronald Firbank's novels, Waugh compared them to "cinema films in which the relation of caption and photograph is directly reversed; occasionally a brief vivid image flashes out to illuminate and explain the flickering succession of spoken words."[56] Henry Green described his novel, *Living* (1929), to a correspondent as "written in a very condensed kind of way in short paragraphs ... A kind of very disconnected cinema film."[57] According to his friend and fellow Etonian Anthony Powell, Henry Green, or Henry Yorke (to use his real name), did very little work as an undergraduate, but made "a point of watching a film every afternoon and every evening of his Oxford life, changes of programme in the city's three cinemas making this just possible."[58] Even if this is only half true, it is still impressive testimony of film-addiction. Evelyn Waugh, in spite of his often declared scorn for the modern world in general, and Hollywood in particular, retained the habit of attending the local cinema every week in his postwar existence as a country gentleman.

Christopher Isherwood famously described his narrative stance in *Goodbye to Berlin* as, "I am a camera, with its shutter open, quite passive, recording, not thinking." It is not clear whether he was alluding to still or moving pictures in this image. But he says in his lightly fictionalised autobiography *Lions and Shadows,* "I had always been fascinated by films . . . I was a born film fan"; and that "if you are a novelist and want to watch your scene taking place visibly before you, it is simplest to project it on to an imaginary screen."[59] In due course Isherwood became a screenwriter himself in Hollywood.

The emphasis on dialogue and external appearances in these novelists, leaving thought and feeling to be implied, was not the only effect of cinema on the novel. It also brought story back into literary fiction. The novel of consciousness tended to neglect story, or diminish its importance, for obvious reasons. The deeper you go, as a writer, into the minds of your characters—the more detailed and refined your registration of their thoughts, feelings, sensations, memories, scruples—the slower the narrative tempo becomes, and the less action there is. Moreover, the machinery of the traditional plot may be seen as a distraction from the true business of the literary novelist, to create the sense of "felt life." That of course was Henry James's aim, and his phrase, and he himself was painfully aware that his work suffered in popularity because it was perceived to lack narrative interest. There is something poignant and slightly desperate in his argument, in the preface to the New York edition of *The Portrait of a Lady,* that it is the character and sensibility of Isabel Archer that makes what happens to her interesting. In comparison to "the moving accident, of battle or murder and sudden death," he admits, "her adventures are . . . mild. Without her sense of them, her sense for them, as one may say, they are next to nothing at all; but isn't the beauty and the difficulty just in showing their mystic conversion by that sense, conversion into the stuff of drama or, even more delightful word still, of 'story'?"[60] The wider reading public, alas, was never convinced. Even in a writer like Conrad, who actually dealt with "accident . . . battle . . . murder and sudden death," the gratifications of the conventional adventure story are deliberately frustrated, inverted, problematised, by complex time shifts, shifts of point of view, elaborate framing devices, and a densely written, syntactically complicated, metaphorically rich prose style—all of which together retard and obstruct the delivery of simple narrative excitement. In Joyce and Woolf, narrative is pared down to a minimum; the great crises in the lives of the characters are alluded to fragmentarily in memory, while the immediate focus is on the habitual and the quotidian. It is not surprising that the action of the greatest of all stream-of-consciousness novels takes place on one ordinary day.

The cinema, however, was from the beginning a popular narrative medium which told exciting stories of a traditional kind. Far from slowing down the normal tempo of human existence to make room for psychological depth, as the literary novel of consciousness does, the cinema, and especially the early silent cinema, artificially speeded it up, keeping its characters in a continuous state of thrilling or farcical jeopardy. Continual exposure to this kind of material must have had its effect on the writers who came of age in the 1920s, and encouraged them to see no necessary contradiction between writing literary fiction and telling a good story.

The fascination of this generation of writers with film, and its influence on their imaginations, did not mean however that their novels always translated successfully to the screen. Graham Greene is an interesting case in point. He too frequented the cinema from an early age; he was for several years in the 1930s a film critic in London, and so saw hundreds of films in the line of professional duty. He wrote numerous screenplays, some original, some adaptations of his own fiction, and almost every one of his novels has been made into a feature film. But in this considerable body of cinematic work, there is only one really great film, *The Third Man*, which Greene scripted himself and originally conceived as a movie, though he later published a novella based on his film treatment.

The influence of the cinema on Greene's fictional technique has been noted often enough: the fast cutting from scene to scene, his eye for the telling synecdochic detail (the rhetorical equivalent of the close-up shot), his preference for exciting plots derived from popular cinematic subgenres—the gangster movie, the spy thriller, the whodunit, the Western. Even his religious novels have these structures. *The Power and the Glory* is a spiritual Western. *The End of the Affair* is a detective story with a Divine culprit. But unlike the other novelists of his generation I have mentioned, the Catholic Greene did not turn away entirely from depth in order to render the surface of life; he remained interested in representing the consciousness of his characters, partly because he regarded them very literally as having "souls," capable of salvation and damnation. And he saw no contradiction in aiming at both social and psychological realism. His compliment to François Mauriac is an implicit manifesto for his own fiction:

He is a writer for whom the visible world has not ceased to exist, whose characters have the solidity and importance of men with souls to save or lose, and a writer who claims the traditional and essential right of a novelist, to comment, to express his views.[61]

Greene's most powerful novels are those in which the implied author identifies with characters who have transgressed the limits of normal civilised society, and are racked with moral and metaphysical anxiety. He takes us inside their minds in free indirect style, but lends them some of his own eloquence, using the privilege of the traditional "omniscient" narrator. For example, here is a passage about the Catholic teenage gangster Pinkie Brown, in *Brighton Rock,* driving the pathetically devoted waiflike Rose to what she supposes to be a suicide pact, but which he intends to be a murder by which he will cover the traces of an earlier crime:

The car lurched on to the main road; he turned the nose to Brighton. An enormous emotion beat on him; it was like something trying to get in, the pressure of gigantic wings against the glass. *Dona Nobis pacem.* He withstood it, with all the bitter force of the school bench, the cement playground, the St Pancras waiting room, Dallow's and Judy's secret lust, and the cold, unhappy moment on the pier. If the glass broke, if the beast—whatever it was—got in, God knows what it would do. He had a sense of huge havoc—the confession, the penance and the sacrament—an awful distraction, and he drove blind into the rain.[62]

Pinkie is experiencing here what Mauriac called "the good temptation"—the temptation to repent. His thoughts are dominated by religious imagery: the wings of the Holy Spirit,

conventionally portrayed as a dove, magnified and fused with
Francis Thompson's figure of the Hound of Heaven, and
mixed up with echoes of the Latin mass and synecdochic flashbacks to Pinkie's violent, deprived childhood and youth.
There's no way this rich matrix of allusion and association
could be conveyed through visual imagery or spoken dialogue
alone. One reason why so many of the films of Greene's novels disappoint is that without the powerful and persuasive rhetoric of his narrative voice, the stories can seem contrived and
melodramatic.

Writing in 1956, the French novelist Alain Robbe-Grillet
invoked the cinematic adaptation of novels to advocate art
that stays on the surface and to denounce what he called "the
old myths of depth."[63] "We know that the whole literature of
the novel was based on these myths," he says. "The writer's
traditional role consisted in excavating Nature, in burrowing
deeper and deeper to reach some ever more intimate strata."
But, "not only do we no longer consider the world as our own
. . . we no longer even believe in its 'depth' . . . the *surface* of
things has ceased to be for us the mask of their heart, a sentiment that led to every kind of metaphysical transcendence."
Robbe-Grillet was an agronomist before he was a novelist or a
screenplay writer, and perhaps his scientific training lies behind his uncompromising materialism, which is antihumanist
as well as atheistic. Even existentialism is dismissed as sentimental and self-indulgent. The world, he says, "is neither significant nor absurd. It *is*, quite simply . . . Around us, defying
the noisy pack of our animistic or protective adjectives, things
*are there.*" And film can remind us of that fact even against its

own intentions. In narrative films, as in the novels on which they are often based, the images are laden with human meanings: "the empty chair becomes only absence or expectation, the hand on the shoulder becomes a sign of friendliness, the bars on the window only the impossibility of leaving." But in the cinema you actually *see* these things, and the effect, Robbe-Grillet claims, is to make the human significations attached to them seem superfluous. "What affects us, what persists in our memory, what appears as essential and irreducible . . . are the gestures themselves, the objects, the movements, and the outlines, to which the image has suddenly (and unintentionally) restored their *reality*." To capture this reality, the novel, according to Robbe-Grillet, must purge itself of language of a "visceral, analogical, or incantatory character." Instead, "the visual or descriptive adjective, the word that contents itself with measuring, locating, limiting, defining, indicates a difficult but most likely direction for a new art of the novel." In short, Robbe-Grillet is calling for a literature without qualia. It's a bracing argument, though the kind of fiction that Robbe-Grillet himself wrote in accordance with it seems to me almost unendurably tedious, except when the human emotions he tried to expunge manage to insinuate themselves back into the text. And I would say the same of the celebrated film he made with Alain Resnais, *Last Year at Marienbad.*

As I observed earlier, there are many postmodernisms, and they are not all experimental. Some were simply anti-modernist. The dominant British novelists of the 1950s, for instance—Kingsley Amis, John Wain, C. P. Snow, William Cooper, John Braine, Angus Wilson, Alan Sillitoe—used fictional forms which harked back to the Victorian or Edwardian novel of social realism, and several of them mounted critical attacks on modernist literary experiment. Their representation of consciousness was entirely traditional in method, and they aimed at originality only in the experience with which they dealt and the distinctive verbal styles in which they described it. The novelists of the previous generation also tended, as their careers lengthened, to revert to the norm in terms of narrative technique. The later work of Waugh, Powell, and Isherwood, for instance, maintains a conservative balance between surface and depth. Graham Greene's work always did; and so, after some unhappy Joycean experiments in *The Clergyman's Daughter*, did the novels of George Orwell. Of this group, only Henry Green persevered with the dialogue novel to the end of his writing life, in books like *Nothing* (1950) and *Doting* (1952). In two radio talks broadcast at about that time, he defended this method, and criticised the fictional convention by which the narrator claims a privileged knowledge of the consciousness of the characters: "Do we know, in life, what other people are really like?" he asked. "I very much doubt it. We certainly do not know what other people are thinking and feeling. How then can the novelist be so sure?" Henry Green was not always faithful to his own prescription. His *Concluding,* for instance, published in 1948, is notable for sudden interventions by the authorial voice telling us what lies behind the speech and actions of the characters, often in bizarre extended metaphors, for example:

"Adams won't like this," she said, and turned with a smile which was for him alone to let him take her, and helped his heart find hers by fastening her mouth on his as though she were an octopus that had lost its arms to the propellers of a tug, and had only its mouth now with which, in a world of the hunted, to hang on to wrecked spars.[64]

One could say that the baroque extravagance of the image exposes and undermines the pretence of authorial omniscience, that it is therefore a metafictional gesture, what the Russian Formalists called a "baring of the device." Certainly metafiction has been a favourite resource of many postmodernist novelists, as different as John Fowles, Muriel Spark, Malcolm Bradbury, John Barth, and Kurt Vonnegut. By openly admitting and indeed drawing attention to the fictionality of their texts, they free themselves to use all the conventions of the traditional novel, including omniscient insights into the consciousness of their characters, without laying themselves open to accusations of bad faith.

Henry Green's argument that, because in real life we can't know what other people are thinking and feeling, novelists shouldn't pretend to do so in writing fiction, is actually voiced by my cognitive scientist, Ralph Messenger, in the passage from *Thinks* . . . that I quoted in the second part of this essay. It may seem simplistic, but it perhaps helps to explain the increasing popularity of first-person narration in fiction in the postmodern period. Both the classic novel and the modernist novel took on the challenge of telling a story from several points of view, representing the consciousness of more than one character, and doing so in what was basically a third-person narrative discourse, even if it might contain some elements in the form of interior monologue. If you jot down a list of classic fiction of the nineteenth and early twentieth centuries, first-person novels modelled formally on the confession or autobiography

are in a distinct minority. But in the second half of the twentieth century it seems to become an increasingly favoured narrative method. It can, of course, take many different forms, and
can be applied to many different aesthetic ends. There is, for
instance, the autobiographical *roman fleuve* for which Proust
provided the great model, imitated later by English writers like
Anthony Powell and C. P. Snow, though they were more interested in the surface of social life, and less interested in the
exploration of psychological depth than was Proust. In *A
Dance to the Music of Time* and the *Strangers and Brothers* series,
the autobiographical narrator acts primarily as an observant
reporter of other people's lives, and is a kind of surrogate for
the old omniscient authorial narrator of classic nineteenth-
century fiction. (Sometimes indeed C. P. Snow's Lewis Eliot
claims an implausibly certain knowledge of the motivation of
his friends and colleagues.) At the opposite aesthetic pole from
these panoramic social novels are the disturbing monologues
of the late Beckett, in which the narrator seems to be a consciousness almost totally deprived of sensory input, and with a
fading memory, condemned to go on narrating without anything tangible to narrate:

> . . . if only there was a thing, but there it is, there is not, they
> took away things when they departed, they took away
> nature, there was never anyone, anyone but me, anything
> but me, talking of me, impossible to stop, impossible to go
> on, but I must go on, I'll go on, without anyone, without
> anything, but me, but my voice . . .[65]

The most common kind of first-person novel is still the fictitious autobiography or confession: Orwell's *Coming up for Air*,
Salinger's *Catcher in the Rye*, Nabokov's *Lolita*, Sillitoe's *Saturday*

*Night and Sunday Morning,* Kazuo Ishiguro's *The Remains of the Day,* and Tim Parks's *Europa* are some notable examples from different decades. Some of the narrators of these novels are transparently sincere, some are unreliable and self-betraying. Sometimes their prose style is elaborately literary, and sometimes racily colloquial. When first-person narration is combined with a focus on "surface" rather than "depth"—when, that is, the consciousness that is revealed by the first-person narrative contains none of the emotions and values that we expect to find there—a peculiarly disturbing effect of alienation can be produced, especially when violent death is involved. Camus's *The Outsider* is a classic instance of this kind of novel, which has inspired many others. Striking contemporary examples are *The Butcher Boy* (1992) by Patrick MacCabe and *Morven Callar* (1996) by the young Scottish writer Alan Warner.

Nicholson Baker's *The Mezzanine* (1988) is an original and highly entertaining postmodernist variation on the Proustian autobiographical novel. The anonymous narrator recalls a trivial action that took place five years earlier, namely, going out in his lunch break from the office where he worked to buy a shoelace to replace one that had snapped. This exiguous story is expanded to the length of a short novel partly by long digressions and footnotes in the tradition of *Tristram Shandy,* and partly by the immense detail with which the narrator describes very ordinary objects and processes. For example:

> Attempting to staple a thick memo, and looking forward, as you begin to lean on the brontosaural head of the stapler arm, to the three phases of the act—
>
> *First,* before the stapler arm makes contact with the paper, the resistance of the spring that keeps the arm held up; then, *second,* the moment when the small independent

unit in the staple arm noses into the paper and begins to force the two points of the staple into and through it; and *third*, the felt crunch, like the chewing of an ice cube, as the twin tines of the staple emerge from the underside of the paper and are bent by the two troughs of the template in the stapler's base, curving inwards in a crab's embrace of your memo, and finally disengaging from the machine completely—

but finding, as you lean on the stapler with your elbow locked and your breath held and it slumps toothlessly to the paper, that it has run out of staples. How could something this consistent, this incremental, betray you? (But then you are consoled: you get to reload it, laying bare the stapler arm and dropping a long zithering row of staples into place; and later, on the phone, you get to toy with the piece of the staples you couldn't fit into the stapler, breaking it into small segments, making them dangle on a hinge of glue.[66]

Baker's verbal descriptions of such qualia are remarkable for several reasons. They combine a scientific grasp of the mechanical with a poetic gift of metaphor, so they are both exact and lyrical, literary equivalents of pop-art's celebration of consumer goods. And whereas in Proust the evocation of qualia is always a route to the recovery of personal emotions and personal history by association, in *The Mezzanine* the emphasis is insistently on the qualia themselves, on the repeatable sensations afforded by manufactured physical objects like staplers. The shoelace that breaks, the narrator tells us, belonged to a pair of shoes bought for him by his father some years previously, "so the breakage was a sentimental milestone of sorts" (p. 15). This offhand reference to the past is not followed up by a nostalgic portrait of the father, or an account of the narrator's relationship with him. The narrator is much more interested in the fact that the other shoelace on the same pair of shoes had snapped the previous day—"the near simultaneity was very exciting—it made the variables of private life seem suddenly graspable and law-abiding" (p. 15)—and speculates about what causes laces to break: walking or pulling? "It was conceivable, though scary to imagine, that the pull-fray and the walk-flex model mingled their coefficients so subtly that human agency would never accurately apportion cause" (p. 28). There is a suggestion in the novel that the narrator is emotionally retarded or immature, but he could equally well be regarded as a kind of comic equivalent of Camus's Outsider. Just as Meursault finally accepts his imminent and meaningless death and lays his "heart open to the benign indifference of the universe," so the "I" of *The Mezzanine* realises that

> I was now permanently arrested at an intermediate stage of personal development . . . I was the sort of man who stood in a subway car and thought about buttering toast—buttering raisin toast, even: when the high, crisp scrape of the butter knife is muted by occasional contact with the soft, heat-blimped forms of the raisins, and when, if you cut across a raisin, it will sometimes fall right out, still intact though dented, as you lift the slice. I was the sort of person whose biggest discoveries were likely to be tricks to applying toiletries while fully dressed. I was a man, but I was not nearly the magnitude of man I had hoped to be. (p. 54)

In one sense *The Mezzanine* is a novel almost entirely about consciousness, since almost nothing happens in it; but the consciousness it reveals is totally absorbed by the surfaces of things, even the surface of a piece of toast.

I haven't done any statistical analysis, but my impression is that a majority of literary novels published in the last couple of decades have been written in the first person. This first struck me in 1989, when I was chairman of the judges of the Booker Prize. We read (or partly read) over a hundred novels and finally chose a shortlist of six. Only after the shortlist meeting did I realise that five of them had "I" narrators: Margaret Atwood's *Cat's Eye*, John Banville's *The Book of Evidence*, Sybille Bedford's *Jigsaw*, Rose Tremain's *Restoration*, and the winner, Kazuo Ishiguro's *The Remains of the Day*. (The exception was *A Disaffection* by James Kelman.) A. S. Byatt, writing recently about the historical novel, observed: "It is perhaps no accident that my exemplary 'modern' texts are all written in the first person—a first person preoccupied with the desirability and impossibility of objectivity and truthfulness," and felt obliged to defend her own preference for the "unfashionable Victorian third-person narrator."[67]

There does seem to be an increasing reluctance among literary novelists to assume the narrative stance of godlike omniscience that is implied by any third-person representation of consciousness, however covert and impersonal. Instead they prefer to create character as a "voice," reporting his or her experience in his or her own words. Where third-person and first-person narration are combined, the latter usually has the last word. In *Atonement* (2001), Ian McEwan, who has tended to favour first-person narration in his previous novels and stories, seems to be telling his story in a rather old-fashioned way, entering into the consciousness of several different characters, and rendering their experience in third-person discourse that makes extensive use of free indirect style. But an epilogue written in the first person reveals that the whole book up to that point has been written by one of the characters, who is herself a novelist, and who admits to having departed from the "facts" in certain crucial respects. What seemed to be a conventional realistic novel turns out after all to be a postmodernist metafiction. Margaret Atwood performed a similar trick in *The Blind Assassin* (2000).

Even Philip Roth, who in his impressive trilogy *American Pastoral, I Married a Communist,* and *The Human Stain* addresses the social and political history of postwar America with something of the scope and ambition of classic nineteenth-century fiction, prefers to use his alter ego Nathan Zuckerman as narrator, rather than claim direct authorial knowledge of the minds and hearts of his characters. Zuckerman reports, reconstructs, imagines the inner lives of the characters just as a novelist would—because he *is* a novelist. But he is also an alibi that the author can claim if held to account for any of the opinions stated in the text. Roth's latest work, *The Dying Animal* (discussed below in Chapter 9), is another ingenious variation on the first-person novel, this time a dramatic monologue.

In a world where nothing is certain, in which transcendental belief has been undermined by scientific materialism, and even the objectivity of science is qualified by relativity and uncertainty, the single human voice, telling its own story, can seem the only authentic way of rendering consciousness. Of course in fiction this is just as artful, or artificial, a method as writing about a character in the third person; but it creates an illusion of reality, it commands the willing suspension of the reader's disbelief, by modelling itself on the discourses of personal witness: the confession, the diary, autobiography, the memoir, the deposition. And it is not coincidental that the boundary between first-person literary fiction and autobiography is becoming increasingly blurred. Some of the most interesting and widely acclaimed books of recent years in Britain and America have been of a kind sometimes called "life writing"—memoirs or confessions that read like novels, that use many of the techniques of novels, that are often written by novelists, or writers who subsequently became novelists, using material that in earlier times would probably have been converted into third-person fiction. Recent examples are Blake Morrison's *And When Did You Last See Your Father?* Nick Hornby's *Fever Pitch,* Nicholson Baker's *U and I,* Martin Amis's *Experience,* Tobias Wolff's *This Boy's Life,* Paul Theroux's *Sir Vidia's Shadow,* Lorna Sage's *Bad Blood,* and Dave Eggers's *A Heartbreaking Work of Staggering Genius.*\*

"Postmodernism" is sometimes used in a very broad sense to include a whole range of cultural styles, attitudes, and arguments: deconstruction, post-industrialism, consumerism, mul-

---

\*The most talked-about American novel of 2001, however, Jonathan Franzen's *The Corrections,* interestingly bucks this trend. In telling his story of the fraught relations between an elderly American couple and their three grown-up children, set against the febrile economic boom of the nineties, Franzen moves confidently between the five principal characters, rendering their divergent points of view with the authorial amplitude and eloquence of classic fiction, while drawing knowledgeably on the concepts and language of contemporary neuroscience to describe and defamiliarise mental processes. This ambitious and impressive novel, together with Ian McEwan's *Atonement,* may conceivably herald, or encourage, a return to the third-person novel of consciousness in postmodern literary fiction.

ticulturalism, quantum physics, cybernetics, the Internet, and so on. Most of these phenomena and ways of thinking deny the existence of universals in human nature. They regard the concepts of "soul" or "spirit," and even the secular idea of the "self" which humanism developed from the Judeo-Christian religious tradition, as culturally and historically determined. The anthropologist Clifford Geertz, for instance, says:

> The Western conception of the person as a bounded, unique, more or less integrated motivational and cognitive universe, a dynamic center of awareness, emotion, judgment and action organized into a distinctive whole and set contrastively against a social and natural background is, however incorrigible it may seem to us, a rather peculiar idea within the world's cultures.[68]

Well, maybe it is; but how many of those cultures have produced great novels that were not formally derived from the Western literary tradition? In a backhanded way, Geertz has provided an exemplary definition of "character" as we encounter it in the classic novel, and in most modern literary fiction.

This idea of the person, whether in real life or in fictional representations, has come under attack from both the humanities and science in recent times. There is, for instance, a certain affinity between the poststructuralist literary theory that maintains that the human subject is entirely constructed by the discourses in which it is situated, and the cognitive science view that regards human self-consciousness as an epiphenomenon of brain activity. Daniel Dennett discovered this when he happened to read a novel of mine in the course of developing the thesis of *Consciousness Explained:* "It is certainly an idea whose time has come. Imagine my mixed emotions when I discovered that before I could get my version of it properly published in a book, it had already been satirized in a novel, David Lodge's *Nice Work*. It is apparently a hot theme among the deconstructionists."[69] He then quotes the following passage about the heroine of the novel, a young lecturer in English Literature called Robyn Penrose:

> According to Robyn, (or, more precisely, according to the writers who have influenced her thinking on these matters), there is no such thing as the "Self" on which capitalism and the classic novel are founded—that is to say, a finite, unique soul or essence that constitutes a person's identity; there is only a subject position in an infinite web of discourses—the discourses of power, sex, family, science, religion, poetry, etc. And by the same token, there is no such thing as an author, that is to say, one who originates a work of fiction *ab nihilo* . . . in the famous words of Jacques Derrida (famous to people like Robyn, anyway) *"il n'y a pas de hors-texte,"* there is nothing outside the text. There are no origins, there is only production, and we produce our "selves" in language. Not *"you are what you eat"* but *"you are what you speak"* or, rather, *"you are what speaks you,"* is the axiomatic basis of Robyn's philosophy, which she would call, if required to give it a name, "semiotic materialism."[70]

Dennett observes that he doesn't subscribe to all of these views: "I wouldn't say there is *nothing* outside the text. There are, for instance, all the bookcases, buildings, bodies, bacteria . . ." This insistence on the objective reality of the material world defines an important difference between most scientists and the post-structuralist/postmodernist theorists who hold that all knowledge, including science, is provisional because culturally constructed. The former get particularly angry when the latter invoke quantum physics and the uncertainty principle to support their arguments, as a celebrated intellectual hoax recently demonstrated.[71] Still, there is enough convergence between Dennett's theory of consciousness and Robyn's theory of the subject to constitute a formidable challenge to the idea of human nature on which most literary fiction is based.

One must concede that the Western humanist concept of the autonomous individual self is not universal, eternally given, and valid for all time and all places, but is a product of history and culture. This doesn't, however, necessarily mean that it isn't a good idea, or that its time has passed. A great deal of what we value in civilized life depends upon it. We also have to acknowledge that the individual self is not a fixed and stable entity, but is constantly being created and modified in consciousness through interaction with others and the world. It may be, therefore, that every time we try to describe the conscious self we misrepresent it because we are trying to fix something that is always changing; but really we have no alternative, any more than the physicist has any alternative to bringing about the collapse of the wave function when he makes an observation, or the deconstructionist has any alternative to using language which she claims is bound to undermine its ostensible claims to meaning. My novels are the products of numerous revisions, and I know that I could have gone on revising them indefinitely, but a published novel is simply more useful as information than a collection of its various drafts would be, and certainly more useful than a novel which is never published because its author never stopped revising it.

# chapter two

# LITERARY CRITICISM & LITERARY CREATION

The word "criticism" covers a great many types of reflection on literature, from the most private and casual to the most public and systematic. It includes the activity of reading itself, inasmuch as reading a literary text is a process of continuous interpretation and evaluation. The mere decision to go on reading a novel or poem to its end is a kind of critical act. In this large sense, criticism is, as T. S. Eliot observed, "as inevitable as breathing."[1] But for the most part I am concerned here with criticism as the written articulation of the reading process in the form of reviews, essays, books, which may themselves take many different forms and have many different objectives: descriptive, prescriptive, polemical, theoretical, and so forth. Criticism covers a huge variety of discourses, and when generalizations are made about the relation between it and creative writing, or between it and scientific discourse, it is usually a particular type of criticism that is being referred to, implicitly or explicitly.

There are, I suggest, four main ways in which the relationship between creative writing and criticism has been perceived:

1. Criticism as *complementary to* creative writing.
2. Criticism as *opposed to* creative writing.
3. Criticism as *a kind of* creative writing.
4. Criticism as *a part of* creative writing.

The first of these perspectives—criticism as complementary to creative writing—is the classical, commonsense view of the matter. It may be expounded as follows. There are writers and there are critics. Each group has its task, its priorities, its privileges. Writers produce original works of imagination. Critics classify, evaluate, interpret, and analyse them. This model usually accords priority to literary creation. The conventional bibliographical distinction between primary and secondary sources implies that creative writers could do without critics—indeed, they seemed to manage very well without them until the Renaissance—but that critics are axiomatically dependent on creative writers for something to criticise. Subscribing to this hierarchical distinction does not, however, necessarily make critics humble.

The absence of anything much resembling literary criticism before the Renaissance, apart from a few treatises on rhetoric and general poetics, does not imply that the critical activity, "something as inevitable as breathing," did not go on then. Of course it did. But when the production of manuscript books was slow, costly, and laborious, few people felt it was worthwhile recording their responses to literary texts in permanent form. The invention of printing, and its development into a very cost-effective industrial process, encouraged the publication and circulation of literary criticism on a vast scale. Much of it has been trivial and ephemeral. But the invention of printing also encouraged the production of much trivial and ephemeral creative writing. In this situation good criticism is seen to have a vital cultural function, namely, filtering out the good literature from the bad, defining and preserving the literary canon. This has been the traditional view of the function of criticism in the academy.

Matthew Arnold was perhaps the first English writer to formulate in an influential way the idea of criticism having this high cultural mission. But he was not just concerned with policing the canon. He stressed the value of criticism in creating a climate conducive to the production of good new writing. In his essay "The Function of Criticism at the Present Time," he says:

> Life and the world being in modern times very complex things, the creation of a modern poet, to be worth much, implies a great critical effort behind it.[2]

And he goes so far as to say that in a period of creative sterility or mediocrity, such as he perceived the second half of the nineteenth century to be in English literature, it might be more useful to be a critic than to be a creative writer. For Arnold, criticism was more or less synonymous with the pursuit of humane knowledge. It was, he said, "a disinterested endeavour to learn and propagate the best that is known and thought in the world."[3] T. S. Eliot, writing his own "Function of Criticism" essay with Arnold's very much in mind, used criticism in a more restricted and more familiar sense, to mean "the eluci-

dation of works of art and the correction of taste."[4] Speaking
of his experience of teaching adult education classes, he says,
"I have found only two ways of leading any pupils to like anything with the right liking: to present them with a selection of
the simplest kind of facts about a work—its conditions, its setting, its genesis—or else to spring the work on them in such a
way that they were not prepared to be prejudiced against it."[5]
Eliot thus gave his blessing to two very different schools of
academic criticism which have often been at war with each
other—on the one hand, traditional historical scholarship, and
on the other hand, the close reading of unattributed poems
pioneered by I. A. Richards at Cambridge under the name of
Practical Criticism, from which evolved the so-called New
Criticism in England and America. Both these schools claimed
to be trying to make criticism more "scientific": historical
scholarship by focusing on hard empirical facts about the literary text, and the New Criticism by focusing on the verbal
structure of the literary text itself. What Eliot most distrusted
was what he called "interpretation": "for every success in this
type of writing there are thousands of impostures. Instead of
insights, you get a fiction."[6] This is a slightly puzzling observation—what were his students supposed to do with the poems
he sprung on them except interpret them? To read a poem is to
interpret its meaning. By interpretation Eliot seems to mean
something more personal and assertive: the effort to explain
an author or a work in terms provided by the critic; criticism
that offers itself as a kind of key that unlocks a mystery.

The theorists of the New Criticism were always struggling
with the problem of how to define the limits of legitimate
interpretation. Wimsatt and Beardsley's 1946 article entitled
"The Intentional Fallacy" is a classic case in point. They assert:

"Judging a poem is like judging a pudding or a machine. One demands that it work."[7] One can see in this analogy the desire to put criticism on a quasi-scientific footing, to make its judgements objective by viewing the literary text in terms of functions. But clearly a poem is not like a pudding or a machine in many important respects. It is a verbal discourse, not a material object, and discourses have complex and multiple meanings. The meaning of a pudding or a machine (a clock, say) is inseparable from its utilitarian function, but a poem does not have a utilitarian function. You could discover how a clock was made by taking it apart, and with this knowledge make yourself another clock which was just as useful; but if you take a poem apart, you may learn something about how it was made but you cannot infer a set of instructions for making an equally good poem—unless it is a replica of the poem you started with.

Wimsatt and Beardsley continue: "It is only because an artifact works that we infer the intention of an artificer." True enough. Literary texts are obviously intentional objects—they do not come into existence by accident. The critics then quote Archibald MacLeish's famous line, "A poem should not mean but be," and comment: "A poem can *be* only through its *meaning*—since its medium is words—yet it *is*, simply *is*, in the sense that we have no excuse for inquiring what part is intended or meant. Poetry is a feat of style by which a complex of meaning is handled all at once."[8] Some lyric poems may give that illusion, but we know that they were produced in time, and we certainly experience a poem's meaning in time, not "all at once"—and differently every time we reread it. This is even more obviously true of long complex works like novels.

Wimsatt and Beardsley's article was a brave and salutary, if ultimately unconvincing, attempt to situate the literary text in some public space unconditioned either by its creative origins or by its individual readers:

> The poem is not the critic's own and not the author's (it is detached from the author at birth and goes about the world beyond his power to intend about it or control it). The poem belongs to the public. It is embodied in language, the peculiar possession of the public, and it is about the human being, an object of public knowledge.[9]

This is a more abstract formulation of the idea of the impersonality of artistic creation which Eliot expounded in his enormously influential 1919 essay, "Tradition and the Individual Talent," where he said that "the more perfect the artist, the more completely separate in him will be the man who suffers and the mind which creates," and that "honest criticism and sensitive appreciation are directed not upon the poet but upon the poetry."[10] Eliot's cultivation of the idea of "impersonality," however, like his attack on "interpretation," was in part a manoeuvre designed to conceal the very personal sources of his own poetry from inquisitive critics.

Here we begin to touch on the second view of the relation between creation and criticism: that they are not complementary but opposed, even antagonistic. As the case of Eliot reveals, it is quite possible for one writer to hold both views, according to what kind of criticism is in question; or to hold both at different times, with different hats on. I must admit to this inconsistency—one might almost call it schizophrenia—myself. For instance, I generally avoid reading criticism about my own work, especially academic criticism of the kind I used to write myself, and taught students to write, because I find it hinders rather than helps creation.

Academic criticism is the demonstration of a professional mastery. It cannot help trying to say the last word on its subject; it cannot help giving the impression that it operates on a higher plane of truth than the texts it discusses. The author of those texts therefore tends to feel reduced, diminished by such discourse, however well meant it is. In a way, the more approving such criticism is in its own terms, the more threatening and unsettling it can seem to the writer who is its object. As Graham Greene said, there comes a time when an established writer "is more afraid to read his favourable critics than his unfavourable, for with terrible patience they unroll before his eyes the unchanging pattern of the carpet."[11]

Academic criticism may pretend, may even deceive itself, that its relation to a creative work is purely complementary. But it also has its own hidden agenda: the demonstration of a professional skill, the refutation of competing peers, the claim to be making an addition to knowledge. The pursuit of these ends entails a degree of selection, manipulation, and re-presentation of the original text so drastic that its author will sometimes have difficulty in recognizing his or her creative work in the critical account of it. But it is not only in relation to criticism of their own work that creative writers often feel alienated by academic criticism. Inasmuch as it aspires to a scientific, or at least systematic, knowledge of its subject, criticism can be seen as hostile to creativity itself. D. H. Lawrence took this view of the matter:

Criticism can never be a science: it is, in the first place, much too personal, and in the second, it is concerned with values which science ignores. The touchstone is emotion, not reason . . . All the critical twiddle-twaddle about style and form, all this pseudo-scientific classifying and analysing of books in imitation-botanical fashion, is mere impertinence and usually dull jargon.[12]

On such grounds it is sometimes argued that it is a bad idea for an aspiring writer to do a university degree in literary studies. I came across a remark to this effect in a newspaper interview with the Irish filmmaker and novelist Neil Jordan (director of *Michael Collins*). Jordan went to University College Dublin because he wanted to write, the interviewer reported, but quoted Jordan as saying: "I found the academic study of English very depressing, and strange that something so personal could be analysed so coherently." It is interesting that whereas Lawrence was scornfully dismissive of the pretensions of academic criticism, it was the very *power* of the critical process, its analytical coherence, that Jordan found intimidating. He accordingly switched to medieval Irish history, which he found more conducive to creativity, since almost nothing for certain is known about it. "You're studying a society where history is invention, a kind of fiction really."

This issue has been raised in a new form by the proliferation, first in America, and increasingly in Britain, of creative writing courses in universities, often pursued in tandem with courses in literary criticism. Is this healthy, is this wise, is it likely to nourish the production of high-quality writing? I can only say that it all depends on what kind of writer you are or want to be. I have certainly never regretted studying English at university and making an academic career in that field. There were sometimes problems in reconciling the social roles or personae of professor and novelist, but I never found any intellectual or psychological incompatibility between the two activities. If I had done, I would have retired much sooner from academic life. Neil Jordan undoubtedly made the right decision for him. It would not be the right one for everybody.

I have been focussing on the relationship between creative writers and academic critics, but tension is just as likely—perhaps more likely—to occur between the creative writer and his *journalistic* critics, since they have a more direct impact on the writer's career—his status, his financial prospects, and his self-esteem. Reviews are the first independent feedback the writer gets on his or her work, as distinct from the reactions of friends, family, agent, and publisher. But of course they are not totally objective or disinterested. Reviewers, like scholars, have their own hidden agenda, which explains why their judgements are often so extreme. Extravagant praise, especially of some obscure or exotic work, is often a means by which literary journalists assert their professional mastery, attempt to steal a march on their peers, and draw attention to their own eloquence. Extravagant dispraise can have the same effect when directed at a well-established reputation. When the reviewer is also a practising or aspiring writer there may be a political motive—political in the literary sense—with one generation of writers seeking to oust its seniors, as in the speculative anthropology of Freud. The reviewing by the Angry Young Men writers of the 1950s, for instance—Kingsley Amis, John Wain, and others—had behind it a determined effort to displace the existing literary establishment, the faded remnants of prewar Bloomsbury and cosmopolitan modernism.

There has always been this Oedipal drama played out on the review pages of newspapers and magazines; but today—at least in Britain—its tone seems particularly spiteful. Salman Rushdie—who has, of course, been subjected to a much more lethal form of criticism—has described the public discussion of contemporary literature in Britain as "the culture of denigration." I think this has something to do with the extent to which the literary novel has recently become big business and the object of intense interest to the mass media. That didn't seem to be the case earlier in the century. It is clear from Virginia Woolf's wonderful diaries, for instance, that she never expected to make much money out of her novels, and that she cared more about her standing among her peer group than about her success or failure with the reading public. "I have made up my mind that I am not going to be popular,"[13] she says at one point. But she is plunged into deep depression and loses faith in her novel in progress because at a party T. S. Eliot seemed to neglect her claims as a writer and spent the whole evening raving about James Joyce. In those days literary reputations were made first among a small elite, and through the medium of small-circulation literary magazines. Structural changes in the economics of publishing and the insatiable appetite of the mass media for information have made it possible in our own day for a gifted literary writer to become rich and famous quite quickly. This then provokes a backlash of envy and spite in the media against the very figure they created, which can be an uncomfortable experience for the subject. Whereas post-structuralism has asserted the impersonality of creative writing in the most extreme theoretical terms—the so-called "death of the author"—literary journalism has never been so obsessed as it is now with the personality and private life of the author.

"The worst of writing," Virginia Woolf observed in her diary, quoting a friend, "is that one depends so much upon praise."[14] Which is to say that a writer, like any other artist, is continually offering his or her work for public assessment, and it is only human to want to be praised for one's efforts rather than blamed. Virginia Woolf's diaries give a wonderfully vivid account of this side of a writer's life—the way her spirits go up and down, in spite of her efforts to remain detached, as favourable and unfavourable verdicts on a new book are received from friends, colleagues, and reviewers. She notes that George Eliot "would not read reviews, since talk of her books hampered her writing," and Woolf sounds envious of such self-control. But one can't help wondering whether George Eliot's partner, George Henry Lewes, didn't make sure that she saw or knew about the favourable reviews.

My own ideal review was exemplified when a former publicity director of my publishers reviewed one of my books under the simple headline, "Literary Genius Writes Masterpiece." Unfortunately it was published in an English-language Hong Kong newspaper of very small circulation.

I turn now to the third of my perspectives on the relation between creation and criticism: that criticism is itself creative, or that there is essentially no difference between the two activities. T. S. Eliot considers this idea only to dismiss it. "No exponent of criticism . . . has I presume ever made the preposterous assumption that criticism is an autotelic activity," he wrote in

"The Function of Criticism."[15] But of course the preposterous assumption has often been made—by, for instance, Gilbert, the speaker in Oscar Wilde's dialogue called "The Critic as Artist," who seems to be a mouthpiece for Wilde himself:

> Criticism is in fact both creative and independent . . . The critic occupies the same relation to the work of art that he criticizes as the artist does to the visible world of form and colour, or the unseen world of passion and of thought.[16]

This view is antithetical to the view of criticism as complementary to creative writing, aiming at objectivity, striving "to see the object as it really is," as Matthew Arnold urged, or discovering its hidden meaning by what Eliot disapprovingly called "interpretation." Criticism, Wilde's Gilbert says, is "in its essence purely subjective, and seeks to reveal its own secret and not the secret of another."[17]

Criticism as the expression of subjective response is of course an essentially romantic idea and implies a romantic theory of literary creation as self-expression. It is often associated with the lyrical and impressionistic, musing-in-the-library style of critical discourse, which I. A. Richards and F. R. Leavis, and the American New Critics, sought to discredit and expunge from academic criticism from the 1920s to the 1950s. But more recently the idea that there is no essential difference between creation and criticism has been given a new academic respectability, and a new sophistication, under the aegis of poststructuralism, and especially the theory of deconstruction, which questions the very distinction between subjective and objective.

A fundamental tenet of deconstruction is that the nature of language is such that any discourse, including a literary text, can be shown under analysis to be full of gaps and contradictions which undermine its claim to have a determinate meaning. If poems and novels have no fixed, stable, recuperable meaning, then clearly criticism cannot pretend to have a duty or responsibility of truth-telling towards them, but is inevitably involved in *producing* their meaning by a process to which Jacques Derrida gives the name "play."[18] In this perspective, criticism is not complementary to creative writing, but supplementary to it, with "supplement" used in a double sense to denote that which replaces what is missing, and that which adds something to what is already there. The absence that criticism fills up is precisely the illusory fixed stable meaning of traditional criticism, and what it adds is the product of the critic's own ingenuity, wit, and resourcefulness in the exercise of semantic freeplay. It is not surprising that Derrida has admitted to being a creative writer *manqué*. His work is a kind of avant-garde literary discourse—punning, allusive, exhibitionistic, and teasingly provocative to those who are not simply baffled and bored by it. Harold Bloom has developed his own idiosyncratic version of creative criticism based on the idea that the apparent misreading of texts by "strong" critics (like himself) replicates the process by which strong poets struggle with the intimidating example of their precursors and liberate themselves from the anxiety of influence. No wonder that in reading Bloom we are so often reminded of Wilde, to whom he refers in *The Western Canon* as "the sublime Oscar Wilde, who was right about everything."[19]

It is, I think, possible to concede that there is a creative element in criticism without collapsing the distinction between creative and critical writing entirely. A good critical essay should have a kind of plot. Some of T. S. Eliot's most celebrated essays were critical whodunits which investigated such mysteries as "Who murdered English poetic diction?" (The culprit turned out to be Milton.)[20] Modern critics of the antifoundationalist school, like Paul de Man or Stanley Fish, are masters of the critical peripeteia, by which the conclusion of the essay turns upon and undermines its own arguments. And there is no reason why criticism should not be written with elegance and eloquence. I try to do so myself. But when I write criticism I feel that I am involved in a different kind of activity from when I write fiction, and part of that difference is that everything in writing a novel has to be decided—nothing is given—whereas in the case of criticism the prior existence of the work or works to be criticised, and the prior existence of other critical opinion about them, places limits on the development of the critical discourse, and makes it on the whole an easier and less anxiety-provoking process.

Roland Barthes suggested in a pregnant little essay called "Criticism as Language," published in 1963, that

> the task of criticism . . . does not consist in "discovering" in the work of the author under consideration something "hidden" or "profound" or "secret" which has so far escaped notice . . . but only in fitting together . . . the language of the day (Existentialism, Marxism, psychoanalysis) . . . and the language of the author . . . If there is such a thing as critical proof it lies not in the ability to *discover* the work under consideration, but on the contrary on the ability to *cover* it as completely as possible with one's own language.[21]

Criticism must face the fact that it can only be "true" by being tautological—that is, by repeating what the text says in the text's own words; and it can only escape from tautology by representing the text in other words, and therefore *mis*representing it. As Professor Morris Zapp says, in my novel *Small World*, "every decoding is another encoding." But this need not entail surrendering all responsibility to the original text. Criticism can be a useful, as well as a merely playful, activity. For reasons I have already suggested, creative writers are apt to find the experience of having their language covered by somebody else's language rather unsettling, and would prefer not to know about it; but for readers, especially of classic texts, this kind of criticism can do for literature, what literature does for the world—defamiliarising it, enabling us to see its beauty and value afresh.

Finally I come to criticism as a part of creation. This is something well-known to creative writers who are also critics. Wilde's Gilbert, for instance, says: "Without the critical faculty, there is no artistic creation at all worthy of the name."[22] Graham Greene said, "An author of talent is his own best critic—an ability to criticise his own work is inseparably bound up with his talent: it *is* his talent."[23] T. S. Eliot wrote:

> Probably . . . the largest part of the labour of an author in composing his work is critical labour; the labour of sifting, combining, expunging, correcting, testing: this frightful toil is as much critical as creative. I maintain even that the criticism employed by a trained and skilled writer on his own

work is the most vital, the highest kind of criticism; and that . . . some creative writers are superior to others solely because their critical faculty is superior.[24]

Like so many of Eliot's critical pronouncements, this one puzzles as well as illuminates. In saying "the criticism employed by a trained and skilled writer on his own work" did he mean *published* criticism of this kind, such as Henry James's Prefaces to his collected novels? If so, Eliot gave us remarkably little of such criticism himself. If he meant the "critical labour" involved in creation, then it would seem that the "most vital, the highest kind of criticism" is for the most part only experienced by writers themselves. Perhaps that is why, as readers, as critics, we are so interested in the genesis of works of literature, in authors' notebooks and draft manuscripts, and in their comments on their own work—it is a way of reconstructing and sharing the "critical labour" that is part of creation.

But Eliot's main point seems to me entirely right. Most of the time spent nominally writing a creative work is actually spent reading it—reading and rereading the words one has already written, trying to improve on them or using them as a kind of springboard from which to propel oneself into the as yet unwritten part of one's text. There are exceptional writers who seem able to produce high-quality work very quickly, with hardly any hesitations or revisions, but for most of us writing is an absurdly labour-intensive activity. Few modern novels, for example, take more than ten hours to read, but the novelist will work for hundreds, perhaps thousands of hours to make that experience enjoyable and profitable, and most of those hours will be taken up with work that is essentially critical, as Eliot describes it. It is not work that necessarily goes on at the writer's desk, but at all times and places: in bed, at the table, while showering or cooking, or walking the dog.

Does this mean that writers are always the best critics of their own work in a public sense? No, of course it does not. They are far too involved to assess the value of their work, or to generalise about its meaning and significance. Where the writer has an advantage over her critics is in explaining how a book came to be written, what its sources were, and why it took the form that it did. But few writers are eager to use this privilege. Even Henry James, in his famous Prefaces, conceals much more than he reveals, as does Graham Greene in the introductions to his books gathered together in *Ways of Escape*. Eliot always politely declined to reveal the sources and describe the genesis of his notoriously obscure poems. Personally, I rather enjoy explaining how I write my novels, and have published a number of essays describing the problems, choices, revisions, and discoveries involved. But I would not claim that this is the most vital, the highest kind of criticism that I or anyone else could write, nor would I claim that the picture of composition it gives bears more than a highly selective and artificially tidy resemblance to the actual process. There are many facts about the composition of my work that I could never recover and many that I would never divulge.

There are several reasons why writers are generally reluctant to engage publicly in analytical criticism of their own work. They may fear they will lose their gift if they analyse it too closely. They may be reluctant to restrict the reader's response by imposing an "authorised" interpretation on the text, knowing that sometimes works of literature mean more than their authors were conscious of. Very often, I believe, the motive for silence is that the writer has tried to give his work the effect of an effortless inevitability, and is understandably reluctant to destroy that illusion by revealing too much about the choices, hesitations, and second thoughts involved in composition. As W. B. Yeats put it:

> A line will take us hours maybe
> Yet if it does not seem a moment's thought
> Our stitching and unstitching has been naught.[25]

The paradox is not confined to poetry. The American short story writer Patricia Hampl has written:

> Every story has a story. This secret story, which has little chance of getting told, is the history of its creation. Maybe the "story of the story" *can* never be told, for a finished work consumes its own history, renders it obsolete, a husk.[26]

One reason why literary creation continues to fascinate us and elude our attempts to explain it is that it is impossible to, as it were, catch oneself in the act of creation. It is not as if one just comes up with an idea for a poem, say, and then puts it into words. The idea, however vague and provisional, is already a verbal concept, and expressing it in more precise, specific words makes it different from what it was. Every revision is not a reformulation of the same meaning but a slightly (or very) different meaning. This was one reason why Wimsatt and Beardsley questioned the idea that a work of literature is the realization of an intention that exists prior to it.

> There is a sense in which an author, by revision, may better achieve his original intention. But it is a very abstract sense. He intended to write a better work, or a better work of a

certain kind, and now has done it. But it follows that his original concrete intention was not his intention. "He's the man we were in search of," says Hardy's rustic constable, "and yet he's not the man we were in search of. For the man we were in search of was not the man we wanted."[27]

Writers discover what it is they want to say in the process of saying it, and their explanations of why they wrote something in a particular way are therefore always retrospective extrapolations, working back from effect to cause—wisdom after the event. It is this inevitable deferral of meaning in discourse that the deconstructionists seized upon to destabilise the whole concept of meaning.

The difficulty of understanding the nature of literary creation is part of the larger problem of understanding the nature of consciousness, which is currently preoccupying specialists in a wide range of disciplines—philosophers, linguists, cognitive scientists, sociobiologists, neurologists, zoologists, and many others. It is said that consciousness is the last great challenge to scientific inquiry, but if you browse through the more accessible literature in this field it is interesting to note how often it touches on questions and phenomena that concern literary critics. For example, I came across Patricia Hampl's suggestive quote about the "story of the story" in a book by the philosopher and cognitive scientist Daniel C. Dennett, *Consciousness Explained*. Dennett relies heavily on the analogy of literary creation for his model of consciousness. He used to believe, he tells us, that there had to be "an awareness line separating the preconscious fixation of communicative intentions from their subsequent execution,"[28] but he came to reject this idea on grounds similar to those on which Wimsatt and Beardsley rejected the intentional fallacy. In its place he formulated the "multiple draft" model of consciousness, which proposes that all thought is produced through a process of expansion, editing, and revision, like a literary text, although unlike literary creation it is so fast that it seems experientially to be instantaneous. To Dennett the mind is like a hugely powerful parallel-processing computer that operates itself, and this is his description of how a particular thought or utterance is produced:

> Instead of a determinate content in a particular functional place [in the brain], waiting to be Englished by sub-routines, there is a still-incompletely-determined mind-set distributed around in the brain and constraining a composition process which in the course of time can actually feed back to make adjustments or revisions, further determining the expressive task that set the composition process in motion in the first place . . . It's just as possible for the content-to-be-expressed to be adjusted in the direction of some candidate expression, as for the candidate expression to be replaced or edited so as better to accommodate the content-to-be-expressed.[29]

This is a phenomenon familiar to anyone who has tried to write formal verse: the search for a rhyming word, or a phrase with the required metrical structure (the "candidate expression"), will affect the semantic development of a poem, and since this happens many times in the process of composition, the final version of a poem may be almost unrecognizable from the first draft. It is rather unsettling to imagine that this may be equally true of every utterance we make, and yet the more one thinks about it the more intuitively plausible it seems.

Dennett pursues the analogy between consciousness and literary creation even further. The very idea of the individual self, he argues, is constructed, like a novel. Unlike other animals, we are almost continually engaged in presenting ourselves to others, and to ourselves, in language and gesture, external and internal. "Our fundamental tactic of self-protection, self-control and self-definition is not spinning webs [like a spider] or building dams [like a beaver] but telling stories"— especially the story of who we are.[30]

There are many different competing theories of consciousness, and Dennett's is only one of them. Basically, if I understand him correctly, he thinks that consciousness is the accidental consequence of *homo sapiens* developing through evolution a huge brain and vocal organs which allowed the species to acquire language, and making selves is what we do with this equipment, which is much more than we need for mere survival. At the opposite pole are religious theories of consciousness, which identify the self with the individual immortal soul which derives from God. Philosophically this is regarded as dualism—the fallacy of the Ghost in the Machine— though the idea of an immaterial self is so deeply ingrained in our language and our habits of thought, whether we are religious believers or not, that it seems to me doubtful that it will ever be completely expunged. Somewhere between the two poles are those thinkers who reject the Ghost in the Machine but deny that the concept of mind can be equated with neurological brain activity, and suggest that consciousness will always be ultimately a mystery, or at least not explainable by or reducible to scientific laws.

The distinguished neurobiologist Gerald Edelman, in his book *Bright Air, Brilliant Fire,* says: "We cannot construct a phenomenal psychology that can be shared in the same way that physics can be shared"—because "consciousness is a first person matter,"[31] because it exists in and is conditioned by history and therefore every individual's consciousness is unique, because linguistically based consciousness is "never self-sufficient, it is always in dialogue with some other, even if that interlocutor is not present."[32] These observations will ring all kinds of bells with anyone who is familiar with modern literary criticism, notably the work of Mikhail Bakhtin. It is not therefore surprising to find Edelman saying, towards the end of his book: "what is perhaps most extraordinary about conscious human beings is their art."[33]

# chapter three

# DICKENS
# OUR
# CONTEMPORARY

Charles Dickens is arguably the greatest of all writers in the English language after Shakespeare, and so has attracted almost as much critical and scholarly attention; but whereas, for historical reasons, comparatively few facts are known about Shakespeare, which places severe constraints on the biographical approach to his work, Dickens lived at the beginning of the Industrial Age, when information itself became industrialised—recorded, reproduced, and (even when hidden) preserved for recuperation by subsequent generations. We know more about Dickens's life, especially his early life, than his own family did, because he concealed from them facts of which he was ashamed, or which he found distressing to contemplate, but which were disinterred posthumously. There have been at least three major biographies published in modern times—by Edgar Johnson, Fred Kaplan, and Peter Ackroyd—and the multi-volume edition of Dickens's letters is approaching completion. But as Jane Smiley observes in her short biography of Dickens in the Penguin Lives series, although "the literary sensibility of Charles Dickens is possibly the most amply documented . . . in history," his character and genius remain almost as mysterious and difficult to comprehend as Shakespeare's.[1]

Although new facts are still being discovered about Dickens, it seems unlikely that any such discovery will fundamentally alter our view of his character and work. The only significant originality attainable by the biographer or critic, and the only excuse for adding to the mountain of secondary literature already heaped on his reputation, is in interpretation of the given facts. Jane Smiley, however, explicitly dissociates herself from those critics and biographers who claim to understand an author and his work better than he did himself. "Writing is an act of artistic and moral agency," she asserts firmly, "where choices are made that the author understands, full of implications and revelations that the author also understands." If this attitude somewhat underestimates the contribution of a writer's unconscious in the creative process, it also enables Smiley to make us see Dickens's achievement afresh without deploying any of the heavy theoretical artillery of modern academic criticism. What inspires her book is her ability to identify *professionally* with Dickens, drawing on her own experience of writing and publishing fiction. Its foundation is her acute perception that Dickens was "a true celebrity (maybe the first true celebrity in the modern sense)"—the first writer, therefore, to feel the intense pressure of being simultaneously an artist and an object of enormous public interest and adulation. In this, and in other related respects, his life and work prefigured much in our own literary culture. If Smiley's book had a title other than the bare name of its subject, it might be (by analogy with Jan Kott's influential study of Shakespeare, though for very different reasons) *Dickens Our Contemporary*.

---

Celebrity is not the same thing as fame. There were English writers before Dickens who were famous in their own lifetime—Samuel Richardson, Dr. Johnson, Lord Byron, for example. But they did not cultivate or exploit their fame, nor did it take over their entire lives as celebrity always threatens to do. Celebrity entails a certain collaboration and complicity on the part of the subject. It can bring great material rewards and personal satisfactions—but at a cost, a kind of commodification of the self. It requires conditions which did not exist before the Industrial Revolution got into its stride: fast and flexible means of production, transportation, and communication, which circulate the work widely and bring the author into actual or virtual contact with his or her audience.

The two greatest novelists of the generation before Dickens, Jane Austen and Walter Scott, both published their novels anonymously: "By the Author of *Waverley*" and "By the Author of *Pride and Prejudice Etc. Etc.*" Scott achieved fame (and a baronetcy) as a poet, but he did not avow authorship of his novels until relatively late in his career; Jane Austen's identity was known only to a small circle of family and friends until her death. How unthinkable such self-effacement seems in our own personality-obsessed, publicity-conscious age! Even Dickens began by writing under a pseudonym ("Boz"), but he discarded it fairly quickly. It is Dickens who stands symbolically on the threshold of the modern literary era, and whose career embodies the difference between being famous and being a celebrity. The very word "celebrity" as a concrete noun, applied to persons, only entered the language in the mid-nineteenth century. The first citation in the Oxford English Dictionary is dated 1849, the year when Dickens published *David Copperfield* and stood unchallenged as the greatest and most popular writer of his age.

Dickens not only wrote novels which became classics of English literature in his own lifetime; he transformed the methods of publishing fiction and thus changed the possibilities of authorship for his contemporaries and their successors. He was a brilliant entrepreneur as well as an artist, driven by painful memories of what it was like to be poor, and the excitement of making money by his own efforts. The story of his first meteoric success is worth recalling. In his early twenties, without private wealth or a conventional gentleman's education behind him, he was eking out a meagre living as a Parliamentary reporter and freelance journalist. Some "sketches" of contemporary life among the lower classes, published under the nom-de-plume "Boz," attracted enough attention to win him a commission that another writer might have treated as hackwork: providing narrative copy to accompany the monthly publication of a series of sporting prints by a popular artist of the day, Robert Seymour. Dickens seized the opportunity to create *The Pickwick Papers*. Very soon the artist found himself playing a subordinate role, obliged to take instructions from the courteous but determined young writer. The unfortunate and mentally unstable Seymour apparently couldn't bear the humiliation, and blew his brains out while working on the second number. He was replaced by Hablôt Knight Browne ("Phiz"); and the sales of *The Pickwick Papers*, which had been sluggish at first, suddenly took off on the wings of Dickens's comic genius. Only 400 copies of the first issue had been published. Before the end, the print run was 40,000.

The success of the monthly publication of *Pickwick* encouraged Dickens to use the same or similar methods for his subsequent novels, from *Oliver Twist* onwards, before issuing them in volume form. He launched a miscellany called *Master Humphrey's Clock* in which *The Old Curiosity Shop* and *Barnaby Rudge* were published in weekly installments. Later he founded a magazine, *Household Words,* which provided a platform for serialization of his own and other novelists' work. Publication in parts and magazine serialization, pioneered by Dickens, became the standard form for the initial publication of novels in the Victorian age, and is one reason why he and other writers of high literary quality, like Thackeray, George Eliot, and Elizabeth Gaskell, commanded a huge popular audience. Smiley is not the first to draw a parallel with modern television drama. The serialised Victorian novel was something between a mini-series and a soap opera, its installments often appearing over a period of more than a year. The audience absorbed the story and became familiar with the characters in a rhythm almost as slow as their own lives. And because Dickens and some of his contemporaries started publishing their novels serially before they had finished writing them, feedback from the audience could affect the development of the story and the roles of the characters. Dickens, for example, sent young Martin Chuzzlewit to America in an effort to revive flagging sales, and wrote more and more scenes for Mrs. Gamp as she proved more and more popular with his readers.

Towards the end of the century this solidarity between literary novelists and the reading public began to disintegrate.

Some writers—Hardy was a notable example—fell foul of the prudish constraints imposed by magazine editors on the representation of sexuality. Others, like Henry James, found that the pursuit of formal beauty and psychological subtlety in their fiction made it less marketable. It is recorded that in 1900 the business manager of the *Atlantic Monthly*, which had serialised several of James's novels, "begged the editor . . . 'with actual tears in his eyes' not to print another 'sinker' by him lest the *Atlantic* be thought 'a high-brow periodical.'"[2] The plea was revealing and prophetic. In the modern period a split developed between cutting-edge literary fiction and middle-brow entertainment fiction. Practitioners of the former, like James, Conrad, Joyce, D. H. Lawrence, Ford Madox Ford, Dorothy Richardson, and Virginia Woolf, resigned themselves, with good or ill grace, to addressing a small but discriminating readership, and were often exiles from their own society in either a literal or a metaphorical sense; while exponents of the traditional, page-turning novel, with well-made plots and an unproblematic rendering of social reality, like Arnold Bennett, John Galsworthy, Compton Mackenzie, and J. B. Priestley, were the commercially successful literary "celebrities," interviewed in, reported by, and themselves contributing to the mass media. Towards the end of the twentieth century, however, this divide became less evident, indeed almost invisible. For a variety of reasons, some cultural, some socioeconomic, literary fiction became more reader-friendly and an object of exploitative interest to the mass media and big business. The "literary best-seller" (that is, an artistically ambitious and innovative book that also sells in huge numbers, like *Midnight's Children* or *The Name of the Rose*)—a concept that would have seemed a contradiction in terms in the period of high modernism—once again became an achievable goal, as it had been in the era of Dickens, and the authors of such books are now celebrities. Even the modestly successful literary novelist today is expected to take part in the marketing of his or her work by giving interviews, appearing on TV and radio, taking part in public readings, book signings, and other meet-the-author events, and thus experiences, in a pale form, the phenomenon of author-as-celebrity that Dickens's career inaugurated, and the stresses and contradictions that go with it.

Dickens was of course "the Inimitable"—it was the epithet he most liked to be applied to himself—and he experienced both the gratifications and the penalties of celebrity on a heroic scale. The success of his early novels was phenomenal. By the age of thirty, Smiley observes, he was already the most famous writer of his day. "He had achieved not simply literary success, but something else, a separate status. His voice and his vision had become *beloved*; as Ackroyd puts it, he was 'public property.'" A letter to his friend and confidant John Forster about a public dinner given for him in Edinburgh in June 1841 shows his awareness that there was something unprecedented about the position he had attained in English life. "The tone of his letter was exultant, pleased, and, at least to some degree, amazed. He seems to have been especially struck by the fact that he was so young and the men who came to celebrate him were old and established."

The exceptional popularity of his books extended to the New World. The story of the crowds waiting on the quays in New York for the ship carrying the latest installment of *The Old Curiosity Shop* to dock, calling out to the passengers and crew, "Is Little Nell dead?" is well known. But it was on his first visit to America in 1842, not long after that triumphal dinner in Edinburgh, that Dickens discovered celebrity could be a curse as well as a blessing. He was lionised, feted, royally entertained, and at first delighted by all the attention. But soon the relentless glare of publicity, the intrusiveness of American journalists, and the impossibility of securing any peace and privacy for himself and his wife Catherine (who had reluctantly accompanied him) became too much. "We can recognize it," says Smiley, the seasoned modern pro, "as a nightmare book tour, the author and his wife unprotected by publicists or any sort of previous experience." Dickens became uneasy, irritable, and openly critical of the host country. His bitter complaints about American publishers' pirating of his work, however justified they might now appear to us, were not well received. The euphoria of his initial reception turned sour, with disillusionment on both sides. Smiley comments shrewdly:

> The new machinery of capitalistic publishing had carried his work far and wide, bringing a single man, a single voice, into a personal relationship with huge numbers of people whom he had never met, and yet who felt intimate with him, because the novel is, above all, an intense experience of prolonged intimacy with another consciousness. But both the author and the readers had misread the relationship from either side.

The same kind of misreading would in due course occur in England; but there, because of its stratified class system, and more complex code of manners, the line between public and private life was still implicitly understood and respected. American society in the 1840s, brash and democratic, prefigured our own Age of Publicity, in which anyone in public life is deemed to be a legitimate object of public curiosity, all the time. Politicians and film stars have learned to cope with this by performing their private lives in public while actually living them in secret, in the company of other celebs, protected by walls and security guards. But the professional lives of politicians and film stars do not entail the kind of self-disclosure that seems inherent in writing novels. As Smiley emphasises, the novel is, among all the literary genres and artistic forms, peculiarly focussed upon consciousness, on the representation of the thoughts and feelings that most of us, most of the time, keep to ourselves: "the intimacy [Dickens's readers] felt through the work came from the natural power of the novel to cross the boundaries of appearance and reveal the inner life . . ." That is to say, not only the inner lives of the characters, but also the inner life of the man who created them. "Authors live in a dialogue with their work, and their work is their inner life made concrete." Modern novelists have developed various defences and disguises—limited point of view, impersonal or unreliable narrators, metafictional tricks of all kinds—to deter readers from making simplistic inferences about the author from his work; but the convention of the omniscient authorial voice favoured by Dickens and most other Victorian novelists encouraged their readers to feel that the text they held in their hands was a direct line to a real human being—that the "Charles Dickens" whose name appeared on the title page of the novel was identical with the person who actually wrote it. But the authorial persona is a rhetorical construction, a "second self," as Wayne Booth called it in *The Rhetoric of Fiction*. When the real author encounters real readers, it can be an uncomfortable experience on both sides.

It is important to recognize, however, that Dickens's celebrity was not forced upon him. He invited it and, most of the time, enjoyed it. It satisfied an element in his character that delighted in public performance and role-playing. Smiley rightly emphasises Dickens's love of the theatre, and his enthusiasm for acting. While writing *Pickwick* he sometimes went to the theatre every night of the week. As a young man he seriously considered becoming a professional actor, and only indisposition prevented him from attending an audition that might have set him on a different career path. As it was, he somehow found time, amid all his writing and editing and business and philanthropic enterprises and domestic responsibilities, to produce and act in elaborate amateur theatricals which were often performed in public theatres, before large audiences. A painting by a Royal Academician portrays him in magnificent costume as Bobadill in Ben Jonson's *Every Man in His Humour,* which he also directed. This fascination—one might almost call it an obsession—with the theatre left its mark on Dickens's novels, not only in those that deal directly with the stage (the Crummles in *Nicholas Nickleby* or Wopsle's Hamlet in *Great Expectations*) but in his distinctive way of creating characters and making them speak and interact. Ackroyd notes his remark to a friend, that "he believed he had more talent for the drama than for literature, as he certainly had more delight in acting than in any other work whatever." It seems obvious that if the Victorian theatre had been as receptive to the literary imagination as the Elizabethan was, Dickens would have been a playwright like Shakespeare rather than a novelist, but the Victorian theatre was in fact trivial and philistine, reducing tragedy to melodrama and comedy to farce. Indeed, even its melodrama frequently degenerated into unintentional farce, as Dickens recognized:

> The plot was most interesting. It belonged to no particular age, people, or country, and was perhaps the more delightful on that account, as nobody's previous information could afford the remotest glimmering of what would ever come of it. An outlaw had been very successful in doing something somewhere, and came home in triumph, to the sound of shouts and fiddles, to greet his wife—a lady of masculine mind, who talked a good deal about her father's bones, which it seemed were unburied, though whether from a peculiar taste on the part of the old gentleman himself, or the reprehensible neglect of his relations, did not appear. This outlaw's wife was somehow or other mixed up with a patriarch, living in a castle a long way off, and this patriarch was the father of several of the characters, but he didn't exactly know which, and was uncertain whether he had brought up the right ones in his castle, or the wrong ones, but rather inclined to the latter opinion, and, being uneasy, relieved his mind with a banquet, during which solemnity somebody in a cloak said, "Beware!" which somebody was known by nobody (except the audience) to be the outlaw himself, who had come there for reasons unexplained, but possibly with an eye to the spoons.

The sublimely funny episode of *Nicholas Nickleby* from which this is extracted shows that Dickens was well aware of the absurdity of much of the popular drama of his day, but he drew directly on melodramatic diction and gesture at the emotional climaxes of his stories, and this can create problems for modern readers. Dickens does not mean us to smile when, in the same novel, the young hero prevents the tyrant school-master Squeers from beating the boy Smike in this kind of language:

> "Wretch," rejoined Nicholas, fiercely, "touch him at your peril! I will not stand by and see it done; my blood is up, and I have the strength of ten such men as you. Look to yourself, for by Heaven I will not spare you, if you drive me on!"

In the winter of 1856–57 Dickens collaborated with his friend and fellow-novelist, Wilkie Collins, on a melodrama entitled *The Frozen Deep.* The story was loosely based on the British Arctic expedition of 1845 to find the North West Passage, in the course of which all the participants lost their lives. Collins wrote the script, but Dickens worked on it as well, and took the role of the leader of the expedition, Richard Wardour. Collins had represented him as the villain of the piece, but Dickens rewrote the part, making him into a more complex individual who redeems himself by a final act of self-sacrifice. This inspired the character of Sydney Carton ("It is a far, far better thing that I do . . .") in Dickens's next novel, *A Tale of Two Cities*; but the play was to have other, more private and personal consequences. In portraying Wardour as a man "per-petually seeking and never finding affection," Dickens was act-ing out (in the psychoanalytical sense) his own increasing dissatisfaction with his marriage, and the play was eventually to bring into his life a woman who would apparently satisfy that longing.

By all accounts *The Frozen Deep* is a typical melodrama of its period, a creakily contrived vehicle for extravagant displays of emotion and overblown rhetoric. It was first performed privately at Dickens's London home as a Twelfth Night entertainment for friends, with Dickens's sister-in-law Georgina and two of his daughters in the cast. But an indication of the importance Dickens attached to this production is that he invited newspaper reviewers to watch it. They, and the rest of the audience, were stunned by the intensity of Dickens's performance. Later that year he arranged public performances of the play in Manchester, to raise money for a deceased friend's family. Realising that his own womenfolk would not be able to hold the stage in a large auditorium, he hired the services of a family of professional actors: Frances Ternan, a widow, and her three daughters, Fanny, Maria, and Ellen ("Nelly"). The first night was a sensation. Dickens reported to a friend: "It was a good thing to have a couple of thousand people all rigid and frozen together in the palm of one's hand . . . and to see the hardened Carpenters on the sides crying and trembling at it." Maria Ternan, an experienced actress, could not restrain real tears as she cradled the dying Wardour in her arms at the climax of the piece.

Obviously something very extraordinary was happening in these performances. Like a great professional actor, Dickens was transmuting dramatic base metal into gold, but he was doing so by drawing deeply on all kinds of conflicted personal emotion. The frozen deep of his own psyche was melted, and the experience was a kind of therapy. He wrote to Collins subsequently, "I have never had a moment's peace or content since the last night of *The Frozen Deep.*" But perhaps that remark also reflected his growing attachment to Nelly Ternan and the trouble it caused in his domestic life. As he began to see more and more of her, Dickens also began proceedings to obtain a legal separation from Catherine, but he indignantly denied that there was any connection between these developments, and insisted, in rather embarrassing and undignified public pronouncements, that his friendship with an unnamed "young lady" was entirely proper and her character irreproachable. In due course he set up Nelly and her mother (who conferred a kind of respectability on the arrangement) in various houses in England and France, and visited them discreetly, but whether she was actually his mistress, and, as was rumoured, bore him a child, no one has been able to ascertain, including Claire Tomalin, who has written the definitive study of the relationship. Dickens had by this time learned to protect his private life with great skill, and Nelly, who outlived him by forty-four years, kept their secret.

Dickens's attitude towards love, marriage, and sexuality, in his life and in his work, is a complex and puzzling subject. Most of his biographers have been baffled by his choice of Catherine Hogarth as a wife. His letters to her written during their courtship give no clue, conveying little sense of real passion. She was rather dull, and not particularly good-looking. Gamely as she tried, she was quite incapable of responding adequately to her husband's intelligence, wit, imagination, and energy. What did he see in her? Perhaps the simplest explanation is that he was a virile but idealistic young man who wished urgently to satisfy his sexual drive in a morally and socially approved fashion, and she was the first woman to accept him. He had courted the love of his youth, Maria Beadnell, for four frustrating years, only to be rejected by her and her family because of his uncertain prospects. When he met Catherine these were improving, and he married her on the strength of the *Pickwick* commission. He claimed later that he realised after only two years that the marriage had been a mistake, yet he went on sleeping with Catherine, and impregnating her, until, after twenty-one years, ten children, and several miscarriages, he instructed her maid to erect a partition in their bedroom so that they could sleep apart. That was in 1857, the year he met Nelly Ternan.

The regular pregnancies imply a certain frequency of intercourse, but Dickens plainly stopped desiring Catherine fairly early in the marriage, complaining that she had grown fat and clumsy and was continually unwell. It seems unlikely that she herself invited or insisted on conjugal sex, since it was the continual childbearing that undermined her health. (There was, of course, no question of using contraception.) One can only suppose that for Dickens it was the equivalent of those twenty- or thirty-mile walks that he was fond of taking, at an average speed of 4.5 miles an hour—a way of releasing and relieving the extraordinary energy and nervous tension pent up in his small, neat body, while the dutiful wife lay back and thought of England (or perhaps *The Pickwick Papers*). The novels throw no direct light on the subject, because they contain not a single word about physical sexuality. Extreme reticence on this aspect of human behaviour was of course compulsory for all Victorian novelists, but Dickens, unlike many of his peers (Thackeray, for example), does not seem to have chafed under this constraint. His imagination was exceptionally chaste. There is not a risqué joke, or a single scene that would "bring a blush into the cheek of the young person" (Podsnap's phrase), in his entire oeuvre. For an essentially comic writer, this is a remarkable achievement.

He seems to have subscribed to the view, widely held (or at least professed) among the Victorian middle classes, that normal women didn't have sexual appetites, and put up with men's for the sake of matrimony and motherhood. His heroines are either childlike or saintly, presexual or asexual (Dora and Agnes in *David Copperfield* are prime examples of each type, and Amy Dorrit combines both). In life Dickens's most intense emotional relationships were with younger, virginal women, notably Mary Hogarth, Catherine's younger sister, who lived with them at the beginning of their married life, and died suddenly and tragically in Dickens's arms, aged only seventeen. He wore one of her rings for the rest of his life, kept a lock of her hair and her clothes, and said it was impossible to exaggerate her influence on him. In due course his sister-in-law Georgina came to occupy a similar place in the household. She was a more intimate companion to Dickens than Catherine, and rumours that she was his mistress were quashed only when she submitted to a medical examination that confirmed she was a virgin. Perhaps with Nelly he finally achieved a relationship that was both emotionally and erotically satisfying. One rather hopes so.

In the 1850s Dickens was going through what we would call a midlife crisis. Jane Smiley does not attempt to excuse his treatment of Catherine, which was deplorable, but by viewing the episode in the perspective of our own "divorce culture," and by empathising with the peculiar psychological pressures that Dickens suffered as artist, entrepreneur, and celebrity, she makes his behaviour comprehensible. She follows Edmund Wilson (in his classic essay, "Dickens: the Two Scrooges") in seeing the novelist's imagination as essentially dualistic— constantly affirming the necessity of virtue, love, altruism, but constantly attracted to the portrayal of evil, cruelty, and hypocrisy. It is a critical commonplace that his most memorable characters are all morally flawed, if not outright villains. The unregenerate Scrooge is much more entertaining than the reformed one. Wilson traced this deep, dark vein in the novelist's work back to the traumatic episode in his childhood when his father was imprisoned for debt and the twelve-year-old boy was abruptly ejected from home and school and sent to work sticking labels on bottles in a blacking factory on the bank of the Thames, in the company of rats and a young orphan called Bob Fagin. Dickens kept this episode a secret from family and friends for most of his life. Around 1850 he wrote down the story for his own eyes only, and later showed it to Forster, who published it posthumously in the first biography of the novelist. "The deep remembrance of the sense I had of being utterly neglected and hopeless," Dickens wrote, "of the shame I felt in my position; of the misery it was to my young heart to believe that, day by day, what I had learned, and thought, and delighted in, and raised my fancy and my emulation up by, was passing away from me, never to be brought back any more; cannot be written." Of course it *was* written, indirectly, in Dickens's incomparable rendering of oppressed and helpless children in his fiction, which confirms Wilson's thesis. But Smiley cautions us against a too reductively Freudian interpretation of Dickens when she points out that novelists do not merely draw on personal experience of conflict in creating their work—they also in a sense discover it in the process of writing. "Art that has a revelatory effect upon the reader had its first revelatory effect upon the writer; the process of working out the plots and relationships in an ambitious novel is always a learning process."

Writing fiction, in Jane Smiley's view, is a way of imposing
order upon the chaotic flux of experience, to make it comprehensible and to project a vision of what it should or might be,
and she offers the interesting suggestion that Dickens tried to
make the real world correspond to his fictionally ordered version of it. She argues that the extraordinary amount of time
and energy that he expended on nonliterary activities of a
social and philanthropic nature—the good works, the fund-
raising, the consciousness-raising, the speeches and dinners
and parties and Christmas festivities and amateur theatricals—
is best explained as an effort to embody in his own life the
vision of the good society implicit in his books. To outward
appearances he succeeded to an astonishing degree; but
inwardly he was disappointed and unfulfilled in one aspect of
his life: the affective and erotic. In Nelly Ternan he saw a last
chance to make up for this absence, and seized it, putting the
whole edifice of bourgeois respectability that he had labori-
ously constructed in jeopardy. That is Smiley's analysis of the
affair, and it is persuasive, as is her account of its effect on his
professional career.

In spite of the smokescreen Dickens created around his relationship with Nelly, the rumours and journalistic coverage
damaged his reputation as a model Victorian public man. "His
ties with the mainstream . . . loosened." He no longer embod-
ied unproblematically the values and aspirations of the
middle-class reading public in his novels, which became darker
and less reader-friendly. Younger readers found him eccentri-
cally old-fashioned; older readers regretted the passing of the
genial, cheerful, reassuring tone of the early books. In his own
life he cultivated "the sort of relationships that are primary in

our century—one-to-one intimacies on the one hand, joined with star-to-audience performances on the other."

These performances were the public readings which occupied more and more of Dickens's time and energy in the last decade of his life, and which undoubtedly hastened his death in 1870, at the age of 58. They were by all accounts extraordinary events. Without the aid of artificial amplification, he held huge audiences (2,000 in Birmingham, 3,700 in Bradford) spellbound. Listeners fainted at his rendering of the murder of Nancy by Bill Sikes. It was a natural extension of his enthusiasm for amateur theatricals, but now Dickens was the complete professional. He revised the extracts from his novels to make them dramatically more effective, rehearsed every nuance of his delivery, and supervised every detail of the staging and lighting. He made a good deal of money from these performances, but that was not the primary motive for undertaking them. He was addicted to the high that comes from thrilling and controlling an audience. Smiley is also surely right to argue that it was a way of maintaining his unique and unprecedented relationship with the public. His readings consisted mostly of "golden oldies" from his early novels—*A Christmas Carol, Oliver Twist, Martin Chuzzlewit*. The appropriate modern analogy is not the more or less competent reading by a more or less nervous novelist in a bookshop or at a literary festival, but the triumphal tour of an aging, still charismatic pop star.

Although Dickens was the greatest of Victorian novelists, his work did not flow in the same direction as the strongest literary current of the time, which was towards greater and greater realism in the rendering of the social world and individual psychology. In that respect the somewhat younger George Eliot was much more representative, and it is significant that in an article written in 1856, at the threshold of her own literary career, she criticised Dickens's depiction of human beings because "he failed to give us their psychological character." Henry James (who as a child hid under a table to listen to his father reading *David Copperfield*, and was discovered when he was unable to restrain his sobs at the pathos of the story) put the boot into *Our Mutual Friend* in the same year when he published his own first tale, complaining in a review that it was "wanting in inspiration" and its characters "lifeless, flat, mechanical." Jane Smiley, on the contrary, regards it as "Dickens's perfect novel, seamless and true and delightful in every line."

The prestige of the Jamesian poetics of fiction in the modern period, reinforced in England by the rather humourless and puritanical school of F. R. Leavis (who famously dismissed Dickens as "a great entertainer" in *The Great Tradition* [1948], though he offered a more generous estimate later), inhibited critical appreciation of Dickens. Smiley suggests that our postmodernist age is more receptive to his kind of "flat," larger-than-life, often grotesque characterization:

> Dickens appeals to that part of the reader that recognises that much is left undiscussed by reasonable discourse, that people and institutions often do populate our inner lives not as who they are but as what they mean to us, and that we often do not see them whole and complex, but simple and strange. This view, of course, has an affinity with childhood, as Dickens had an affinity with childhood, but it also has an affinity with many states of consciousness throughout life,

including madness or obsession and exalted states of love or spiritual transcendence. That Dickens submerged into his style many good, useful and humane ideas is a testament to the fact that his vision did not prevent him from living and working in the world, but simply intensified his experience of it. As he said to Forster, "Only think what the desperate intensity of my nature is."

That desperately intense nature produced an imagined world of extraordinary vividness, variety, and life-enhancing humour—but at a certain human cost, which Jane Smiley's book helps us to measure: the awesome expenditure of energy, the unremitting demands made upon himself and others, and the eventual abbreviation of life itself. Charles Dickens was indeed "the Inimitable." Few other writers have possessed his willpower, never mind his genius.

# chapter four

# FORSTER'S
# FLAWED
# MASTERPIECE

Ever since Lionel Trilling's seminal *E. M. Forster: A Study* (1943), which argued persuasively for Forster's canonical status, and focused special attention on *Howards End,* that novel has been required reading for serious students of modern English fiction. It has been exhaustively discussed and analysed in innumerable periodical articles and books. The details of its genesis, composition, and reception have been painstakingly recuperated, and the author's manuscript pored over for evidence of changes of authorial intention. And yet very few of the critics and scholars who have devoted so much time and attention to *Howards End* have concurred with Trilling's judgement that it is Forster's masterpiece. Most would award that accolade to *A Passage to India* (1924). Many have expressed dissatisfaction with the earlier novel, for a variety of reasons: its design is excessively schematic, its plot relies on improbable coincidences, the behaviour and motivation of the main characters are sometimes implausible, and its verbal style is prone to sudden, and not always happy, shifts of tone.

How can we explain or resolve the paradox, of a novel apparently so deeply flawed and yet so inexhaustibly fascinating to literary critics? There are, I suggest, two reasons. First, the good things in *Howards End* are very good indeed. Second, even when it does not fully convince as fiction, it is always intelligently engaged with issues of the deepest interest and concern to the kind of people who teach the humanities in universities, and to the much larger number of people whose values and beliefs have been largely formed by such an education. *Howards End* fingers with unparalleled precision a sensitive spot in the consciousness, or conscience (in French the word *conscience* has both meanings), of the liberal literary intelligentsia. In one of the best recent essays on *Howards End,* Daniel Born has argued persuasively that it provides "the most comprehensive picture of liberal guilt in this century."[1] The issue it addresses, and dramatises in an absorbing human story, is whether culture in the large sense defined by Matthew Arnold, as the pursuit of "a *harmonious* perfection, developing all sides of our humanity; and as a *general* perfection, developing all parts of our society,"[2] is ultimately dependent on the availability of money; and if so, what stance should those who subscribe to that view of culture adopt towards those who make money and towards those who have little or none.

Of course, the question does not present itself in quite the same terms at the beginning of the twenty-first century as it did in the first decade of the twentieth. For Margaret Schlegel (and for Forster) the possibility of bad faith arose when people of her type and class refused to recognize that their way of life, with its priorities, attitudes, and values, depended on the possession of private incomes, inherited and invested. "You and I . . . stand upon money as upon islands," she says to her aunt. "It is so firm beneath our feet that we forget its very existence . . . I stand each year upon six hundred pounds, and Helen upon the same . . . And all our thoughts are the thoughts of six-hundred-pounders."[3] One reason she respects the Wilcoxes is that they make no hypocritical pretence of despising the money that supports their life-style, and another is that they work hard for it. Today there are fewer intellectuals living on unearned income, but most of us are enmeshed in capitalist economies, uncomfortably aware (or complacently unaware) that the quality of our lives depends ultimately upon economic structures which entail injustice and inequality on a global scale.

Like all classics, *Howards End* is both revealing of its own time and yet of more than "period" interest. The manners and morals of middle-class English society in the decade before the Great War are preserved in its pages like a collection of perfect fossils. Some features of this world have gone forever: for example, the existence of a huge pool of cheap labour for domestic service; or the repressive and hypocritical sexual code which made pregnancy outside marriage the ultimate disgrace for a respectable woman. But in other respects, *Howards End* seems surprisingly relevant to our own contemporary concerns, especially in the debate it stages between the values of the liberal intelligentsia and those of the capitalist bourgeoisie. The Schlegels belong to the Edwardian equivalent of what an inspired anonymous British journalist in the 1980s called "the chattering classes," while the Wilcoxes are Thatcherites *avant la lettre*. When Henry Wilcox says to Margaret, "You can take it from me that there is no Social Question—except for a few journalists who try and get a living out of the phrase," he anticipates Mrs. Thatcher's notorious assertion (to a journalist) that "there is no such thing as Society." In her effort to make a connection between these two opposed social groups and their value-systems, Margaret Schlegel anticipates the ideological shift of the "soft left" towards acceptance of market economics following the collapse of Communism.

Edward Morgan Forster was born in 1879. His father died in the following year, and he was brought up by his mother, assisted by numerous female relatives. He later recalled the ambience of his childhood as "a haze of elderly ladies."[4] Notable among these was his great-aunt, Marianne Thornton, whose father had been a leading member of the so-called "Clapham Sect," an influential group of high-minded Evangelical Anglicans in the first decades of the century. She left Forster £8000 in trust on her death in 1887, enough to assure him of a modestly comfortable private income in adult life. But the most intense and important emotional tie in his childhood, and for long afterwards, was with his widowed mother, who never remarried. In psychoanalytical terms it was a classic scenario for the development of a homosexual temperament.

The happiest years of Forster's childhood were those between 1883 and 1893, when he lived with his mother at Rooksnest, a house in the country near Stevenage in Hertfordshire, about twenty-five miles north of London, that was to be the model for "Howards End." Later they moved to Tonbridge, in Kent, where Forster attended Tonbridge School. In spite of being protected from the full rigours of a British public school by virtue of being a day pupil rather than a boarder, Forster was deeply miserable at this establishment. His gentle, shy, feminized personality was at odds with the aggressively masculine, athletic, and imperialistic ethos of the school (of which the Wilcoxes might have been products).

In 1897, however, Forster went up to Kings College Cambridge to read classics, and was happy once more. He came under the influence, indirect rather than direct, of the philosopher G. E. Moore, whose *Principia Ethica* (1903) argued that affectionate personal relations and the contemplation of beauty are the supremely good states of mind. This teaching was enthusiastically adopted by some of the cleverest young men in Cambridge, such as Lytton Strachey and Maynard Keynes, who in due course carried it to London, where, stripped of Moore's own austere moral code, it became the hedonistic philosophy of the Bloomsbury Group. It would be difficult to exaggerate the influence of Cambridge on Forster's personal and intellectual development. As an undergraduate he found there a kind of ideal society—privileged but not ostentatiously affluent, steeped in tradition, and housed in beautiful ancient buildings. It was at that time an almost exclusively male society, in which intense friendships could and did develop. It was at Cambridge that Forster recognized his homosexual orientation, though some years passed before he experienced his first physical relationship.

After graduating Forster travelled extensively in Italy (with his mother as companion) and later took a cruise to Greece, acquiring experience of the English abroad that he would use to good effect in his early novels. On his return to England he began to write for the *Independent Review,* a new journal founded by a group of his friends and aimed at the liberal intelligentsia. It published his first short story, "The Story of a

Panic," in 1904. In the following year he published his first novel, *Where Angels Fear to Tread*. *Howards End* (1910) was Forster's fourth published novel, and the one that firmly established his reputation among his contemporaries as an important writer.

The first seed of *Howards End* seems to have been planted in Forster's consciousness by a return in the summer of 1906 to his old haunts near Stevenage. He called at Highfield, a house owned by a wealthy stockbroker named Poston, where he and his mother had been frequent visitors in his youth. Mr. Poston had lost his wife and recently married a new one, whom Forster found "pretty, pleasant and clever" but incongruously matched with her philistine and boastful husband. "Like all such he talks incessantly," Forster reported to his mother in a letter. "The rooms are full of Fra Angelicos, etc., and [Poston] shows them off just as he used to show off his fields, though in this case he cannot always recollect the names . . . I cannot think that such an unusually charming person can love him deeply."[5] Here we seem to recognize the unsuspecting models for Margaret Schlegel and Henry Wilcox. But it was two years before Forster sketched the first outline of *Howards End:*

> Idea for another novel shaping, and may do well to write it down. In a prelude Helen goes to stop with the Wilcoxes, gets engaged to the son and breaks it off immediately, for her instinct sees the spiritual cleavage between the families. Mrs Wilcox dies, and some years later Margaret gets engaged to the widower, a man impeccable publicly. They are accosted by a prostitute. M. because she understands and is great, marries him. The wrong thing to do. He,

because he is little, cannot bear to be understood, and goes to the bad. He is frank, kind and attractive. But he dreads ideas.[6]

Interestingly absent from this synopsis is any hint of the reconciliation between Margaret and Henry Wilcox, and between the values they respectively represent, which is implied by the conclusion of the finished novel, and signalled by its epigraph, "Only connect." Forster evidently discovered this theme in the process of writing the novel, which occupied him until well into 1910. It was published in October of that year.

Forster's involvement with the *Independent Review* had focused his attention on social, political, and economic questions. One of the contributing members of the editorial board of this journal was C. F. G. Masterman, Fellow of Christ's College Cambridge, who became a Liberal Member of Parliament in 1906 and later served in government as a minister. In 1902 he enterprisingly rented a tenement flat in south London, and wrote a book of amateur sociology entitled *From the Abyss: Of Its Inhabitants, by One of Them.* (A year later Jack London published a similar account of his experiences in London's East End, *The People of the Abyss*.) "The abyss" is a phrase used in connection with Leonard Bast in *Howards End*: "The boy, Leonard Bast, stood at the extreme verge of gentility. He was not in the abyss, but he could see it, and at times people whom he knew had dropped in, and counted no more" (p. 58). The fear of falling into poverty through misfortune is the fate worse than death that haunts the genteel mind in the late nineteenth and early twentieth centuries. "The abyss" was the Victorian and Edwardian equivalent of what we call the Underclass, but before the institution of state welfare it was a bottomless pit of misery and degradation—hence the lurid and infernal name. We can be confident that Forster had read this book of Masterman's. Born observes that his description of Leonard and Jacky's flat in chapter 6 of *Howards End* "seems lifted straight out of *From the Abyss*."[7] Interestingly, when asked later in life if he had ever written about a situation of which he had no personal experience, Forster cited "the home-life of Leonard and Jacky in *Howards End*."[8]

In 1909, when Forster was writing his novel, Masterman wrote a series of articles in *The Independent Review* which he published as a book in the following year, entitled *The Condition of England*. *Howards End* is often called a "Condition of England novel." Forster would certainly have read Masterman's work as it appeared in serial form, and was evidently influenced by it; but the phrase itself had a much older provenance. It first became current in the 1840s, the "Hungry Forties" as they were called, a decade of great poverty, suffering, and social unrest. "The condition of England question," Thomas Carlyle wrote in 1843, ". . . is justly regarded as one of the most ominous, and withal one of the strangest, ever seen in this world."[9] In his novel *Coningsby* (1844) Benjamin Disraeli refers to "that Condition of England Question, of which our generation hears so much."[10] The question was explored in other novels, including Disraeli's own *Sybil* (1845), Mrs. Gaskell's *Mary Barton* (1848) and *North and South* (1855), and Charles Dickens's *Hard Times* (1854). Most of these novels dealt with the gap between the rich and the poor, the "two nations" of *Sybil*, and the problem of reconciling the interests and rights of capital and labour. In *The Condition of England* and *Howards End*, the emphasis falls somewhat differently. There are still two nations of haves and have-nots in Edwardian England, but there is also deprivation of a spiritual, cultural, and psychological kind which cuts across class divisions. By this date, the brutal, life-threatening poverty which the Victorian writers depicted had been, if not abolished, considerably reduced, as Masterman observes:

> A proportion of the population is raised well above the privations of poverty larger than ever before in history . . . It is rather in the region of the spirit that the doubts are still disturbing . . . Is the twentieth century to advocate a scheme of life which will itself provide a consolation in the loss of the older faiths, and redeem mankind from a mere animal struggle for the apparatus of material pleasure?[11]

This is a question Forster addresses in *Howards End,* sometimes through the reflections and observations of his heroine Margaret Schlegel, sometimes in his own authorial voice, and sometimes in a fusion of the two. There is a quasi-religious, certainly a mystical strain in this level of the text which is worth examining.

Forster described himself as "a child of unbelief,"[12] meaning that, to his generation of intellectuals, atheism and agnosticism came very easily, with none of the traumas suffered by their Victorian predecessors over the loss of Christian faith. Churchgoing and collective prayer were mainly social rituals in his childhood and youth; as an undergraduate at Cambridge he soon ceased to pretend that he was a believing Christian. But, as Frederick Crews has pointed out, Forster had "a thwarted fascination with the Absolute," a "theological preoccupation without a theology to support it."[13] Though he found Christianity unappealing, he was not a materialist, and recoiled from any reductively scientific account of human nature. In *Howards End,* sometimes through the authorial voice, and sometimes using the Schlegel sisters as mouthpieces, he frequently states the claim of the Unseen against the Seen. He is fond of the words "soul" and "eternity." His heroine Margaret seems not to be a believing Christian, or to subscribe to any other religious faith, but she is confident of her own immortality (p. 323). The railway station of King's Cross suggests infinity to her (p. 27). Her views on the relationship between sexual desire and human love are shared by the author:

> She knew that out of Nature's device we have built a magic that will win us immortality. Far more mysterious than the call of sex to sex is the tenderness that we throw into that call . . . We are evolving, in ways that Science cannot measure, to ends that Theology dare not contemplate. "Men did produce one jewel," the gods will say, and saying, will give us immortality. Margaret knew all this . . . (p. 238)

Neither Margaret nor Forster actually believes in the existence of these lowercase "gods," of course—they are a rhetorical flourish, to give life to a rather vague abstract idea. But Forster was always more sympathetic towards paganism than towards Christianity. One of the reasons he found Italy and Greece so congenial was that you didn't have to scratch far beneath the surface Catholicism of Mediterranean culture to find the traces of ancient nature worship. The wych elm at Howards End, with the pigs' teeth embedded in its bark, points to the ancient pagan past of the place, which is very much part of the house's symbolic significance.

Both Masterman and Forster were liberals whose deepest instincts were, in a nonpolitical sense, conservative. Both deplored the environmental damage caused by "progress," especially the increasing dominance of the motor car. Both regretted the loss of traditional rural customs, occupations, and amenities caused by spreading urbanization and suburbanization. Underlying the vision of both men's books is what we may call a pastoral myth, which associates all that is most valuable in human life with the country and all that is most threatening and corrupting with the city, and maintains that what looks like material progress is actually a process of spiritual decline. As Raymond Williams pointed out in his book *The Country and the City* (1973), the most striking thing about these views is that they have been firmly believed by some people (especially literary people) in every age or generation as far back as you care to trace them (eventually you end up in the Golden Age of classical pastoral, or the Garden of Eden before the Fall). Things were always better in the past, before they were damaged or destroyed by the internal combustion engine, or the industrial revolution, or land enclosure, or the dissolution of the monasteries, or whatever. Many of Forster's strictures on the decline in the quality of modern life, in a novel published more than ninety years ago, could have been written yesterday—except that the ruined England he describes despairingly is one we look back on as comparatively unspoiled. For example:

> Month by month the roads smelt more strongly of petrol, and were more difficult to cross, and human beings heard each other speak with greater difficulty, breathed less of the air, and saw less of the sky. Nature withdrew: the leaves were falling by midsummer; the sun shone through dirt with an admired obscurity. (p. 115)

*Howards End* is almost allegorical in design, and for this reason it is impossible to discuss the novel without summarising the plot in some detail. The Schlegel sisters, Margaret and Helen, are clever, cultured, and idealistic. Their surname inevitably evokes Romantic literature and philosophy, by association with the famous German brothers Friedrich and Wilhelm von Schlegel. The sisters are in fact half-German in extraction and have an easy familiarity with Continental Europe. They have private incomes which allow them to pursue their interests in high culture and personal relations without having to work for their living. There are differences of temperament and attitude between them which remind us of other pairs of sisters in classic English fiction (Elinor and Marianne in Jane Austen's *Sense and Sensibility,* for instance; Dorothea and Celia Brooke in George Eliot's *Middlemarch;* and Ursula and Gudrun in D. H. Lawrence's *Women in Love*). Margaret is more earnest, clear-sighted, and selfless than the volatile, egocentric, impulsive Helen, and is consequently favoured by the author. But they agree on many fundamental principles and differ mainly about how to put these into practice. Their London ménage is essentially feminine, even feminist up to a point, and they enjoy a degree of independence unusual for unmarried women of the period, both their parents being dead and their younger brother Tibby signally lacking in virile assertiveness.

The Wilcoxes, in contrast, belong to the prosperous commercial bourgeoisie. Henry Wilcox has lifted himself and his family to the top of their social class by his success as a businessman. He acquired the house, Howards End, through his wife's inheritance, but it does not satisfy his social ambitions, and throughout the story he is restlessly seeking some more pretentious abode. As a family the Wilcoxes are antithetical to the Schlegels: politically conservative, patriotic, insular (they have "very little faith in the Continent"), but imperialist, patriarchal (both syllables of the name have strongly masculine connotations), work-oriented, philistine, materialistic, conventional in manners, addicted to motor cars and sports in their leisure time. Mrs. Wilcox dutifully conforms to these values, though her heart seems to beat to a different tune.

After the two families meet on holiday abroad, the Schlegel sisters are invited to Howards End, but only Helen is able to go (there is a hint that Mrs. Wilcox really wished to invite Margaret alone). Helen is at first impressed by the energy and self-confidence of the Wilcoxes, and charmed by Mrs. Wilcox. She is physically attracted to the youngest Wilcox son, Paul, and imagines that she is in love. But she is quickly disillusioned, feeling "that the whole Wilcox family was a fraud, just a wall of newspapers and motor-cars and golf-clubs, and that if it fell I should find nothing behind it but panic and emptiness" (p. 40). This last phrase is one of several, like "telegrams and anger," "the Seen and the Unseen," "the prose and the passion," which Forster uses frequently in the course of the novel as a kind of shorthand for its cultural and metaphysical themes. We might detect here the influence of Matthew Arnold, who had a similar knack of coining and repeating key phrases ("sweetness and light," "Hebraism and Hellenism," "culture and anarchy") in his social and literary criticism.

Helen's efforts to disentangle herself from her brief involvement with Paul, compromised by Aunt Juley's clumsy intervention, generate the excellent social comedy of the novel's opening sequence. It is Ruth Wilcox who provides the necessary

calm and balm at the crucial moment. Though a loyal and obe-
dient wife, she is not a Wilcox in spirit. Her biblical given name
suggests a woman who has married into a foreign tribe, and
the fact that she dies quite soon in the story from a long-
concealed illness suggests that she has in some sense been
"killed" by the marriage. But she is not a spiritual Schlegel
either, being essentially conventional in her views and lacking
intellectual curiosity. She is identified with her house, Howards
End, and she embodies the pastoral myth referred to earlier.
We first see her like a figure in an allegorical masque:

> She approached . . . trailing noiselessly over the lawn, and
> there was actually a wisp of hay in her hands. She seemed to
> belong not to the young people and their motor, but to the
> house, and to the tree that overshadowed it. One knew that
> she worshipped the past, and that the instinctive wisdom
> the past can alone bestow had descended upon her . . . High-
> born she might not be. But assuredly she cared about her
> ancestors, and let them help her. (p. 36)

It is a crucial passage, in which, as so often in this novel, the
narrator's voice adopts a slightly archaic literary diction ("be-
stow," "assuredly," "high-born") to give solemnity and weight
to the sentiments expressed—and perhaps, the sceptical reader
may sometimes think, to disguise their lack of philosophical
foundations.

A second character essential to the thematic design of the
novel, Leonard Bast, is introduced in another consummately
managed piece of social comedy, when his umbrella is accidentally purloined by Helen at the symphony concert. Leonard is
an office clerk. "We are not concerned with the very poor,"
says the narrator. "They are unthinkable, and only to be ap-

proached by the statistician and the poet" (p. 58). This observation has irked many readers of *Howards End,* and indeed
there is something objectionable about it. Like several authorial asides in the novel, it seems to be trying to "have it both
ways"—to be both ironically self-deprecating and at the same
time flippantly patronising. The "very poor" are simultaneously elevated into the realm of tragedy and reduced to the
level of dull social statistics. In fact Forster had no direct
knowledge of the very poor and would never have risked
attempting to depict them in his fiction. But a white-collar
worker like Leonard Bast, clinging to the bottom rung of the
lower-middle class by his fingertips, and struggling hopelessly
to improve his lot and his mind, was for this novelist's purposes a more interesting example of the underprivileged in
Edwardian England than, say, a factory worker, or a miner, or
an agricultural worker such as Bast's grandparents were. The
Bast family history epitomises what Masterman called "the
largest secular change of a thousand years: from the life of
the fields to the life of the city. Nine out of ten families have
migrated in three generations."[14] The authorial voice of
*Howards End* speculates that Leonard Bast would have been
happier in the more static society of the past, when he would
have had a settled place and role in society. As it is, he lacks the
education, leisure, and funds to fulfill his aspirations to high
culture.

The eagerness of the Schlegel sisters to be nice to Bast, his
bafflement by their skittish chatter and free-and-easy manners,
the unbridgeable gap of experience, assumptions, and economic status between him and them—all these things are
captured and communicated by Forster with an exquisite
lightness of touch and economy of means. The whole of

chapter 5 indeed displays Forster's skill as a writer at his best: from the famous commentary on Beethoven's Fifth Symphony at the beginning, to its quiet, meditative conclusion, as the Schlegel sisters' drawing room darkens with the evening, and the talkative women fall silent at last and reflect uneasily on their brief, unsatisfactory encounter with Leonard Bast:

> It remained as a goblin footfall, as a hint that all is not well in the best of all possible worlds, and that beneath these super-structures of wealth and art there wanders an ill-fed boy, who has recovered his umbrella indeed, but who has left no address behind him, and no name. (p. 57)

In the next stage of the narrative, the Wilcoxes take one of the new flats overlooking the house occupied by the Schlegels, causing the latter some irritation and embarrassment. Margaret writes a discourteous letter to Mrs. Wilcox, of which she is immediately ashamed (one is reminded of Emma Wood-house's snub of Miss Bates in Jane Austen's *Emma*). Making up for her rudeness, Margaret befriends Ruth Wilcox, though ostensibly they have little in common. Ruth is about to show Margaret her beloved house, but the expedition is aborted by the return of her husband and son from a motoring holiday. Shortly afterwards, Ruth Wilcox dies, leaving a note expressing a wish that Margaret should inherit Howards End. The Wilcoxes decide to ignore it. Henry Wilcox begins to woo Margaret, and she accepts him, to the dismay of Helen. The sisters seek Henry's advice on improving Bast's situation, but the result is that he loses his job and is cast into the abyss. The outraged Helen seeks to embarrass Henry into making repa-ration, but her ill-conceived plan has far-reaching and fatal consequences. Henry's hypocrisy is exposed and Margaret's marriage jeopardised; Helen herself spends a night with Bast and becomes pregnant; Bast is chastised by Charles Wilcox and dies of heart failure; Charles is sent to prison; Henry, "broken" by this misfortune, throws himself on Margaret's mercy (rather like Rochester at the end of *Jane Eyre*). At the end of the novel, Margaret and Henry are sharing Howards End with Helen and her child, who will inherit it. Thus Ruth Wilcox's wish is fulfilled, and the possible reconciliation of the divided classes, ideologies, and interests displayed in the story is suggested in the hopeful figure of the child and the traditional seasonal activity of hay-making, both symbolic of fertility and renewal. This pastoral idyll, of course, hardly constitutes a viable solution for post-industrial society at large, as Forster perhaps acknowledges in the ominous reference to the "red rust" of a housing development only eight meadows distant from Howards End (p. 329).

Forster set himself a difficult task: to tell a convincing story of personal relationships in which every character and every action also carries a heavy freight of representative significance and contributes to the thematic design. Opinions differ about how far he succeeded. Personally I am not bothered by his reliance on coincidence at several crucial points in the story (for example, Jacky's connection with Henry Wilcox, and Leonard Bast's untimely appearance at Howards End). These events are a legitimate exercise of a novelist's licence, and Forster handles them deftly. Helen's brief sexual relationship with Leonard Bast, which seemed gratuitously shocking to some contemporary readers, and excited the derision of Katherine Mansfield ("I can never be perfectly certain whether Helen was got with child by Leonard Bast or by his fatal forgotten umbrella. All things considered, I think it must have been the umbrella"),[15] seems to me not inconsistent with her character, though it can be seen as a displaced and disguised version of a more plausible homosexual encounter between two men from different classes.

The main stumbling-block for me, and for many readers, is Margaret's motivation in marrying Henry Wilcox. We see clearly what this signifies on the thematic level of the text: an effort to "connect" the wealth-creating energy of the Wilcoxes with the humanising idealism of the Schlegels. It arises out of Margaret's (and Forster's) conviction that liberal intellectuals are in bad faith in despising and dissociating themselves from the capitalist economic system which supports their life-style; and in failing to recognize the industry, dedication, and enterprise of those who keep the system going. "More and more do I refuse to draw my income and sneer at those who guarantee it," says Margaret (p. 178). There is nothing inherently improbable or inconsistent about this as an attitude. The problem is that Margaret is required by the plot to act it out by marrying Henry Wilcox, and nothing he says or does persuades us that she would do so. The best that can said for him is that he is a kind and efficient host on social occasions, but he values his friends as friends hardly at all. We never see him exhibit his skills as a man of business—the only piece of professional advice he gives turns out to be wrong. Intellectually he is prejudiced, arrogant, and conformist. He never engages in real debate with Margaret, and never changes his opinions about anything. He is a sexual hypocrite, who cannot see that his affair with Jacky was an offence against Ruth Wilcox, to whom he was married at the time, not to Margaret. One must agree with F. R. Leavis's magisterial verdict: "Nothing in the exhibition of Margaret's or Henry Wilcox's character makes the marriage credible or acceptable."[16] For this strand of the novel to work, it would have been necessary to present some new and more favourable view of Henry to the reader, but instead Forster continues to make him condemn himself by every word and action.

Sexual attraction might have provided the required motivation—and seems to do so, at first: Margaret's enjoyment of the novel experience of being wooed is plausible. But Henry proves to be a clumsy lover in courtship, snatching a wordless kiss and leaving Margaret upset and dissatisfied:

> . . . the incident displeased her. Nothing in their previous conversation had heralded it, and worse still no tenderness had ensued . . . he had hurried away as if ashamed. (p. 186)

As to their sexual life after marriage, Forster was prevented both by the reticence of the age and by his own ignorance of heterosexual love from giving us any direct account of that, but there isn't any indirect hint, either, of a sexual awakening or fulfillment on Margaret's part. Her thoughts on the subject all emphasise the sublimation of sexual desire in human love; and when Miss Avery shows her the nursery at Howards End, with Tibby's bassinet in place, as if awaiting a baby, Margaret turns away "without speaking" (p. 268), suggesting that she does not expect, for one reason or another, to have a child herself.

E. M. Forster has always occupied a problematic position in the literary history of the twentieth century. He is generally recognized as a major modern novelist, with a place in the same pantheon as Henry James, Joseph Conrad, James Joyce,

Virginia Woolf, and D. H. Lawrence. But even the admiring Trilling observed, shrewdly, that "he is sometimes irritating in his refusal to be great"[17]—something those other writers consistently strove to be; and in form his work has little in common with theirs, with the partial exception of D. H. Lawrence. The kind of fiction we call modern*ist,* or sometimes symbolist, exemplified by those writers, reacted strongly against the form of the nineteenth-century novel, in which, typically, a complex plot is narrated and commented on by an omniscient authorial voice. Instead it sought to represent the world as experienced in the individual consciousness or unconscious, using limited viewpoints, or unreliable narrators, and frequent time-shifts which disrupt the temporal logic of cause and effect. Narrative cohesion is to a large extent replaced by symbolic patterning and intertextual allusion in these often difficult and ambiguous works. Forster, however, in many ways perpetuated the nineteenth-century tradition. He tells an entertaining, well-made story in chronological order, frequently intrudes to comment on the action in his authorial voice, and switches the narrative point of view freely from one character to another. But his authorial intrusions are knowingly self-conscious, sometimes calling attention to their own artificiality in metafictional asides, for example:

> To Margaret—I hope that it will not set the reader against her—the station of King's Cross had always suggested infinity . . . Those two great arches, colourless, indifferent, shouldering between them an unlovely clock, were fit portals for some eternal adventure . . . If you think this is ridiculous, remember that it is not Margaret who is telling you about it . . . (p. 27)

Furthermore, Forster grafted onto the form of the well-made traditional novel a subtle use of symbolic patterning, the repetition-with-variation of resonant phrases and images, which he himself called, in his *Aspects of the Novel* (1927), "pattern and rhythm."[18] Another critic has called this technique "spatial form," and identified it as a key characteristic of modernist literature.[19] The combination of traditional and modern elements in Forster's fictional technique is signalled by his naming, as the novelists from whom he had learned most, Jane Austen and Marcel Proust.[20] The first name is no surprise; the second perhaps is, until we read what Forster has to say about the quasi-musical structure of *A la recherche du temps perdu* in *Aspects of the Novel*.

As an example of Forster's fictional technique in *Howards End* we might look at chapter 11, about Mrs. Wilcox's funeral and its aftermath. It begins with an authorial descriptive passage. "The funeral was over. The carriages had rolled away through the soft mud, and only the poor remained" (p. 97). We could be reading George Eliot—or Thomas Hardy, as the narrator goes on to describe the reactions of the local country people, and then adopts the point of view of one of them, a woodcutter pollarding the elms overlooking the churchyard. The woodcutter's thoughts convey the traditional, semi-pagan, in-tune-with-nature response to death, which soon gives way to a renewed commitment to life, as he goes off to "mate," stealing a chrysanthemum from the graveside for his girl. Then follows an authorial description of the deserted churchyard at night: "Clouds drifted over it from the west; or the church may have been a ship, high-prowed, steering with all its company towards infinity" (p. 98). This metaphor, which has a purely descriptive function here, is recalled for a serious thematic purpose in a crucial passage much later in the novel, in chapter 19. That chapter begins with Margaret and her companions standing on the ridge of the Purbeck hills with the south of England spread out before them, and ends with Margaret and Helen arguing about the differences between their values and those of the Wilcoxes. The authorial voice sums up:

> England . . . For what end are her fair complexities, her changes of soil, her sinuous coast? Does she belong to those who have moulded her and made her feared by other lands, or to those who have added nothing to her power, but have somehow seen her, seen the whole island at once, lying as a jewel in a silver sea, sailing as a ship of souls, with all the brave world's fleet accompanying her towards eternity? (p. 178)

This is very poetic prose, echoing a famous piece of Shakespearean patriotic rhetoric ("this precious stone set in the silver sea"—*Richard II*), and seeking to go even higher up the scale of the Sublime in the striking image of England as a ship of souls sailing towards eternity. If Forster persuades us to accept such high-flown language in what is essentially a prosaic tragi-comedy of manners (and I think he does here), it is partly because he has already planted the trope in our minds in a more subdued form in the earlier chapter. He is not always so successful. Some of the purple passages towards the end of the novel sound like George Meredith on a bad day (for example: "Let squalor be turned into tragedy, whose eyes are the stars, and whose hands hold the sunset and the dawn" [p. 321]).

Returning to chapter 11: after the brief reappearance of the woodcutter early next morning, the narrative focus shifts to

the Wilcox family "attempting breakfast" at Howards End.
First we get a rendering of Henry's thoughts about his
deceased wife, using free indirect style to convey his state of
mind with considerable intimacy and immediacy: "He had
been told of the horror by a strange doctor, whom she had
consulted during his absence from town. Was this altogether
just? Without fully explaining, she had died. It was a fault on
her part, and—tears rushed into his eyes—what a little fault! It
was the only time she had deceived him in those thirty years"
(p. 99). Then we get a description of Henry's physiognomy
from the narrator's point of view, with the narrator's implied
judgements on his character: "the chin, though firm enough in
outline, retreated a little, and the lips, ambiguous, were cur-
tained by a moustache" (p. 100). Then we have a sequence of
short scenes consisting mainly of dialogue, involving Henry
Wilcox, his daughter Evie, her brother Charles, and his bride
Dolly. We are briefly admitted to Dolly's thoughts, but in a
much more summary and therefore dismissive style than that
used for Henry Wilcox: "she wished that Mrs Wilcox, since
fated to die, could have died before the marriage, for then less
would have been expected of her" (p. 101). Charles and Evie
complain pompously about the pollarding of the elms, as a
way of not referring to their real feelings. "They avoided the
personal note in life. All Wilcoxes did," comments the narrator
(p. 101). The point of view shifts again, to Charles, and we
share his thoughts in free indirect style as he goes out to check
on his motor car. Then another dialogue scene: Charles has an
altercation with his father's chauffeur which is interrupted by
Dolly in a state of panic, summoning him back to the house
for a reason she cannot reveal in front of the servant (a frequent dilemma for Forster's characters). The reason is that

Henry Wilcox has discovered his wife's note about leaving Howards End to Margaret. A family council ensues in which they reproach the woman for whom they were grieving a few moments earlier, and rationalise their determination to ignore her wish. The ironies are worthy of Jane Austen. But Forster wants to be fair to the Wilcoxes. "It is . . . a moment when the commentator should step forward. Ought the Wilcoxes to have offered their home to Margaret? I think not" (p. 107). In ten pages the narrative discourse has shifted in perspective and voice at least ten times.

In *Aspects of the Novel* Forster took issue with the critic Percy Lubbock's insistence, following the precept and practice of Henry James, that a consistent and disciplined "method" in the handling of point of view was crucial to the craft of fiction. What is really crucial, Forster says, is "the power of the writer to bounce the reader into accepting what he says . . . Look how Dickens bounces us in *Bleak House* . . . Logically, *Bleak House* is all to pieces, but Dickens bounces us, so that we do not mind the shiftings of the viewpoint."[21] Clearly, this is a tacit defence of his own narrative method.

The reception of *Howards End* on its first publication in 1910 was enthusiastic. The consensus of reviewers was that with this book Forster had fulfilled the promise of his earlier work and established himself as an important literary novelist. The *Daily Mail* described it as "The Season's Great Novel," and the *Daily Telegraph* roundly declared: "Mr E. M. Forster is one of the great novelists."[22] The *Times Literary Supplement* described it as "a very remarkable and original book . . . What gives Mr

Forster's writing its quite unique flavour is . . . [the] odd vein of charming poetry which slips delicately in and out of his story."[23] *The Daily News* described it as "the most significant novel of the year," and commented on its intriguing combination of traditional and modern qualities: "Mr Forster's method is a sort of bridge between that of Mr Conrad and that of Mr Galsworthy."[24] Several reviewers expressed what subsequent generations of readers have felt—that the book's power and appeal somehow triumphantly survive its flaws. "Mr E. M. Forster has written a very remarkable book, though he has hardly achieved an altogether satisfactory novel," opined the anonymous reviewer in *The Westminster Gazette.*[25] Edward Garnett claimed in the *Nation* that "Mr Forster has sacrificed the inflexibility of artistic truth to the exigences of his philosophical moral," but was otherwise generous in his praise of a book that "says most effectively those very things that the intelligent minority feel, but rarely formulate."[26]

Forster found that he had suddenly become a literary celebrity—fêted, interviewed, the recipient of invitations and fan mail. But he did not have the temperament to really enjoy this success. His biographer P. N. Furbank plausibly suggests that its main long-term effect was to make him afraid of future failure.[27] Certainly he took many years to produce his next novel, *A Passage to India* (1926), and that proved to be the last one he published in his long lifetime. This barrenness was a matter of regret and puzzlement to his admiring readers. Some light was thrown on it after his death by the public disclosure and discussion of his homosexuality. To friends he had confessed to being bored and frustrated by the impossibility (for a writer of his generation) of dealing openly and directly in his fiction with the only kind of sexual love which really interested him. In old age he even turned against *Howards End* for this reason, recording the following judgement in 1958:

> *Howards End* my best novel and approaching a good novel. Very elaborate and all pervading plot that is seldom tiresome or forced, range of characters, social sense, wisdom, colour. Have only just discovered why I don't care for it: not a single character in it for whom I care . . . Perhaps the house in *Howards End,* for which I did once care, took the place of people . . . I feel pride in the achievement, but cannot love it, and occasionally the swish of the skirts and the non-sexual embraces irritate.[28]

This comment is characteristically honest, witty, and perceptive, but it has something of the weariness and impatience of old age. In middle life Forster wrote a number of stories and a novel, *Maurice,* with homosexual content, which he circulated privately. Some of these writings have been published posthumously, but they cannot be regarded as masterpieces of gay literature. Forster's literary reputation rests on the novels he wrote, not for a coterie, or for himself, but for the literary public at large, and among them *Howards End* will always have a high place.

# WAUGH'S
# COMIC
# WASTELAND

The early novels of Evelyn Waugh have probably given more pleasure to more readers than any comparable body of work from the same period of English fiction (1928–1942). I discovered these books myself in adolescence. I was, I think, fifteen when my father put into my hands a tattered Penguin edition of *Decline and Fall*. For most of his life he was a dance musician by profession, and at some time in the 1930s he used to play in a night club frequented by Evelyn Waugh and his friends, whose names figured prominently in the newspaper gossip columns of the day. This had given my father a personal interest in the author, but it was a very tenuous link between *my* world and that of Waugh's early fiction.

We lived in a cramped semi-detached house in a drab suburb of southeast London, our respectable lower-middle-class life-style constrained not only by the income of a jobbing dance musician, but by the climate of Austerity that permeated the whole country in the immediate postwar years: rationing, shortages, rules and restrictions—the fair-minded but somewhat puritanical ethos of the early Welfare State. I attended a local state-aided Catholic grammar school. Nothing could have been further from my experience than the world of Waugh's novels, inhabited by characters who were for the most part upper-class and in some cases aristocratic, educated at public school and Oxbridge, many of them idle, dissolute, and sexually promiscuous or deviant (though much of that went over my adolescent head), seldom seen occupied in useful work, their time mostly spent shuttling from party to party or from country house to country house, with occasional adventurous excursions Abroad. Even the fact that Evelyn Waugh was a Roman Catholic, as I was, provided little basis for identification, partly because Waugh's romantically idealised version of Catholicism (epitomised in *Brideshead Revisited)* was so remote from the religious subculture of the suburban Catholic "ghetto" which I knew, and partly because his religious beliefs were not overtly manifested in the early novels which I most enjoyed. I suppose I found these books fascinating precisely because they opened my eyes to the existence of a milieu wholly different from my own—adult, glamorous, hedonistic, and quintessentially "prewar." By Christmas 1950, when I was a month short of sixteen, I was sufficiently hooked to request as a seasonal present from my mother copies of *Vile Bodies, Black Mischief,* and *Scoop* in the Chapman and Hall Uniform Edition—books which I still possess and frequently reread with undiminished pleasure.

So what sort of books are these novels, and what is the secret of their enduring and catholic (with a small "c") appeal? The first thing to be said about them is that they are funny. Very funny. Laugh-out-loud funny. Laughter, as we know (intuitively, and lately from medical science), is highly therapeutic; and the ability to provoke it, in generation after generation of readers, is a rare gift, always cherished. But to call these books "comic novels" might suggest that they belong to a sub-genre of light fiction designed merely to divert and amuse. Waugh's early novels certainly do that—but they do much more. They disturb and challenge as well as entertain the reader. P. G. Wodehouse wrote "comic novels"—with great skill and verve, which Waugh greatly admired. But they are essentially escapist and formulaic; they do not grapple with the dark side of human nature. As Waugh himself eloquently observed, late in life, "For Mr. Wodehouse there has been no Fall of Man . . . the gardens of Blandings Castle are that original garden from which we are all exiled."[1] The world of Waugh's fiction, in contrast, is definitely a fallen one, in which people act with appalling disregard for fidelity, honesty, and all the other virtues. The fact that this behaviour is often very amusing does not make it any less shocking.

For this reason these books are sometimes described as satires. Waugh himself disclaimed this description, asserting that satire "flourishes in a stable society and presupposes homogeneous moral standards."[2] In fact it is doubtful whether there ever was such an era—it is a historical construction or a nostalgic myth. But the idea was of the utmost importance to Waugh's imagination. His work is saturated in the idea of decline—that civilization is in a state of terminal decay. The title of his first novel, *Decline and Fall*, could stand as the title of almost all of them, and the hymn sung by Uncle Theodore in *Scoop*, "Change and decay in all around I see," could be their signature tune. Satire in any era is a kind of writing that draws its energy and fuels its imagination from an essentially critical and subversive view of the world, seizing with delight on absurdities, anomalies, and contradictions in human conduct. It is not the disposable wrapping around a set of positive moral precepts. Evelyn Waugh's early novels therefore have an essentially satirical motivation. They turn an impartial and comprehensive ironic vision upon the pretensions and follies of every class, profession, race, and even religion. They gave offence to some readers in their own day, and undoubtedly they still do in the era of Political Correctness. We all have a desire or need to protect some things from irreverent scrutiny. But in these novels nothing is immune.

In combining elements of comedy, often of a robustly farcical kind, with satirical wit and caricature, in order to explore social reality with an underlying seriousness of purpose, Evelyn Waugh belonged to a venerable and peculiarly English literary tradition which one can trace back through Dickens and Thackeray, Smollett, Sterne, and Henry Fielding. Lewis Carroll was also a perpetual source of inspiration. But Waugh's early novels were distinctively modern—indeed, they were significantly innovative in form; though it was some time before this was fully perceived or appreciated. Could novels so effortless to read, so funny and so accessible, really belong to the history of modern literature? The academic critics of the time certainly didn't think so. Reviews apart, there was virtually no serious criticism written about Evelyn Waugh until after

World War II (and then, ironically, the usual complaint was that he was not as good as he had been before the War).

One reason for this neglect was that in the perspective of the dominant critical orthodoxy, that of the New Criticism, modern fiction was identified with modern*ist* fiction, that is to say the symbolist novel of subjective consciousness as represented variously by the work of Henry James, Ford Madox Ford, Joseph Conrad, James Joyce, Virginia Woolf, and D. H. Lawrence. Modernist fiction was difficult, obscure, experimental. It sacrificed story to the representation of subjective experience. It heightened and distorted language to imitate the workings of the consciousness and the unconscious. The generation of writers to which Waugh belonged (it includes Christopher Isherwood, Graham Greene, Henry Green, Ivy Compton-Burnett, and Anthony Powell) were of course well aware of this body of work, and of its poetic equivalents (Waugh's familiarity with T. S. Eliot's *The Waste Land* is particularly obvious). In many ways they shared the assumptions on which it was based—that modern life was peculiarly chaotic, disorderly, and unstable, and that the conventions of the Victorian or Edwardian realistic novel were inadequate to represent it truthfully. But like every new generation of writers, they had to free themselves from "the anxiety of influence" by their literary father-figures; they had to find a new way to "make it new." They developed a fictional technique that was antithetical to that of modernist fiction, without being a mere reversion to Victorian or Edwardian models. Instead of the over-plotted, over-moralized traditional novel, and instead of the almost plotless stream-of-consciousness novel, they wrote novels which declined either to comment or to introspect, which told interesting but often unsettling stories mainly through dialogue and objective description of external behaviour.

Of course nothing is ever entirely new in the development of literary form. There is always a precursor, a source of inspiration, for every innovation. In Waugh's case it was Ronald Firbank, that late-flowering bloom of the Decadence. Waugh's description of Firbank's eccentric but original fiction, in an essay published in 1929, is worth quoting at length:

> [Firbank's] later novels are almost wholly devoid of any attribution of cause to effect; there is the barest minimum of direct description; his compositions are built up, intricately and with a balanced alternation of the wildest extravagance and the most austere economy, with conversational nuances . . . His art is purely selective. From the fashionable chatter of his period, vapid and interminable, he has plucked, like tiny brilliant feathers from the breast of a bird, the particles of his design . . . The talk goes on, delicate, chic, exquisitely humorous, and seemingly without point or plan. Then, quite gradually, the reader is aware that a casual reference on one page links up with some particular inflexion of phrase on another until there emerges a plot; usually a plot so outrageous that he distrusts his own inferences.[3]

This, written by Evelyn Waugh between his first and second novels, would do very well as a characterization of his own technique. But great writers do not merely copy other writers; they borrow and transform the tricks they admire. Firbank's novels, amusing in short, infrequent samplings, are fatally limited by the author's narrow interests and camp sensibility. Waugh applied Firbank's techniques to a broader and more recognizable social world and combined them with other methods of fictional representation. From Firbank he derived the technique of evoking a scene and implying a plot through a mosaic of fragmentary, often unattributed, direct speech, but he does not entirely eschew "direct description." Indeed, passages of carefully wrought descriptive prose are often the source of his most effective comedy—as in, for example, the arrival of the Welsh Silver Band at the school sports in *Decline and Fall*:

> Ten men of revolting appearance were approaching from the drive. They were low of brow, crafty of eye and crooked of limb. They advanced huddled together with the loping tread of wolves, peering about them furtively as they came, as though in constant terror of ambush; they slavered at their mouths, which hung loosely over their receding chins, while each clasped under his ape-like arm a burden of curious and unaccountable shape.

Unfair to Welsh rustics? Of course—but the description of the upper-class members of the Bollinger Club mustering for their Oxford reunion on the first page of the novel is scarcely more flattering:

> . . . epileptic royalty from their villas of exile; uncouth peers from crumbling country seats; smooth young men of uncertain tastes from embassies and legations; illiterate lairds from wet granite hovels in the Highlands; ambitious young barristers and Conservative candidates torn from the London season and the indelicate advances of debutantes . . .

The comic surprise of that last phrase, attributing indelicacy to the putative virgins rather than their suitors, is very typical of Waugh's style, depending as it does on both the artful positioning of the words and the inversion of a presumed natural order.

Who was the young man who composed this droll, poised, irresistibly readable prose? Born in London in 1903, he belonged to a very literary family. His father, Arthur Waugh, was a publisher and man of letters; his elder brother, Alec, wrote a novel, *The Loom of Youth,* when he was only seventeen, and went on to become a professional writer and popular novelist. Alec had left his (and his father's) public school, Sherborne, under something of a cloud—the source material for *The Loom of Youth*—and in consequence Evelyn was sent to Lancing College, an establishment which prided itself on its atmosphere of Anglican piety. By the time Evelyn went up to Oxford, in 1922, however, he had become an agnostic.

Evelyn Waugh's adolescence was inevitably overshadowed by the Great War and the patriotic emotions it aroused, heightened by the fact that Alec was fighting in the trenches of Flanders. Evelyn's generation, the young men who had been just too young to fight in the War themselves, felt an irrational guilt about this, and a certain resentment at having been denied the opportunity to prove themselves in action. But in retrospect the War itself seemed more and more to have been a catastrophic folly, which completely discredited the older generation who had presided over it, and the values and assumptions to which they clung. In due course many of the younger generation, including Evelyn Waugh, would find ways of testing themselves by adventurous foreign travel, and would seek an alternative system of values in Communism or Catholicism. But in early youth they asserted themselves by the reckless and anarchic pursuit of pleasure. By the time

Waugh went up to Oxford, the sobering presence of Great War veterans in the student body had almost disappeared, and undergraduate life was, for many at least, a continuous party. Waugh certainly did little academic work. He mixed with a fast, smart set, lived above his income, got frequently drunk, and amused himself with student journalism. He was, in his own words, "idle, dissolute and extravagant." He left Oxford with a third-class degree in History and scant prospects of employment that would enable him to keep up with his fashionable friends. He enrolled for a while in an art course (he was a skillful draughtsman, as his illustrations to his own early novels attest), taught in two private schools of the kind classified by the teaching agency in *Decline and Fall* as "School" (as distinct from Leading School, First-Rate School, and Good School), was briefly a probationary reporter on the *Daily Express,* and even contemplated an apprenticeship as a carpenter. This was a period of great frustration and depression for Waugh, and according to his volume of autobiography, *A Little Learning,* he actually tried to drown himself off a Welsh beach in 1925, but was driven back to shore, and the will to live, by the stings of jellyfish. This story, at once shocking and amusing, reminds us how much *angst* and despair lie under the urbane comic surface of his early novels.

In 1927 he obtained a commission to write a book about Dante Gabriel Rossetti, and became engaged to Evelyn Gardner, daughter of Lord Burghclere. In 1928 they married, and at first fortune seemed to smile on the union of "He-Evelyn" and "She-Evelyn" (as they were known to their friends). *Decline and Fall* was published shortly afterwards to enthusiastic reviews, and they had a belated honeymoon on a Mediterranean cruise which He-Evelyn was offered free, as part of a travel-book deal (*Labels*, 1930). Rather ominously, he took Spengler's *The Decline of the West* with him to read on this trip. On their return to England in the spring of 1929, the novelist retired to the country to write *Vile Bodies*, leaving his wife in London. A few months later she informed him that she was in love with another man; the couple separated; and civil divorce proceedings began.

This, needless to say, was a heavy blow to Waugh, a private agony and a public humiliation. It seems that he had no inkling that anything was amiss with his marriage, and the suddenness and completeness of his wife's infidelity, so early in their life together, left a permanent scar on his psyche. It also left its trace in his fiction, most powerfully in *A Handful of Dust*, where the heartless sexual betrayal of a man by a woman epitomises the general collapse of values and morals in modern society. Shortly after this experience Waugh began taking instructions from a Jesuit priest and was received into the Church in 1930, the year when *Vile Bodies* was published. The character of Father Rothschild, S.J., who pops up here and there in that novel, often in the most exalted political circles, with a false beard and heavily annotated atlas in his suitcase, parodies the Protestant stereotype of the Jesuit as devious conspirator. But he makes a serious comment on the decadence of the Young Generation which seems to reflect Waugh's own views: "Don't you think," said Father Rothschild gently, "that perhaps it is all in some way historical? I don't think people ever *want* to lose their faith in religion or anything else. I know very few young people, but it seems to me that they are all possessed with an almost fatal hunger for permanence. I think all these divorces show that."

Although *Decline and Fall* and *Vile Bodies* are obviously the work of the same writer, there are interesting differences, both formal and thematic, between them. Paul Pennyfeather, the hero of the earlier book, is, as has often been observed, a kind of latter-day Candide, an innocent *naïf,* who is both victim and observer of the folly, villainy, and corruption of modern society. Expelled, with monstrous injustice, from Oxford, he is condemned to work as the lowest form of pedagogic life, an unqualified schoolmaster at a bad private school. From this fate he is rescued by the whim of Margot Beste-Chetwynde and suddenly installed at the glittering apex of high society. But the financial basis of this luxurious life-style is a prostitution racket for which Paul chivalrously takes the rap, and he is sent to prison. He is not altogether unhappy there: "anyone who has been to an English public school will always feel comparatively at home in prison." The absence of any pity for the hero's plight is entirely typical of these novels: it is left to the reader to supply the moral outrage which events invite. But he is rescued once again by his rich friends, and given a new identity, under which he returns to Oxford to study theology. Paul thus ends up where he began—but not quite the same person. He has had enough of liberty and licence. We leave him studying early Christian heresies in a spirit of intolerant orthodoxy—perhaps a premonition of the author's later conversion to Roman Catholicism.

Adam Fenwick-Symes, the hero of *Vile Bodies,* is also the victim of duplicity and betrayal, but he is less innocent and more knowing than Paul Pennyfeather; and by the end of the story he has become a deceiver himself. The plot, such as it is, charts his constantly frustrated attempts to raise enough money to marry Nina. Promises of riches are constantly being pressed upon him—by the drunk Major, by Nina's father, by Fleet Street—only to be snatched away again, or prove worthless. Eventually Nina callously jilts Adam to marry his friend Ginger, but soon regrets her decision. While Ginger is fighting in the war which has just broken out in Europe, Adam impersonates him at the Christmas festivities in Nina's family home. This adulterous episode, framed by all the domestic sentiment that belongs to a traditional English Christmas, is richly ironic—funny, shocking, and oddly poignant, all at once.

*Vile Bodies* is my personal favourite among these novels, for its daring mixture of the comic and the serious, and for the brilliance of its technique. There are unforgettable comic set-pieces, like Agatha Runcible's appearance at breakfast at Number 10 Downing Street in her Hottentot fancy dress costume, or Colonel Blount's absent-minded reception of Adam at Doubting Hall. But there is also a seemingly effortless evocation and deployment of a large cast of characters on a broad social stage. The novel might be described as a kind of comic prose equivalent to *The Waste Land*. Like Eliot's poem, it had painful personal sources (Adam's relationship with Nina obviously derives in part from Waugh's courtship and the breakup of his marriage), but, like Eliot, Waugh managed to objectify this material and embed it in a panoramic picture of the decadence and confusion of English society in the aftermath of the Great War, which seems to be spinning faster and faster out of control, like Agatha Runcible in her racing car. The narrative shifts rapidly from social group to social group; Cockney accents contrast with patrician voices, the jargon of motor racing mechanics with the in-group slang of the

Bright Young Things—*so bogus, so sick-making, don't you think? Or don't you?*

The technique owes a lot to cinema, in its fluid cutting from scene to scene, and in making the reader *infer* meaning from brief, telling images and fragments of conversation. Waugh belonged to the first generation of writers to grow up with the medium, and he remained a regular cinema-goer throughout his life. His early fiction does by choice what film is bound by its nature to do—it stays on the surface of things. Perhaps this explains why these novels have proved difficult to adapt successfully as films: what seems experimental on the page seems routine on the screen, and the tension between the two media is somehow lost.

Another development in technology which left its mark on Waugh's fiction was the telephone. He was perhaps the first literary novelist to exploit this instrument on a significant scale to dramatise failures of communication, either deliberate or involuntary, between characters. Much of the courtship between Adam and Nina is conducted by phone, and one short chapter (11) consists entirely of two such conversations. Behind the clipped, banal phrases—*"We aren't going to be married today?" "No." "I see." "Well?" "I said, I see." "Is that all?" "Yes, that's all, Adam." "I'm sorry." "Yes, I'm sorry too. Goodbye." "Goodbye Nina"*—there are depths of unspoken pain and betrayal. The phrases "Well" and "I see," which have a merely phatic function in the conversation, acquire an ironic and poignant resonance, for nothing is well and these interlocutors cannot see each other.

In the 1930s, Waugh's professional life fell into a certain pattern: he would go abroad, write a travel book about his experiences, and then rework the material in a novel. In 1930 he was sent to Abyssinia by a newspaper to report on the coronation of Emperor Haile Selassie I. His nonfiction account of this trip was *Remote People* (1931), and its fictional fruit was *Black Mischief* (1932). Abyssinia is transformed into Azania, an island state off the coast of East Africa, whose young monarch, the Emperor Seth, is infatuated with western ideas of Progress and strives vainly to impose them on his still primitive subjects. He orders his commander-in-chief, General Connolly, to issue boots to the army and equip it with a tank. The tank cannot operate in jungle terrain and is useful only as a punishment cell; the soldiers assume the boots are extra rations and eat them. Seth's campaign to introduce contraception misfires when the people misinterpret his posters, with their before-and-after illustrations of the advantages of using condoms.

> See: on right hand: there is rich man: smoke pipe like big chief: but his wife she no good; sit eating meat; and rich man no good: he only one son.
> See: on left hand: poor man: not much to eat: but his wife she very good, work hard in field: man he good too: eleven children; one very mad, very holy. And in the middle: Emperor's juju. Make you like that good man with eleven children.

It is easy to mistake this comedy for a display of racial prejudice. There is no doubt that Evelyn Waugh, like most Englishmen of his class and time, harboured a measure of such prejudice. But his imagination was more even-handed. It was the *clash* of different cultures in colonial and post-colonial Africa, all seeking to exploit each other, that fascinated Waugh, because it generated so many delicious incongruities, absurdities, and contradictions in human behaviour. In Africa, he found, the comedy of manners bordered on the surreal. Only in *Alice in Wonderland,* Waugh wrote in *Remote People,* could he find a "parallel for life in Addis Ababa . . . the peculiar flavour of galvanised and translated reality."

Seth defines his struggle as "a war of Progress against Barbarism." Waugh shows that progress is usually only another form of barbarism. Certainly its representatives in Azania are hardly to its credit: the sublimely lazy and inefficient British legation, the self-important, self-deceiving French legation, or the Englishman who becomes Seth's right-hand man, Basil Seal. As a novel, *Black Mischief* suffers perhaps from not having a really sympathetic character, unless it is the down-to-earth General Connolly. Instead of a reactive, victimized hero, we have in this book a totally amoral anti-hero, a "corker" but a cad, to whom deception and the double cross are second nature. Basil's romance with Prudence, the British Ambassador's daughter, lacks the underlying poignancy of the relationship between Adam and Nina in *Vile Bodies,* but this absence licences one of the blackest reversals in the history of comedy, when he unknowingly eats her flesh at a cannibal feast.

In the winter of 1932–33, Waugh made a trip to British Guiana and Brazil to gather material for a travel book *(92 Days).* In the course of an otherwise uneventful trek through the jungle, he encountered a lonely settler whose eccentric and slightly sinister demeanour gave him the idea for a short story about an explorer who is held captive by such a man and is made to read the entire works of Dickens aloud at gunpoint. The idea continued to fascinate him, and in due course he wrote a novel, in his own words, "to discover how the prisoner got there, and eventually the thing grew into a study of other sorts of savage at home and the civilized man's helpless plight among them." The novel was *A Handful of Dust* (1934), and the "civilized man" is Tony Last, proud owner of Hetton Abbey, a hideously ugly Victorian fake-gothic country house, happily married (or so he thinks) to Brenda. In fact Brenda, a kind of aristocratic latter-day Emma Bovary, is bored and restless, unable to share Tony's enthusiasm for Hetton and the archaic lord-of-the-manor life-style that he tries to keep up on an insufficient income. She starts an affair with the unremarkable and effete John Beaver because he offers her some escape from the crippling ennui of her domestic life, and re-entry into the shallow, sophisticated pleasures of London high society. Tony is easily deceived because he "had got into the habit of loving and trusting Brenda," but a tragic accident to their son, John Andrew, precipitates an open breach.

Of all Waugh's novels, *A Handful of Dust* draws most deeply on the traumatic breakdown of his own first marriage, which makes the poise of the book—its subtle balancing and tight control of the tragic and the comic, the emotional and the satirical—all the more remarkable. Waugh's technique of staying on the surface, giving the minimum of information about the characters' thoughts and feelings, making the reader draw the appropriate conclusions from what they say and do, prevents the novel from becoming excessively emotional or moralistic. We never, for instance, get direct access to Brenda's mind or heart. The first indication that she is attracted to Beaver comes from a conversation with her sister Marjorie in which she first denies, and then half-admits, that she "fancies" him; and when she fails to mention on returning home to Tony that she met Beaver in London, we realise that she has embarked on a course of deception. Marjorie irresponsibly encourages the affair, then tries to effect a reconciliation—too late and for the wrong reasons. "Of *course* Brenda doesn't love Beaver. How could she?" Marjorie says to Tony. "And if she thinks she does at the moment, it's your duty to prevent her making a fool of herself. You must refuse to be divorced—anyway, until she has found someone more reasonable." The callousness, snobbishness, and arrogance of that afterthought make it a devastating indictment of Marjorie and her set.

The only point at which, it seems to me, Waugh is unfair to Brenda—when, in D. H. Lawrence's phrase, he "puts his thumb in the scale, to pull down the balance to his own predilection,"[4] is the climactic moment when she is told that "John" has been killed in an accident, and presumes it is her lover. When her informant clearly implies that in fact it is her son who is dead, "She frowned, not at once taking in what he was saying. 'John . . . John Andrew . . . I . . . Oh thank God . . .' Then she burst into tears." I don't believe that any mother, however cold-hearted and selfish, would say "thank God" in these circumstances. But I have not encountered any other reader who feels the same, and indeed this scene is often cited admiringly as an example of Waugh's irony.

Our sympathies are naturally drawn to the innocent party in the triangle, Tony Last, and it is hard to suppress a cheer when, by a brilliant narrative reversal, he turns the tables on

Brenda's selfish and grasping family and friends. But it is important to recognize that he is portrayed as a weak and limited man in many respects, and that his cult of Hetton is exposed as a self-indulgent illusion. "A whole Gothic world had come to grief" in the collapse of his marriage, for which he must bear some of the blame. That is why, in the novel's design, he is punished by the grotesque fate that awaits him in the depths of the South American jungle. Both Tony and Brenda are shown to be fundamentally immature, reverting to nursery rituals in times of stress, and both are shown weeping with self-pity, like children, when their fortunes reach their lowest ebb. Waugh later said of *A Handful of Dust* that "it was humanist and contained all I had to say about humanism."[5] What he implied was that, without a transcendental religious faith, humanism was helpless in the face of human weakness, evil, and death. His title was taken from *The Waste Land,* the work of another literary convert to Christian orthodoxy: *"I will show you fear in a handful of dust."* This work, considered by most critics to be one of Waugh's finest achievements, is certainly the most serious and complex of the early novels.

With *Scoop* (1938) Waugh returned to a more purely comic mode. "It is light and excellent," he commented in his diary early in its composition, and he was right. For this novel he drew on the experience of two more visits which he made to Abyssinia in the 1930s, as a correspondent reporting the Italian invasion and occupation of that country for *The Daily Mail.* This campaign was, like the Spanish Civil War, part of the political preliminaries to the Second World War, and in *Scoop* there is a good deal of topical satire at the expense of both Fascist and Communist ideologies. Essentially, however, it is, as its subtitle declares, "a novel about journalists," and has achieved immortality as such. Many journalists consider it the best novel ever written about their profession. The engine of the plot—a case of mistaken identity, which sends the retiring nature columnist of the *Daily Beast,* William Boot, to the war-threatened African state of Ishmaelia instead of the fashionable novelist John Boot—is one of the oldest in comic literature, and is, in the cold light of reason, highly implausible. So are many other events in the story. That doesn't matter in the least. As the very name of the fictitious newspaper implies, the novel is not meant to be soberly realistic. Waugh's comic genius allowed him to invent fantastic incidents which seem only slightly exaggerated in the reading, because they have a *representative* truthfulness. One might cite as an example the embedded anecdote of the legendary ace reporter Wesley Jakes, who started a revolution by accidentally filing a story from the wrong country. The basic message of the book is that newspapers construct the reality they claim to report—not (as modern media studies often claim) for sinister ideological reasons, but because they are so obsessed with the mystique of their trade—the need to entertain their readers, to scoop their competitors, and so on—that they make gross errors of fact and interpretation all the time. It is precisely because he is not a professional journalist that William Boot stumbles on the truth about Ishmaelian politics; but at one exquisitely ironic point in the narrative he is unable to publish a true story about a Russian agent operating in the capital because a false story to the same effect has already been circulated and then denied. The whole novel is a tissue of mistakes, misrepresentations, lies, and evasions. Mr. Salter's formula for dealing with his employer's gross misconceptions, "Up to a point, Lord Copper," has deservedly become proverbial.

*Put Out More Flags* (1942) is a kind of epilogue or *envoi* to the sequence of novels that began with *Decline and Fall*. In it, Waugh revived several characters from the previous books, like Basil Seal, Peter Pastmaster, Alastair and Sonia Trumpington, invented a lot of new ones (notably the homosexual aesthete Ambrose Silk), and exhibited this large cast reacting in various ways to the outbreak of World War II. Most of them are ill-prepared for the crisis—including the soldiers:

> Freddy was in uniform, acutely uncomfortable in ten-year-old trousers. He had been to report at the yeomanry head-quarters the day before, and was home for two nights collecting his kit, which, in the two years since he was last at camp, had been misused in charades and picnics and dispersed about the house in a dozen improbable places. His pistol, in particular, had been a trouble. He had had the whole household hunting it, saying fretfully, "It's all very well, but I can get court-martialled for this," until, at length, the nurserymaid found it at the back of the toy cupboard.

The novel is diffuse and episodic in structure, and somewhat uneven in tone, combining ruthless comic satire in Waugh's old manner with a more affectionate, even at times sentimental attitude towards his characters. One might cite, as examples of the latter, Alastair's altruistic enlistment in the ranks, or Peter Pastmaster's decision to marry and beget an heir before risking his life in the armed struggle. It should be remembered, though, that Waugh himself volunteered for active service with similar idealism, and that his subsequent disillusionment with the political and military conduct of the war had not yet hardened into firm conviction when, in 1941, he wrote *Put Out More Flags* to divert himself on a long and tedious voyage by troopship. And, in spite of its flaws, this novel has many pleasures to offer. The subplot of Basil Seal's commercial exploitation of the awful evacuees, for example, the narrative thread of the lunatic bomber at large in the Ministry of Information, and the unerringly wrong prophecies of Sir Joseph Mainwaring are handled with characteristic skill. The fact is that Evelyn Waugh was incapable of writing badly, and often in this novel he writes as brilliantly as ever. But his great work of fiction about the Second World War, the *Sword of Honour* trilogy, was still to come.

# chapter six

# LIVES IN LETTERS: KINGSLEY & MARTIN AMIS

The *Letters of Kingsley Amis* is a big, thick book: just over 1,200 closely printed pages, including copious and useful footnotes by the meticulous editor, Zachary Leader.[1] Faced with such a tome, readers may be tempted to dip into it, rather than read it from cover to cover. That would be a mistake. First, you might deny yourself much pleasure, especially in the form of humour. I have not laughed aloud at a book so frequently for a very long time—possibly not since reading the *Letters* of Philip Larkin, with which this collection is symbiotically connected. Second, only by reading the Amis letters continuously and in chronological order can you trace the "emotional arc" of the life they reveal.

I quote that phrase from Martin Amis's book *Experience*, which was published at the same time; and to get the most out of the father's letters you must read the son's book too.[2] It describes and meditates on a number of dramatic events in

Martin Amis's life that converged in a period not much longer than a year between 1994 and 1995, namely: the breakup of his marriage to Antonia Phillips, and the beginning of a new relationship with Isabel Fonseca (whom he later married); a long and excruciating course of dental treatment and oral surgery; the revelation that his cousin Lucy Partington, missing since Christmas 1973, was one of the victims of the infamous serial murderer Frederick West; the protracted and much publicised negotiations for a very large advance on his novel *The Information*, entailing an acrimonious parting from his agent Pat Kavanagh and her husband, Amis's close friend, Julian Barnes; the appearance in his life of a daughter, Delilah, now nineteen, whom he had never previously met and who had only just been informed of his relation to her; the life-threatening illness of his literary hero and mentor, Saul Bellow; and the last illness and death of his father, Kingsley.

This was an extraordinary concatenation of trials and tribulations, alarms and excursions, reversals and discoveries, which might seem implausible in a novel; and Martin Amis was wise to write it up in an autobiographical rather than a fictional mode, speaking, as he says, "without artifice"—which is not the same thing, of course, as without art. There is a great deal of art in *Experience*, not only in the style, as one would expect from this writer, but also in the structure. The narrative is notable for elaborate and complex time-shifts back and forth across the author's life, setting up echoes and parallels between incidents, playing variations on the themes of love and death, fathers and sons, innocence and experience. And it too has footnotes, even longer and more copious than Zachary Leader's, which provide a further level of remembrance and reflection.

Since Martin Amis, for reasons which may readily be guessed at, provides very little circumstantial detail about his matrimonial problems, the emotional core of *Experience* is the death of his father, which also provides its narrative climax. On one level, therefore, the book belongs to what has lately become a very popular subgenre—the confessional memoir provoked by the death of a parent or spouse, such as Blake Morrison's *And When Did You Last See Your Father?* John Bayley's *Iris,* and John Walsh's *The Falling Angels.* But Martin Amis's contribution has a special twist, in that his relationship to his father was, from young adulthood onward, always public as well as private, literary as well as familial. Not only were they both novelists; they occupied nearly identical positions as trend-setters in the literary generations to which they respectively belonged, and consequently excited more adulation, imitation, hostility, and media attention than any of their contemporaries. I once described this as "a dynastic succession unprecedented in the annals of English literature," and Martin Amis is well aware of its uniqueness. So indeed was Kingsley. In 1984, the year when both *Money* and *Stanley and the Women* were published, Martin reported that an American friend had said to him, "I bought your book today. I bought your daddy's book too," and Kingsley commented delightedly, "That sentence will only get said once in the history of the world." He was not always so benevolently disposed to his son's success, however. "Of course Martin Amis is more famous than I am now," he grumbles to Philip Larkin in a letter that same year. And in 1979: "Martin is spending a year abroad as a TAX EXILE . . . Little shit. 29, he is. Little shit." There is some irony at his own expense there, but some genuine resentment too.

With the Amises there was, therefore, a doubling of the

ordinary Oedipal tension between father and son. Literary rivalry raised the stakes in the unfolding family romance. When Kingsley left his first wife, Hilary, for Elizabeth Jane Howard in 1963, Martin and his elder brother were as hurt as children usually are in such circumstances. In due course they went to live with their father, but Martin's mild delinquency and resistance to schooling were obviously a form of protest. When, belatedly, he began to take literature seriously, he worked fanatically hard to achieve a first at Oxford, as his father had done, debated reputations and ideas fiercely with him, and developed his own talent under the inspiration of mentors (Nabokov, Bellow) whom his father scorned. In taste and practice, Kingsley was anti-modernist, but Martin is post-modernist.

*Experience* is, then, not just an exploration of the father-son relationship, but also of what it is to be a writer—more specifically, what it is to be a writer in a culture obsessed with the idea of celebrity. The interest of the mass media in literary novelists seemed to intensify suddenly in the 1980s, just as Martin hit his stride as a writer, and he has been in the public spotlight ever since. "I have seen what perhaps no writer should ever see: the place in the unconscious where my novels come from," he says at the outset of his book. "I could not have stumbled on it unassisted. Nor did I. I read about it in the newspaper." The deliberate bathos of the last sentence thinly disguises a deeply felt grievance. In 1994–1995 the obsessive interest of the British press in what another age would have regarded as his private life reached fever pitch. "My teeth made headlines." One of the motives behind *Experience* is a certain settling of scores with the fourth estate, or at least a setting straight of the record. (No journalist, one hopes, who reads Martin's graphic account of what was done to his teeth and jaw will ever make a sneering joke about "cosmetic dentistry" again.)

When Philip Larkin's *Letters,* edited by Anthony Thwaite, were published posthumously in 1992, they caused a good deal of consternation and controversy, duly whipped up by the media, because of the poet's privately expressed illiberal opinions and revealed penchant for soft pornography. Martin, who was reviewing the book, had a conversation with his father at this time which nicely evokes the sparring relationship that existed between them:

> —And I suppose *your* Letters are going to be even worse. From the PC point of view. There'll be even more fuss.
> —But I won't be around for that.
> —I'll be around for that.
> —Yes *you'll* be around for that.

And so he was, but more involved than Kingsley could have guessed. Martin read Zachary Leader's edition of the letters in typescript or proof while he was writing *Experience,* and he occasionally comments on them, as well as on the life events to which they refer, and sometimes comments on his comments in footnotes. On the whole he is relieved that the letters are not as offensive as he had feared they might be, and concludes that in the many fierce, exhausting arguments they had about nuclear disarmament, race, gender, and politics, his father was often deliberately "winding me up" (all's fair in the Oedipal struggle). The letters are certainly going to give offence, however. Kingsley Amis was often brutally dismissive in his comments about people, especially about other writers and their works. Many of them are still alive; some believed they were on friendly terms with him; and all will be hurt to some extent by what they read here. Since it is clear that Amis was writing with posthumous publication in mind ("what a treat is awaiting chaps when we're both dead and our complete letters come out"—Amis to Larkin, September 1956), one infers that he intended this effect, or at least didn't care about it. But then the old devil never went out of his way to be liked.

These *Letters* are not going to change the minds of people who have already decided that the man who wrote them was boorish, bigoted, sexist, and overrated. All the more reason to read them in tandem with the son's memoir, in which exasperation and outrage are tempered by affection and intimate memories. For example, one of the most troubling of Kingsley's character traits in later life was an obsession with Jews and their prominence in public and artistic life. "What's it like being mildly anti-Semitic?" Martin asked him one day. "It's all right," Kingsley answered, in typical sparring mode. But of course it isn't all right, not in the light, or darkness, of modern history, and one is glad to know that Martin harried him on the topic. On another occasion Kingsley found Martin with Primo Levi's *If This Is a Man*. "What's that you're reading? Some *Jew?*" Keeping his back turned as he fixed a drink, Martin summarised Levi's description of being rounded up with other Jews for deportation to Auschwitz. When he turned around, Kingsley's face "was a mask of unattended tears."

> He said steadily,
> —That's one thing I feel more and more as I get older. Let's *not* round up the women and the children. Let's *not* go over the hill and fuck up the people in the next town along. Let's not do any of that ever again.

I for one am grateful for that anecdote.

Reading the *Letters,* one wonders how different the development of postwar English writing might have been if Kingsley Amis and Philip Larkin had not happened to meet as undergraduates in war-time Oxford and become close friends. In due course they introduced a new style, a new tone of voice, a new stance towards reality, in poetry and prose, which quite simply changed the literary landscape and redefined the concept of the writer's vocation. It was very much a collaborative enterprise, in which they tutored and counselled and encouraged each other through the years of apprenticeship and obscurity, but it was conducted mainly by correspondence because, after Kingsley was called up in 1943, they never lived in the same place. As Martin observes of these letters, "It was love, unquestionably love on my father's part." Indeed, many passages could have been lifted from real love-letters. After one of their rare reunions Kingsley "was amazed as I always am to find how much we had to say to each other. I enjoy talking to you more than to anybody else because I never feel I am giving myself away" (14 June 1946). "I have a feeling that what we say to each other is more or less inexhaustible" (24 June 1946). Amis acknowledges and at the same time defuses the intensity of his devotion to Larkin by jokingly addressing him as "dalling," on occasion, while urging his diffident friend to fornicate as enthusiastically as himself and collaborating in the composition of a pornographic serial about lesbian schoolgirls.

It is fascinating to observe in these letters the gradual formation of what might be called the "poetics of the Movement" (do I hear a derisive snort from the spirit world?), using that phrase to cover prose as well as verse; and also to observe the development of Amis's own distinctive verbal style. Looking back in a late (October 1985) letter to Larkin, he said, "I think it's all to do with Mandarin vs. Vernacular, was it, as Cyril C put it?" and indeed Cyril Connolly's celebrated distinction in *Enemies of Promise* is a useful shorthand account of what Amis and Larkin stood for—and against—in literary culture, especially as glossed by Amis in the same letter: "You know, art novel, Pickarso, European thought, bourgeois conscience, Tuscany, Beckett, we haven't got a television set, lesson of the master and nothing happening. (Adapt Kojak's sneer: Who reads ya, baby?)" As Zachary Leader reminds us in one of his exemplary footnotes, Connolly said that Mandarins tend to "make their language convey more than they mean or more than they feel." This precisely sums up Amis's objections to Dylan Thomas and the Apocalyptic school of poets, and to the decadent work of older writers who had once been exponents of Connolly's New Vernacular style. Amis's comment on Stephen Spender in a letter of September 1946 is characteristic:

> I used to think that he knew how to put down good words. And now I have been reading Ruins and Visions, a poetry book. And I find in the words of this book there is a lot of poll lis sill ab bick fuss sin ness ("the total generosity of original unforewarned fearful trust"), and a lot of ad dough less scent sew dough mith oller gee ("Oh, which are the actors, which the audience?"), and a lot of Europe-falling-about-our ears and Oh-my-dearest and playing with abstractions . . . because HE CAN'T THINK WHAT TO SAY.

The youthful Amis may have acquired the habit of sceptical close-reading in part from *Scrutiny*, but the carnivalesque, polyphonic style in which he makes his analysis is worlds away from the earnest severities of Leavisian criticism. (A decade later, it blew like a refreshing breeze through the review columns of the *New Statesman* and *Spectator.*)

Right from the beginning of the correspondence there is a fascination with puns, homophones, misspellings, and mispronunciations of words. When Amis makes a typing error, for instance, instead of emending or crossing it out, he swears typographically, as it were, by fusing an expletive with the misprinted word, before typing the intended word correctly. For example: "Log fog Longmans sent the Legacy back of course" (9 March 1949; *The Legacy* was his first attempt at a novel). This kind of wordplay often seems quite Joycean ("I want to be the . . . *pee-tea* coach at a girls' school" [20 June 1950])—perhaps surprisingly in view of Amis's anti-modernist prejudices; but in fact he always respected Joyce's virtuosity, and in any case the verbal fooling predated his acquaintance with the Irish master's more experimental work. If there was a literary source, it was Frank Richards's Billy Bunter stories.

The Amis "vernacular style," then, was by no means a reversion to the stylized simplicity of Hemingway, or the cool elegance of early Waugh, or the I-am-a-camera realism of Isherwood (though *Goodbye to Berlin* was one of his favourite books, which he reread continually throughout his life). Amis's writing was more ludic, and it made elaborate use of obscenity and scatology. This began as a laddish private game between himself and Larkin, but gradually extended itself into their criticism, verse, and prose. An example would be their habit of concluding letters with a valediction ending with the word "bum." At first "bum" is merely an all-purpose word standing for, and thus mocking, official jargon related to events previously described in the letter, for example, "With reference to your application for the post of Assistant Lecturer in the Department of Bum." But in a more developed form it can have a punning logic or surreal appropriateness to the context, generating hilarious Rabelaisian comedy: "No doubt the matter has escaped your bum." "Amis asked for the Court's discretion in respect of his bum." "There is something disconcertingly unreal about Mr Amis's bum." The trope eventually found its way into Amis's fiction in *I Like It Here* (1958), and its supreme epiphany in the telegram the hero receives from his mother-in-law: "'KEEP PHOTOGRAPHICAL BUM TO SHOW ON RETURN . . .' There is a God, Bowen thought."

Another feature of Amis's fiction that he developed and perfected in his letters to Larkin was the observation and description of human behaviour, especially the mannerisms, meaningless remarks, thoughtless clichés, unconscious self-contradictions, petty pretensions, and the like that pervade all social life and social discourse. He found the father of his first wife, Hilary, Leonard Bardwell, particularly irritating in this respect ("He's gone out to-day to see how much he remembers of the geography of Swansea; those are the *ipsissima verba*. Now why, I wonder does he want to do that? What will he do if he remembers a lot of it? And what will he do if he finds he doesn't remember a lot of it?"). Amis relieved his exasperation by basing the character of Professor Welch in *Lucky Jim* on "Daddy B," while himself taking on the role of Jim. (For example: on meeting him at Swansea station: "As the train drew in I began swearing in a whisper and very fast, like a man about to go to a concert who pisses as much as he can

beforehand, even though he may not want to at the time.")
Some of the funniest passages in the *Letters* express Amis's violent hostility to this harmless and innocent man (whom his
grandson, incidentally, tells us he "loved").

Up to 1954, Amis's letters air two other constant complaints:
his poverty, and his failure to get published. "Oh I'm so poor,
I'm so poor," he wails in June 1952. And, in February of the
same year: "If only someone would *take me up,* or even show *a
bit of interest.* If only someone would publish some books by
me, I could start writing some books." The successful publication of *Lucky Jim* early in 1954 did not make him rich
overnight, but it did initiate a steady improvement in the family's quality of life. More important, he found himself recognized as an original new voice, and quickly began to network
with other young writers of similar orientation. He was
always rather disingenuous on this subject, repudiating the
label of Angry Young Man, and pooh-poohing the idea of a
coherent "Movement" or literary school to which his work
belonged. In practice he plunged into literary politics with
some relish. He befriended John Wain, whom he never really
liked, and whose work he despised (his demolition of *Living in
the Present* in a letter to Larkin in July 1955 might have silenced
Wain forever if he had read it), because he recognized Wain's
power and influence. "With you as general," Amis writes to
him shortly before the publication of *Lucky Jim,* "the boys
could move right into control." And a few weeks later: "It's a
branch of business, that's what it is, the writing game. A
branch of business."

The *Letters* tell a personal as well as a literary story, but, as always with writers, the two were intertwined. Amis's wooing of Hilly in Oxford as reported to Larkin ("We have been arguing for the past week about sleeping in the same bed as each other") was clearly the source for *Take a Girl Like You* (1960). In due course Hilly "yielded" and then became pregnant. Amis arranged an abortion (illegal, of course) but, to his credit, cancelled it at the last moment because of fears for Hilly's safety, and married her instead. The story is told with amazing candour in a long letter to Larkin, and would be told again nearly half a century later, barely altered, in the novel *You Can't Do Both* (1994). A very similar phrase, "You can't have it both ways, you see," occurs in a letter of December 1959, where it refers to the irreconcilability of marital stability and serial adultery, but this was a principle Amis found difficult to put into practice. The enhancement of his life-style, reputation, and self-esteem that came with literary success brought numerous opportunities for dalliance, which he seized greedily. There was something compulsive, and even desperate, about his philandering, as there was later about his drinking and eating. "I found myself at it practically full-time," he told Larkin on returning from a visiting appointment at Princeton. "You have to take what you can get while you can get it, you sam [*sic*]."

Hilly was hurt by his infidelities, but she had affairs of her own, and at one point Amis feared she might leave him for the journalist Henry Fairlie. This provoked a remarkable letter from Amis to Fairlie, tense with controlled anger and anxiety, in which he eloquently argues that a second marriage based on the illusion of romantic "love," and on the destruction of a first marriage, would be inherently unstable and unlikely to last. This proved to be eerily prophetic of his own future. Hilly's affair with Fairlie ended, and the Amises were reconciled; but a few years later, by which time Kingsley had taken up a fellowship at Peterhouse College, Cambridge, he met and fell in love with the novelist Elizabeth Jane Howard (appropriately, the occasion was a seminar on sex in literature). His love letters to Jane at this period, tender and rhapsodic, are like nothing else in the correspondence, and testify to the intensity of his romantic passion. One remark also suggests that there was some psychosexual insecurity behind his previous philandering: "Thanks to you I have dismissed for ever any lingering doubts about my masculinity and all that," he writes to her on 29 April 1963. He still wanted to have it both ways, with a wife and family in Cambridge and a mistress in London; but Hilly's patience finally snapped, and the marriage ended in a rather confused and messy fashion in 1963.

After the divorce, Kingsley married Jane, and for a while all was well in their rather imposing country house on the northern outskirts of London. Martin remembers Lemmons as a house "strong in love" at this time. But after a few years the seams of the marriage began to strain and split under the stress of temperamental differences, Kingsley's drinking, and sexual problems which proved unresponsive to the therapeutic treatment amusingly chronicled in *Jake's Thing* (1978). In December 1980 Amis informed Larkin that Jane had left him: "Not with anyone, just buggered off. She did it partly to punish me for stopping wanting to fuck her and partly because she realised I didn't like her much." The cruelly blunt language seems to imply *"and good riddance,"* but he adds with characteristic honesty, "trying to take in that she never will be around is immeasurably crappier than having her around."

In this mid-life period, Martin believes, Kingsley was in "moral retreat." There was an exceptionally long silence (four years) between *Jake's Thing* and the next novel, which was the designedly misogynistic *Stanley and the Women.* And it was about this time that Kingsley's political opinions, which had been moving to the right ever since the mid-1960s (having been communist as a student, and Fabian socialist in young adulthood), became increasingly rigid and extreme. A certain cooling of the friendship with Larkin is also observable. Robert Conquest takes his place as Amis's favoured correspondent for posterity, but the humour of these letters is coarser and more mechanical, the discourse less dialogical, than in the letters to Larkin. Amis seems at times to be turning into a caricature of himself.

Eric Jacobs's authorised biography of 1995 disclosed that behind the bluff and often aggressive public manner there was in fact a timid man, subject to numerous phobias about flying, travelling on the Underground, being alone in a house, and so on. The *Letters* and *Experience* reveal that this neurotic streak in his character went back further than one might have guessed. Martin recalls his father's panic attacks in the night in their Swansea years, and how Hilly would lead Kingsley to his bedroom to be calmed by his young son. Zachary Leader records in a note that Kingsley was consulting psychotherapists as early as 1946. I can't help wondering whether the source of all this isn't to be found in Kingsley's military service in the Royal Signals. It has always surprised me that he made so little direct use of this experience in his fiction—just three short stories. The letters that Amis wrote to Larkin at the time, like the stories, portray a life of boredom, depression, and petty intrigue which make Amis seem more like a National Serviceman in peacetime than a soldier who joined the Allied forces in Normandy only three weeks after D-day, and followed the advancing British army across northern Europe until the conclusion of the war. Whole literary careers have been launched on the back of such material, especially in America, and yet Amis made no explicit use of it. In a letter to Larkin of May 1953, wondering what to write about after *Lucky Jim,* he says "the Ormy [*sic*] is more or less out of the question—I didn't do any fighting and I've forgotten what I did do." Could there be some denial or repression of traumatic experience in that last clause?

Whatever the source of his neuroses, they made him ill-fitted to survive alone after the split with Elizabeth Jane Howard. The problem was ingeniously solved, through the mediation of Martin and Philip, when Kingsley set up house with Hilly and her third husband Alastair Boyd, Lord Killmarnock, paying the bills in return for being looked after—a development someone in his circle compared to a twist in an Iris Murdoch novel. The arrangement worked well, but Kingsley was in many ways a sad figure by that time—anxious, overweight, impotent, and either bored or angry when he wasn't writing. "Not much news . . .," he wrote to Philip Larkin. "I go to the club and get drunk, or read and get drunk, or watch TV and get drunk." That was actually in 1979, but his habits didn't change much in succeeding years. His literary tastes, never very catholic, narrowed still further. He couldn't get on with the new generation of fashionable British novelists like Salman

Rushdie, Ian McEwan, and Martin Amis, and was reduced to *re*-reading the crime stories of Dick Francis.

In Martin's view, Kingsley pulled himself out of this slough of despond by writing *The Old Devils* (1986). It is, Martin thinks, his masterpiece, but

> what mattered most to me at the time was that it an-
> nounced a *surrender of intransigence* . . . [It] marked the
> end of his willed solitude. He hadn't forgiven Jane, and
> never would, but he had forgiven women, he had forgiven
> love . . . Kingsley's snarl of disappointment had finally run
> out of breath.

*The Old Devils* deservedly won the Booker Prize that year, the prize Martin is famous for *not* winning, but the son rejoiced in the father's success (the Oedipal struggle was over by now); and it seemed to prompt a sudden late spurt of creativity. Several novels followed in quick succession, of varying quality, but always with cherishable and inimitable passages in them. Physically, though, Kingsley went into a steep decline. He began to fall down a lot, and one such fall triggered his final illness.

Martin's account of that illness, a combination of trauma, stroke, dementia, and pneumonia, does full justice to its pathos, its black comedy, and its moments of almost Conradian horror ("I'm in hell," he suddenly says from his hospital bed, to the consternation of his sons). In a particularly poignant scene, Martin tries to penetrate his father's befogged mind by reading to him the wonderfully comic speech of the aphasic stroke victim, George Zeyer, in *Ending Up*.

> —All this, Dad, in the book *you wrote*.
> He is contemplating me with delighted admiration.

—Do you remember?
—*No,* he said.

There is a sense in which watching and waiting for the death of a parent is the same for everybody. It is one of the fundamental rites of passage, an item on what Martin Amis refers to (borrowing the phrase from his friend Christopher Hitchens) as "the pain schedule" we carry about with us all our lives; and it is one that most of us, on reflection, would rather suffer than avoid. Having lost my own father about seven months before reading *Experience,* at a much greater age (ninety-three) but in not dissimilar clinical circumstances, I found this part of the book particularly absorbing and moving. It seemed to me that it got the mixed emotions involved exactly right. (The effect was reinforced by a strange coincidence. In a "Postscript" Martin Amis records that three weeks after the death of his father he went on literary business to Poland, to Warsaw and Cracow, and took the opportunity to visit, for the first time, Auschwitz—where, inevitably, he struggled to make emotional and cognitive connections between the small scale of his personal pain schedule and the immense and incomprehensible suffering memorialised there. Four weeks after the death of my father I made exactly the same journey, with similar thoughts and emotions.)

In concentrating on those parts of *Experience* that are most relevant to Kingsley Amis's *Letters,* I have hardly done justice to its thematic range and complexity. Some readers will be surprised by the personality of the author it reveals: tender, affectionate, even sentimental at times; a doting father, racked with guilt for breaking up his first marriage, thus visiting on his own sons the misery that he and his brother suffered when *their* parents separated; deeply disturbed by the foul murder of his cousin; sincerely delighted by his reunion with his long-lost daughter. I remember somebody in the media seriously suggesting to me at the time that the discovery of Delilah had been engineered as a publicity stunt to help sales of *The Information*. Martin Amis would probably be neither shocked nor surprised to hear that. He has a theory that the journalistic spite he attracts has something to do with the fact that his attackers are in the writing game too. "Valued reader, it is not for me to say that this is envy. It is for *you* to say that it is envy."

I have another theory, not entirely frivolous. Could it be that he acquired his reputation for arrogance because for twenty-five years (as he tells us) he never smiled in public for fear of revealing his teeth? This seems to have been one of the penalties of dynastic succession, like the Hapsburg nose. Kingsley too, we learn, had bad teeth—hence the rather supercilious smirk in the photos of him as a handsome young man, and the tight-lipped jowly stare of the later portraits. And embedded in *Experience* is a wonderful mini-essay about the dental deficiencies of the two literary precursors Martin most admires, James Joyce and Nabokov. "I claim peership with these masters in only one area," he writes. "Not in the art and not in the life. Just in the teeth." The book is full of such delectable humour at the author's own expense, by which he avoids the danger that this kind of writing always courts, of seeming narcissistic, self-justifying, and egocentric. The simultaneous publication of these two richly rewarding and intimately connected books, *Letters* and *Experience,* was a major literary event.

# chapter seven

# HENRY JAMES
# &
# THE
# MOVIES

The heroine of the hit romantic comedy of 1999, *Notting Hill*, is an American movie star who comes to England to make a film. That this film-within-a-film is an adaptation of an (unspecified) novel by Henry James shows how shrewdly *Notting Hill* fingered the pulse of cultural fashion and taste at the end of the twentieth century. Four major motion pictures based on James's novels have been released in recent years—*The Portrait of a Lady* (1996), *Washington Square* and *The Wings of the Dove* (both 1997), and *The Golden Bowl* (2000).

The usual explanation for this phenomenon is that James is the new Jane Austen—that the vogue for his novels in the movie world was triggered by the success of *Sense and Sensibility* and *Emma*. But there were several earlier movie adaptations of James's fiction. In 1974 there was *Daisy Miller*, directed by Peter Bogdanovich. The Merchant-Ivory team made *The Europeans* in 1979 and *The Bostonians* in 1984. There have been three film versions of *The Turn of the Screw,* most recently one in 1992 which updates the action to the 1960s. And going even further back, there was a film of *Washington Square* made by William Wyler in 1949 called *The Heiress* and based on the stage adaptation of that name. Olivia de Havilland won an Oscar for her performance in it.

Over the same period there were several television adaptations of James's books, especially in England in the 1970s, when there must have been a fan of James high up in the BBC's drama department. The BBC produced serial versions of *The Portrait of a Lady* in 1968, *The Spoils of Poynton* in 1970, *The Golden Bowl* in 1972, *The Ambassadors* in 1977, and *The Wings of the Dove* in 1979. A new adaptation of *The Turn of the Screw* was broadcast by the BBC in 2000. Television is arguably a more suitable medium than feature films for the adaptation of James's novels. The small screen lends itself to James's concentration on character and dialogue rather than action and spectacle. Serial form allows the adaptation to move at something like the leisurely pace of the original novels, most of which were in fact written for serial publication in magazines before they were published as books. For these and other reasons television adaptations of James's novels are more likely to be faithful to the original novels, and therefore more likely to please those who have *read* the novels, than movie versions. I am not going to discuss TV adaptations of James here, however, mainly because they are not available for viewing. (For the same reason I omit discussion of the Merchant-Ivory feature film of *The Europeans,* which was not available as a video in Britain when I was writing this essay.)

That Henry James's novels should be so popular with modern filmmakers is both ironic and paradoxical. It is ironic because throughout his literary career James hankered after a great popular and commercial success, and never achieved it. His novels never sold in great quantities, and his effort to become a stage dramatist ended in disaster after a few attempts, when he was booed by the gallery on the first night of *Guy Domville* in 1895, the most humiliating event of his literary career. In his lifetime he was revered by other writers and the more discriminating critics, but was never a best-seller, or anything like one. In recent times, however, his work has reached millions of people all around the world through the medium of the most popular and democratic art form of the twentieth century—the cinema.

James was an uncompromisingly highbrow writer, an innovator in form, whose works, particularly the later ones, are difficult and demanding even for well-educated readers. He was one of the founding fathers of the modern or modernist novel, which is characterised by obscurity, ambiguity, and the presentation of experience as perceived by characters whose vision is limited or unreliable. These are not the usual ingredients of best-selling fiction—and they are equally alien to the cinema. This is why the popularity of James's books with modern filmmakers is paradoxical as well as ironic.

Henry James was supremely a novelist of consciousness. Consciousness was his subject: how individuals privately interpret the world, and often get it wrong; how the minds of sensitive, intelligent individuals are forever analysing, interpreting, anticipating, suspecting, and questioning their own motives and those of others. And consciousness of this kind, which is self-consciousness, is precisely what film as a medium finds most difficult to represent, because it is not visible. If you make the characters put their thoughts into speech, you destroy the essential feature of consciousness in James's world-picture—its private, secret nature; if you have the characters articulate their thoughts in voice-over monologue, you go against the grain of the medium and produce an artificial, intrusive effect. Facial expression, body language, visual imagery, and music can all be powerfully expressive, but they lack precision and discrimination. They deal in broad basic emotions: fear, desire, joy. James's fiction, by contrast, is full of the finest, subtlest psychological discriminations.

An example: in chapter 41 of *The Portrait of a Lady,* Gilbert Osmond is discussing with his wife, Isabel, Lord Warburton's interest in his young daughter, Pansy. Relations between Isabel and her husband are already bad by this point in the story. Osmond says:

> "My daughter has only to sit perfectly quiet to become Lady Warburton."
>
> "Should you like that?" Isabel asked with a simplicity which was not so affected as it may appear. She was resolved to assume nothing, for Osmond had a way of unexpectedly turning her assumptions against her. The intensity with which he would like his daughter to become Lady Warburton had been the very basis of her own recent reflections. But that was for herself; she would recognize nothing until Osmond should have put it into words; she would not take for granted with him that he thought Lord Warburton a prize worth an amount of effort that was unusual among the Osmonds. It was Gilbert's constant intimation that for him nothing in life was a prize; that he treated as from equal to equal with the most distinguished people in the world,

and that his daughter had only to look about her to pick out a prince. It cost him therefore a lapse from consistency to say explicitly that he yearned for Lord Warburton and that if this nobleman should escape his equivalent might not be found; with which moreover it was another of his customary implications that he was never inconsistent. He would have liked his wife to glide over the point. But strangely enough, now that she was face to face with him and although an hour before she had almost invented a scheme for pleasing him, Isabel was not accommodating, would not glide. And yet she knew exactly the effect on his mind of her question: it would operate as an humiliation. Never mind; he was terribly capable of humiliating *her*—all the more so that he was also capable of waiting for great opportunities and of showing sometimes an almost unaccountable indifference to small ones. Isabel perhaps took a small opportunity because she would not have availed herself of a great one.

Osmond at present acquitted himself very honourably. "I should like it extremely; it would be a great marriage."

The corresponding passage in the screenplay of the 1996 film reads simply:

OSMOND: You see, I believe my daughter only has to sit
    perfectly quiet to become Lady Warburton.
ISABEL: Should you like that?
OSMOND: I should like it extremely.[1]

The long paragraph interpolated between Isabel's question and Osmond's answer in the novel is an extraordinarily subtle analysis of the games unhappily married people play when they talk to each other. Isabel pretends not to know how intensely Osmond desires the match in order to make him admit it and thus expose his own pretence of being aloof from such social vanities. This, we are reminded, is only one episode in the long war of attrition, of move and countermove, that their marriage has become. And although Isabel is the weaker party in this struggle, we see that she has learned, as it were, to fight dirty; she has learned how to dissemble for the sake of a small conversational advantage. Osmond, however, escapes by an unusual and graceful display of honesty: "I should like it extremely." James's dialogue is faithfully reproduced in the film, but there is absolutely no way the actors in the film could convey the content of Isabel's unvoiced thoughts or those she imputes to Gilbert Osmond in the text.

Here is a second example, this time from Merchant-Ivory's *The Bostonians,* one of the most faithful feature film adaptations of a James novel. The story concerns the women's movement in late nineteenth-century America. The heroine is a young girl, Verena Tarrant, with a charismatic gift for public speaking, who is befriended by the dedicated feminist—and, by implication, temperamentally lesbian—Olive Chancellor. Verena meets Olive's cousin Basil Ransom, a handsome young man of traditional views from the Deep South, who falls in love with her and courts her, but insists that she must give up her public career in the women's movement if she marries him. The story charts the tug-of-war between Olive and Basil for Verena's allegiance, and between her own divided loyalties. In chapter 39 Basil pursues Verena to a small seaside village where the two women are staying, and calls on her. Verena, who has just reaffirmed her devotion to Olive, tries to dismiss him, but he persuades her to take a walk. Later, Olive receives a message from Verena that they have gone out to sea in a boat. In the novel the sequel is told entirely from Olive's point of view, and represents a kind of dark night of the soul for her. She wanders the shore for hours thinking that Verena has betrayed her, that Verena never cared for her as she has for Verena, and she even doubts the point of her own feminist mission:

> She knew, again, how noble and beautiful her scheme had been, but how it had all rested on an illusion, of which the very thought made her feel faint and sick.

Then these feelings are overtaken by fears for Verena's safety. Olive hurries back to the house and finds Verena returned, huddled on the sofa.

> She didn't know what to make of her manner; she had never been like that before. She was unwilling to speak; she seemed crushed and humbled. This was the worst—if anything could be worse than what had gone before; and Olive took her hand with an irresistible impulse of compassion and reassurance. From the way it lay in her own she guessed her whole feeling—saw it was a kind of shame, shame for her weakness, her swift surrender, the insane gyration, in the morning. Verena expressed it by no protest and no explanation; she appeared not even to wish to hear the sound of her own voice. Her silence itself was an appeal— an appeal to Olive to ask no questions (she could trust her to inflict no spoken reproach); only to wait till she could lift up her head again. Olive understood, or thought she understood, and the woefulness of it all only seemed the deeper. She would just sit there and hold her hand; that was all she could do; they were beyond each other's help in any other way now. Verena leaned her head back and closed her eyes,

and for an hour, as nightfall settled in the room, neither of the young women spoke. Distinctly, it was a kind of shame. After a while the parlour-maid, very casual, . . . appeared on the threshold with a lamp; but Olive motioned her frantically away. She wished to keep the darkness. It was a kind of shame.

In the film we have no way of knowing exactly what either woman is thinking at this or any other point in the whole sequence, which is almost entirely silent, without dialogue, interior monologue, or even music. Olive's behaviour as she wanders along the shore expresses only anxiety about what has happened to Verena (she has a vision of the young girl's body being washed ashore which makes the point, perhaps over-emphatically). We have no way of knowing that she is suffering bitter disillusionment, with women in general and with Verena in particular. Then when Olive returns home to find Verena there, her behaviour in the film expresses only relief, and a sudden release of sexual passion when she embraces Verena. The gesture of waving away the maidservant with the lamp is retained, but we have no way of knowing that this is to conceal Verena's "shame."

The film is for the most part faithful to the novel in showing the episode from Olive's point of view. But it does add a scene not in the book, in which we see Verena and Basil on the shore, beside a rowboat at the water's edge. Verena, who has been wearing Basil's jacket, gives it back to him, and he throws it into the boat in a gesture of frustration and defeat as she walks away. It is not at all clear whether they have just come back from a boat trip in the course of which Verena has told Basil that she does not love him, or whether she is refusing to go out in the boat with him, which he interprets as a gesture of rejection. In either case she appears to change her mind, runs back, and throws herself into his arms. They embrace passionately beside the breaking waves. The next we see of Verena (evidently some hours later, to judge by the change of light) she is discovered by Olive, huddled on the sofa looking traumatised. What has happened in the meantime to cause this extreme reaction? The embrace on the seashore doesn't seem to account for it. If you didn't know the book, and your Henry James, you might think that Verena had been a victim of date rape.

I have given two examples where the film version cannot match the precision and subtlety of the representation of character and motive in the original novel simply because of the nature of the medium. So I come back to the question I raised earlier. Why have filmmakers been so attracted to James, when the difficulties of filming his work are so obvious and so formidable? There are several possible answers.

Period or costume drama is popular with audiences, and the film industry is always looking for suitable books to adapt. Such films are expensive to make, because of all the historical detail that has to be recreated, but the works on which they are based are mostly out of copyright, so movie rights do not have to be paid for. James's novels have great parts for American actors as well as British, which is important in an industry dominated financially by America. They give plenty of scope for sumptuous costumes, as well as visually interesting locations—aristocratic country houses, and "heritage" sites like Rome, Florence, and Venice. But they do not involve expensive set-pieces requiring masses of extras and special effects, as many earlier nineteenth-century classics do—there are no battles, revolutions, and the like in James's novels.

In his use of narrative, James was a transitional novelist, between the elaborately plotted novel of the high Victorian age—Dickens, Thackeray, George Eliot—and the modernist experimental novel of consciousness and the unconscious—Joyce, Woolf, Lawrence—in which plot is minimal. Commercial movies must have a strong narrative line. James's novels do have stories with a beginning, a middle, and an end, and they are about subjects which have always fascinated movie makers and movie audiences: sexual desire and money, and the various ways in which these things can become intertwined. But James's stories—even in the long novels—are fairly simple. There is not a lot of complication and subplotting. The essential narrative content of *The Portrait of a Lady* or *The Wings of the Dove* can be summarised, or "pitched" as they say in the movie industry, in a couple of sentences. This is an advantage in filmmaking. In adapting a Victorian classic, even as a TV mini-series, you have to discard a huge amount of plot, and a lot of characters. All you have to do with James is condense, and what gets left out is not narrative material, but psychological detail. *The Portrait of a Lady* is a very long novel—over 600 pages in my World's Classics edition—but every significant character in it appears in the film, even (fleetingly) Henrietta Stackpole's lover, Mr. Bantling.

James was not an inherently cinematic novelist *avant la lettre* as, for example, Thomas Hardy was.[2] James never describes situations of extreme physical jeopardy like that of Elfride and Knight on the cliff face in *A Pair of Blue Eyes,* nor visualises a scene with the startling detail and unusual perspectives of

Hardy's authorial narrator. That doesn't matter—the film-maker can bring his own heightened visual effects to the story. James's natural affinity was with the theatre, not with the new medium of moving pictures which emerged in the later part of his lifetime. He was a constant theatregoer and tried with very limited success to adapt his novels for the stage and to write original plays. This ambition is not surprising, because he was very good at dialogue—the dialogue of educated, upper-class people, mostly, but also on occasion lower-class American English—and he was good at imagining and orchestrating "scenes"—that is, people interacting in social situations, or confronting each other in private moments of conflict. He himself spoke of this as his "scenic method," and attributed it to his long-standing interest in the theatre. In short, he wrote novels which are full of characters and scenes that can be performed, and which would positively *invite* performance if they weren't so heavily enveloped in introspection and analysis.

It is tempting for filmmakers to suppose, therefore, that all you have to do with a Henry James novel is strip out all the psychologising. Then you will be left with a strong story, some interesting characters, and a lot of good lines, which sounds like a recipe for a satisfactory film. But of course it is not as easy as that. Without the psychologising, the plots can seem melodramatic, or difficult to follow, or simply uninteresting. Transferred from the page to the screen, the original dialogue can seem artificial. Ironically (in view of James's failure as a dramatist), his fiction—at least in the case of the shorter works—has transferred rather more readily to the stage than to the big screen: for example, *The Heiress, The Aspern Papers,* and *The Turn of the Screw.* On the stage, melodrama and artificiality are at home.

For those who know and love the novels of Henry James, the movie adaptations will always be more or less disappointing, because of the medium's inability to do justice to what is arguably the most important component of the books—their detailed and subtle representation of the inner life. Even those who do not know the novels may sense that something is lacking in these films, and wonder why anyone bothered to make them. It is no coincidence that the most critically admired film adaptation, *The Europeans,* was based on a little-known, relatively slight early work, essentially comic and satiric in tone, with a lot of dialogue and relatively little psychological analysis. Of the four recent major film adaptations, the most successful with film critics and the general public was *The Wings of the Dove.* It was also the one which took the most liberties with the original text and is therefore most likely to dissatisfy or outrage devoted readers of Henry James's novels. The films of both *Washington Square* and *The Portrait of a Lady,* in different ways, fall between two stools: trying to be faithful to a classic and trying to make a commercially successful movie for a modern audience. *The Golden Bowl* comes closest to squaring this circle.

The least satisfactory and least interesting of these films in my opinion is *Washington Square,* though it should be the easiest of the three to adapt. It is a short novel with a very dramatic story and lots of good scenes, as its previous adaptations for the stage and then the screen (as *The Heiress*) had shown. Catherine, the plain daughter of the rich Dr. Sloper, is courted by a shallow adventurer, Morris Townsend, abetted by her Aunt Lavinia, and steadfastly opposed by her dominating father. For some inscrutable reason the American producers cast two British actors, Albert Finney and Maggie Smith, for two of these four American characters, and employed a Polish director, Agnieszka Holland, to direct. As one would expect, Finney and Maggie Smith give excellent performances, but there were surely several American actors who would have done just as well. Maggie Smith's character, Aunt Lavinia, has been made less interesting than in the novel, where her vicarious romantic infatuation with Townsend is largely responsible for the tragedy. In the novel she is mischievous, in the film merely comic or pathetic. There is an absurd and totally incredible scene in the film when she arranges to meet Townsend clandestinely in a low dive (it is an oyster bar in the novel) where a couple are actually having noisy sexual intercourse behind a thin, tattered curtain at her back as she talks to Townsend.

The heroine is played by Jennifer Jason Leigh, who is completely miscast in terms of the original novel. Catherine is described in the blurb on the back of the videotape box as "a lovely young woman." The whole point of the story is that she is not lovely, and is entirely lacking in any other obvious charm. "A dull plain girl, she was called by critics," says the narrator. She is not even interestingly ugly or disabled. She is "stolid," strong and healthy. Clearly the film producers could not bring themselves to cast a genuinely plain actress. Jennifer Jason Leigh is good-looking in a rather gamine way, so to make sense of her part in the story she has to play the young Catherine as gauche to the point of imbecility. When she is introduced to Townsend at her cousin's engagement party, she stares at him like a hypnotized rabbit, totally incapable of speech, creating an embarrassing scene. In the novel, however, the scene is described like this:

Catherine, though she felt tongue-tied, was conscious of no embarrassment: it seemed proper that he should talk, and that she should simply look at him. What made it natural was that he was so handsome, or rather, as she phrased it to herself, so beautiful. (chapter 4)

The film also fudges the character of Townsend. In that scene of their first meeting, he seems as spontaneously taken with Catherine as she is with him. In the book it is obvious from the way he artfully ingratiates himself with Catherine's aunt on the same occasion that he is already conducting a calculated campaign to marry Catherine. The film, however, encourages us to think that he genuinely loves Catherine as well as her money. In a crucial scene in the book Dr. Sloper goes to see Townsend's sister, with whom he is living, to try to confirm his suspicions about the young man's true character. It's a brilliantly written scene in which the honest woman tries not to be disloyal to her brother, but cannot in the end conceal his unscrupulousness. Her final word, wrung from her by the force of Sloper's personality, is "Don't let her marry him!" and it settles any lingering doubts the reader may have about Sloper's judgement of Townsend. In the film, this line is moved forward in the scene to become part of a passage of verbal fencing: Sloper says he doesn't consider Townsend a fit husband for his daughter, and the sister says lightly, "Then don't let her marry him." The climax of the scene in the film is an attack by the sister on Sloper for arrogant abuse of his power and wealth. What makes the character of Sloper so interesting is that he is absolutely right about Townsend, but absolutely wrong in the way he treats Catherine. By blurring the first point, the film turns his character into a stereotype of the repressive father.

Both the screenplay and the direction move the story relentlessly towards cinematic cliché. So when Townsend finally breaks off the relationship and drives away from the distraught Catherine in a cab, of course it happens in pouring rain and of course Catherine, running after him, falls flat on her face in the muddy street. The final scene of the film is a particularly gross travesty of the original. In the novel, some years after the engagement was broken off by Townsend, and Sloper has died, he comes back, encouraged by Aunt Lavinia, to ask for a reconciliation, but Catherine, who has not married, tells him he has hurt her too much for her to consider such a thing. Townsend leaves, and in the last few lines there is an exchange between him and Aunt Lavinia in the hall that makes it clear he is as self-seeking as ever:

> "You will not despair—you will come back?" "Come back? Damnation!" And Morris Townsend strode out of the house, leaving Mrs Penniman staring.
>
> Catherine meanwhile, in the parlour, picking up her morsel of fancy work, had seated herself with it again—for life, as it were.

That is the last, eloquent line of the tale. In the film, Townsend calls on Catherine when she is teaching or entertaining a large group of little children (presumably in compensation for or sublimation of frustrated maternal instincts), who are removed so that the interview can take place. Catherine declines his offer. Townsend leaves, subdued, and we glimpse Aunt Lavinia in the hall. There is no exchange of words between them. Catherine sits down at the piano; a little girl comes up and stands beside her, and smiles timidly. Catherine smiles back and continues to play. An operatic soprano sings an aria on the sound track, the background goes dark, Catherine plays on, and she gives a faint reminiscent smile. Blackout.

*The Portrait of a Lady* is a more interesting failure. Great things were expected of it. It was directed by Jane Campion, the Australian director of that remarkable film, *The Piano*. It had a mouthwatering cast: Nicole Kidman, John Malkovich, Barbara Hershey, Martin Donovan, Shelley Winters, Richard E. Grant, and Sir John Gielgud. Yet it was badly received by most of the critics. Here are some review quotes I gathered from the Internet:

> "It's all surface and no depth. There's no heart to this story . . . many of the set-ups just take too long, none of the complications inherent in the plot are shown clearly enough, none of the dialogue does enough to emphasise the real evil involved in manipulating people . . . Poor Henry James. I thought of him rolling in his grave, as I sat squirming in my seat."

> "Campion has sacrificed sense to style, leaving powerful characters only vaguely explored in a story that should be based on emotions, not looks."

> "Very little of this tragedy makes it to our hearts as a result of an inept screen adaptation, inconsistent directing, meaningless camera angles and pointless closeups."

What went wrong? One might begin to answer that question by considering why Campion's *The Piano* went right. It was a director's film through and through. She herself wrote the script, which has relatively little dialogue (partly because the heroine is dumb) and tells a very simple story of basic emotions. The film makes its impact almost entirely by images—juxtapositions of culture and nature. Nobody who has seen the film will forget the opening scene of the piano being unloaded onto the surf-pounded beach, or the climax when the heroine in her Victorian clothing is dragged down into the depths of the sea, tethered to the piano. *The Portrait of a Lady* is a very different proposition: a classic novel, full of subtle psychological twists and turns, in which intense emotions are almost entirely concealed behind a surface of upper-class manners and polite conversation. The film certainly tries to be faithful to James's novel—perhaps the screenplay, written by Laura Jones in collaboration with Campion, tries too hard in this respect. Of course they had to condense drastically, but most of the dialogue is actually James's, and there is no significant deviation from the original story. However, Jones and Campion make spasmodic attempts to escape from this reverential approach with occasional sequences in quite different styles. The film begins with shots of a number of young women of the 1990s lying languorously around on the grass and then fades into a close-up of Nicole Kidman as Isabel—evidently a clumsy attempt to establish the "relevance" of the story to the present day. There is an erotic fantasy sequence in which Isabel imagines herself being caressed simultaneously by the three men who have at that stage been attracted to her—Ralph Touchett, Lord Warburton, and Caspar Goodwood. Isabel's tour of the Middle East prior to her marriage to Osmond is represented by an early silent film pastiche sequence in black and white which also takes on a surrealistic, dreamlike quality. These deviations from naturalism jar both with the basic style of the film and with each other.

Some reviewers thought that John Malkovich played Gilbert Osmond as such a creepy, sinister character that it was impossible to believe that Isabel would marry him. But it has to be said that there is a certain weakness in the original novel here—James never really shows us Isabel's moment of decision, of commitment to Osmond. We see her being quite plausibly attracted to his intelligence, culture, and polished manners; we see him call on her and make his proposal of marriage, which she does not accept or reject. She postpones an answer because she is going abroad. Osmond leaves, and James describes Isabel's feelings thus:

> Her agitation . . . was very deep. What had happened was something that for a week past her imagination had been going forward to meet; but here, when it came, she stopped. The working of this young lady's spirit was strange, and I can only give it to you as I see it, not hoping to make it seem altogether natural. Her imagination . . . hung back: there was a last vague space it couldn't cross—a dusky, uncertain tract which looked ambiguous and even slightly treacherous.

This "last vague space" is surely sexual, and it is not so much Isabel's imagination that cannot cross it as James's. He more or less admits as much, "not hoping to make it seem altogether natural." Then there is a gap in the narrative, and the next time we see her she is engaged. There is never a moment in the text when Isabel acknowledges that she is "in love" with Osmond.

Jane Campion has attempted to deal with this problem by suggesting that Osmond casts a kind of erotic spell over Isabel. She sets the proposal scene not in a drawing room, but in the crypt of the cathedral in Florence. Isabel returns to look for her parasol, which Osmond has found. Its shadows suggest a bat's wing. Isabel seems hypnotised as Osmond circles around her, twirling the parasol as he woos her. His final kiss (not in the novel at all) has a vampirish quality. The scene illustrates a general tendency in film adaptations of James's novels to make explicit the erotic element that James left implicit, because sexual emotions are comparatively easy to convey by nonverbal means. In this case, though, it was a reasonable liberty to take with the given material.

The endings of James's novels often raise problems for film-makers because he favoured open or ambiguous endings, whereas the expectation of a classic period film, especially if it is a love story, is that it will have a closed and preferably happy ending. The fatuous ending of *Washington Square,* which tries to compensate Catherine for her spinsterhood with a vicarious family of adoring children, is a case in point. The film of *The Portrait of a Lady* is more satisfactory in this respect. In James's novel, Caspar Goodwood makes a final appeal to Isabel to leave her hateful husband and live with him. She is tempted, but refuses. In the very last scene of the book, Henrietta Stackpole enigmatically urges Goodwood to "wait." In the screenplay Laura Jones attempts a more affirmative, if no more cheerful, ending by making Isabel's motive for returning to Italy an altruistic determination to protect Pansy from her oppressive father. The last scene in the screenplay—Isabel returning to the convent room where Pansy is incarcerated—is entirely invented:

*The door opens.*
PORTRESS: A visitor to see you.

> **Isabel** *comes into the room.*
> *The door shuts behind her.*
> **Isabel** *steps into the lamplight.*
> **Pansy** *looks at her as if at an apparition.* **Pansy's** *voice out of the shadows:*
> PANSY: You've come back.
> **Isabel**—*eyes dazzled by light*—*finds it hard to see the girl in the shadows beyond the lamplight.*
> ISABEL: Yes, I've come for you.
> *She holds out her hand towards* **Pansy.**
> **Pansy** *sees* **Isabel's** *hand, held out, in the brightest part of the light.*
>
> The End

Apparently this scene was shot, but not used (wisely, I believe). In the final editing Campion chose to end the film earlier than either screenplay or novel. Isabel has her final meeting with Caspar Goodwood in the snow-covered grounds of the Touchetts' country house, Gardencourt (the snow is a detail added by the film). Goodwood makes his passionate appeal, and takes Isabel in his arms. She responds to his kiss, but then breaks away and runs back to the door of the house. She stops with her hand on the door, turns, and looks back at him. Freeze frame: end of film. Isabel's expression and body language in the freeze frame are ambiguous. Is she turning back to Goodwood, deciding not to open the door that leads back to social respectability and emotional sterility? Or is she asserting that she is not running away at all, but courageously "affronting her destiny"? (This is James's phrase in the Preface to the New York edition of the novel, using "affront" in the slightly archaic sense of to confront defiantly.) It is impossible to tell. But this indeterminate conclusion is preferable to the screenplay's sentimental ending.

*The Wings of the Dove* was the best received of the recent James films. Stephen Holden in the *New York Times,* for instance, said: "Few films have explored the human face this searchingly and found such complex psychological topography. That's why *The Wings of the Dove* succeeds where virtually every other film translation of a James novel has stumbled . . . The English director [Iain Softley] has found the equivalent of James's elaborately analytical prose in the shadow play of eagerness, suspicion and self-doubt flickering across the face of its troubled three main characters." Holden put his finger on the fundamental challenge of adapting James for the cinema. Not all of his colleagues were as impressed as this, but the film did well at the box office, and was nominated for two Oscars—for Helena Bonham Carter's performance as Kate Croy and for Hossein Amini's screenplay.

This screenplay has been published, with a short but very interesting introduction by the writer. I happen to know that Amini was commissioned to write the screenplay after the film had been in development for several years, beginning with a script by the biographer and critic Claire Tomalin, which was much more faithful to the original novel. Amini (who had previously scripted *Jude,* a feature film adaptation of Hardy's *Jude the Obscure*), describes his first impression of James's novel as follows:

> . . . an extraordinary book, but very long, very dense, and completely uncinematic. The story telling was internal, the

key scenes were all reported after the event, and each character took on the narrative in a baton structure.[3]

But Amini had always been a fan of *film noir*, the generic term
given by French film theorists to certain Hollywood films of
the 1940s that dealt with stories of illicit love and crime from
the point of view of the transgressors—films like *Mildred
Pierce, The Postman Always Rings Twice,* and *Double Indemnity.* In
*The Wings of the Dove* he perceived a "film noir in costume"
waiting to be made: "two lovers deceive and betray a friend
and corrupt their love in the process. It was irresistible to a noir
buff." Amini candidly admits that "by reducing the novel to its
basic story spine we risked losing much of the texture and
complexity of the original, and there was a danger of drifting
into melodrama." But, he claims, this was the only way to
make a film of James's novel that would engage a modern
mass audience. And he was to a large extent justified by the
result.

"Where the book plays the major confrontations 'off camera,'" Amini says, "I had to reinvent them." In fact most of the
scenes in the film are either invented by Amini, or deviate significantly from the corresponding scenes in the novel. Some
examples of invented scenes: Kate tracking her father to an
opium den; Densher being denied access to Aunt Maud's
house; Kate and Milly giggling over pornographic illustrations
in a bookshop; Milly's first meeting with Densher at a party
which he attends with another woman on his arm—a deliberate provocation to Kate; Kate visiting Densher at his newspaper office; Kate visiting Densher in his lodgings. Lord Mark
is transformed into a drunken villain, and he blunders into
Kate's bedroom in the middle of the night, when she is his

guest, to say that he intends to marry Milly for her money but really desires Kate. The whole Venice carnival sequence, in which Milly excites Kate's jealousy by dancing with Densher, provoking Kate into letting Densher have sex with her standing up against a wall on the canalside, is, needless to say, invented—and incidentally is taking place at the wrong time of year.

Most of these changes have an erotic content, and one could say that the general effect of Amini's screenplay and Softley's direction, like Jane Campion's in *The Portrait,* but even more boldly, is to bring the implied sexuality of James's story to the surface, at the expense of considerable anachronism in the representation of manners. The filmmakers moved the implied date of the action forward by about ten years, but this was done mainly for design reasons and does not make the invented behaviour of the characters any more plausible or consistent. James's Kate Croy would not, for instance, have dreamed of visiting Densher unchaperoned in his lodgings: the essence of the lovers' dilemma in the novel is that they can't marry because of a lack of money and they can't meet in private because they aren't married.

The result of this very free adaptation is a rather vulgar, but very watchable, version of the novel. Two examples follow, from the beginning and the end of the film, both of which derive from scenes in the novel but deviate significantly from them. In the novel James explains, through Kate's internalised reminiscence, that she had met Densher long before her mother's death and before she moved in with her Aunt Maud—first at a party, and then by chance some weeks later, when they caught sight of each other in the crowded carriage of a London Underground train (it is one of the first literary novels in English to use such a setting). As the seats emptied, Densher moved closer to Kate so he could exchange some polite greeting. She guessed that he was staying on past his intended destination to keep her company, and indeed he got out at her stop and accompanied her home. So their mutual attachment began.

The film begins with a moody, atmospheric credit sequence set in the Underground, overlaid with a plangent sound track. Standing in a crowded carriage, Kate catches the eye of a young man who, politely but expressionlessly, gets to his feet to offer her his seat. She takes it wordlessly. At the next stop she gets out and he follows her until they are alone in a lift. As it rises to the ground level they suddenly turn to each other and passionately embrace. The fact that they don't speak to each other up to this point implies that this is their first encounter, and that the embrace must be read as the explosion of some sudden and irrepressible sexual chemistry between two strangers (rather like the first meeting of the lovers in *Last Tango in Paris*). But when Densher's fondling becomes overtly sexual, he murmurs, "Kate," and she says, "No, Densher"—then it is apparent that they know each other, and we can only infer that the way they behaved up to that point was some kind of sexual game to heighten the excitement of the meeting. There was no social reason why they shouldn't have greeted each other in the train, or pretended that they didn't know each other. It goes without saying that James's characters would never have behaved in either of these two ways. In the published script, incidentally, they don't say anything to each other in the lift, maintaining the ambiguity to the very end of the opening sequence. It cannot be denied that this succeeds in the primary task of an opening sequence: to seize the audience's attention, and draw them into the world of the film.

The ending of *The Wings of the Dove* provides one of the great moments in James's late work. There are in fact two key scenes after Milly has died, leaving Densher and Kate feeling unhappy and uneasy. In the first, Densher gets a letter written in Milly's hand which he shows to Kate. Together they burn it without reading it. Then Densher gets a letter from a New York law firm, and sends it to Kate, unopened. She brings it back to him, opened. They both know it contains news of a bequest to Densher—what they had plotted to achieve all along. But now Densher does not feel he can accept the money. Kate won't marry him without it, except on one condition:

> "Your word of honour that you're not in love with her memory."
> "Oh—her memory!"
> "Ah"—she made a high gesture—"don't speak of it as if you couldn't be. *I* could in your place; and you're one for whom it will do. Her memory's your love. You *want* no other."
> He heard her out in stillness, watching her face but not moving. Then he only said: "I'll marry you, mind you, in an hour."
> "As we were?"
> "As we were."
> But she turned to the door, and her headshake was now the end. "We shall never be again as we were!"

In the film these two scenes are conflated. Kate comes to Densher's lodgings because he has been avoiding her. He shows her the unopened letter from Milly. She throws it on the fire. Then she goes into his bedroom, takes off her clothes, and lies down on the bed, curled up like an unhappy child. Heavy rain streams down the windowpane and darkens the room. Densher undresses and joins Kate on the bed. After some verbal fencing about Milly, they make love. After their climax, the screenplay reads as follows:

> *For a moment neither speaks.*
> MERTON: I'm going to write that letter.
> KATE: Do whatever you want.
> MERTON: I want to marry you, Kate. *(There's a long silence.)* Without her money.
> KATE: Is that your condition?
> MERTON: Yes.
> KATE: Am I allowed one too?
> MERTON: Of course you are.
> KATE *buries her face deeper in his chest. She kisses it softly. Her eyes are wet.*
> KATE: Give me your word of honour . . . Your word of honour that you're not in love with her memory . . .?
> MERTON *stares out, he doesn't reply. They stay there a moment longer in each other's arms.*
> KATE *rolls away from him and gets out of bed. She takes her clothes and walks into the next door room.*
> MERTON *doesn't follow her, he lies in bed and listens to her put her clothes back on, he hears her walk out of the door and close it behind her, he hears her footsteps on the stairs. He makes no attempt to follow her.*

> *He lies back and stares at the ceiling, there are tears in his*
> *eyes. He rolls over on his front.*
> EXT. FLASHBACK. VENICE DAY.
> *A black and silver funeral barge moves like a silent arrow*
> *through the water.*
> MERTON *(off)*: "My heart is sore pained within me, and
> the terrors of death are fallen upon me, Fearfulness
> and trembling are come upon me, and horror hath
> overwhelmed me. And I said, Oh that I had wings like
> a dove, for then I would fly away, and be at rest."

This sequence is rather different from the other examples
I have considered in that the problem of rendering consciousness doesn't arise: in James's text the thoughts and motivation
of the characters are all out in the open, articulated in dialogue. Amini has, however, used this dialogue sparingly, has
deliberately discarded the great curtain line of the original,
"We shall never be again as we were" (presumably as too the-
atrical), and has instructed the actors to convey the emotions
they are feeling by their expressions and their body language.
Kate's wordless offering of herself to Densher is a displace-
ment of a sexual consummation that James refers to, but never
of course describes, in the novel: it is the price Densher exacts
from Kate in Venice for pretending to be in love with Milly. So
it is dramatically appropriate, though it would have been even
more effective if it had been their first lovemaking—Kate
keeping her side of the bargain even as the prize slips from her
grasp—and the implausible coupling beside the Venice canal
had been omitted. The scene has a powerful erotic charge, but
it is a sad, doomed kind of sexuality. Helena Bonham Carter's
thin, white, naked torso, writhing above the prone Densher in

what looks more like pain than ecstacy, is reminiscent of the paintings of Egon Schiele.

The finished film omits the quotation from the psalm, and adds another brief scene showing Densher returning to Venice, looking fairly prosperous and cheerful, presumably using Milly's legacy to dedicate himself to her memory. This seems to be another mistaken effort to provide a slightly more upbeat ending than the original, and is certainly much less effective than either Amini's or James's conclusions.

In their long-lasting partnership Ismail Merchant and James Ivory have developed a distinctive, but conservative, style of adapting classic and modern fiction that is sometimes unfairly derided by young cineastes as "heritage" cinema. In commenting publicly on his film of *The Wings of the Dove,* the director Iain Softley cited Merchant-Ivory as a model he *didn't* want to follow, and in that respect he certainly succeeded. I have faint but agreeable memories of Merchant and Ivory's lively version of *The Europeans* (1979). *The Bostonians* (1984) was an honourable failure at adapting what James himself acknowledged is a flawed novel (he excluded it from the New York edition of his work). Their adaptations of Forster's *A Room with a View* and *Howards End,* and of Ishiguro's *The Remains of the Day* are, however, benchmarks of the genre: beautifully acted, ravishing to look at, produced with scrupulous attention to period detail, and intelligently respectful of their sources. All of them were scripted by the novelist Ruth Prawer Jhabvala, as is their production of *The Golden Bowl.*

The first few minutes of this film suggest that the team has deviated drastically from its usual style—either that, or you have taken a wrong turning in the multiplex and are watching a different movie entirely. It seems to be a Websterian melodrama about aristocratic sex and violence in Renaissance Italy: a lady has been discovered in *flagrante delicto* with her stepson by her older (and allegedly impotent) husband and is dragged off, spitting defiance, to summary execution by his soldiers. Cut to 1903, and this lurid tale turns out to be an episode in the family history of Prince Amerigo, which he is relating to Charlotte as he gives her a guided tour of his dilapidated palazzo—and, in the nicest possible way, the push, because of his forthcoming marriage to Maggie.

This invented prologue develops what is a mere hint in James's text—that the Prince's family history has its dark and scandalous passages—into a kind of parallel narrative evoked and alluded to several times in the course of the main action, which takes place in England. For example, a ballet enacting essentially the same story is performed at a private party attended by the principal characters, causing them some discomfiture ("Just like *Hamlet!*" as one of the guests exclaims), and Amerigo and Maggie's little boy dresses up with a toy sword and paper helmet that recall the shadows of the soldiers in the opening sequence. There are several hints (not to be found in James's text) that Adam Verver might take violent revenge on the Prince if sufficiently provoked by jealousy.

This strand in the film was obviously designed to add some extra excitement, colour, and suspense to what is essentially a psychological study of characters constrained by the manners of their time and class from any overt display of violent passion. After the initial surprise (for those who know the book) it doesn't have the disruptive effect of the gestures to modernity in Softley's *Wings of the Dove* or Jane Campion's *Portrait of a*

*Lady,* but is fully assimilated into the period illusionism of the film. To Jamesians it will inevitably seem a distracting and unnecessary embellishment, but others may well find that it enlivens what is otherwise a restrained and deliberately paced movie.

James's novel is divided into two parts, entitled "The Prince" and "The Princess" respectively, and the author, who regarded it as his masterpiece, was particularly proud of the "manner in which the whole thing remains subject to the register, ever so closely kept, of the consciousness of but two of the characters" (Preface to the New York edition). This is not strictly true: we get glimpses into what some of the other characters are thinking and feeling in both parts, and there are choric interludes in which the Assinghams analyse and interpret the enigmatic behaviour of the principals. But it is vital to the effect of the book that in the first half we experience the story mainly from the Prince's point of view, and have *no* privileged access to the Princess's mind, while in the second half the reverse is true.

In the film, because of the nature of the medium, all the characters are equally transparent—or equally opaque. The actors can only reveal their thoughts by what they say, or by their facial expressions and body language. Happily *The Golden Bowl* is extremely well cast, and James Ivory has drawn from his performers ensemble acting of a very high order. Uma Thurman is outstanding as Charlotte—though admittedly the effect of adaptation, as well as the story itself, gives her a wider range of emotions to display than the other principals (Jeremy Northam as Amerigo, Kate Beckinsale as Maggie, and Nick Nolte as Adam Verver) are afforded. Anjelica Huston and James Fox give excellent support as the Assinghams, together with Madeleine Potter as the frisky Lady Castledean. All are adept at acting with their eyes, implying layers of unspoken thoughts. A good example, early in the film, is the quick oblique glance that Charlotte gives the Prince over Maggie's shoulder as the two women embrace at their first meeting after Charlotte and Adam's engagement. It combines triumph with a certain trepidation; it promises discretion about the past as it invites complicity in the future.

Another instance is the scene at Matcham, the country seat of Lord and Lady Castledean, when Charlotte coolly informs Fanny Assingham that she and Amerigo, in spite of the absence of their respective spouses, are going to stay on together at the house party for an extra day. Fanny stares her disapproval, and the Prince has to face down her barbed civilities. What we don't get—what we can't possibly get—is the tumult of emotion he is brilliantly described as feeling in the corresponding passage in the novel, his admiration for the social beauty of Charlotte's perfectly judged tone and his intuition of "some still other and still greater beauty" that it promises for them both:

> She had answered Mrs Assingham quite adequately; she had not spoiled it by a reason a scrap larger than the smallest that would serve, and she had, above all, thrown off for his stretched but covered attention, an image that flashed like a mirror played at the face of the sun. The measure of *everything* to all his sense, at these moments, was in it—the measure especially of the thought that had been growing with him a positive obsession and that began to throb as never yet under this brush of her having, by perfect parity of imagination, the match for it. His whole consciousness had by this time begun almost to ache with a truth of an exquisite

order, at the glow of which she too had, so unmistakably then, been warming herself—the truth that the occasion constituted by the last few days couldn't possibly, save by some poverty of their own, refuse them some still other and still greater beauty. (chapter 21)

This is a good example of how James's late style achieves a kind of slow-motion representation of consciousness, enabling us to follow and relish every nuance in a complex interweaving of thought and feeling that occupies only a few fleeting seconds in real time.

The few hours which the lovers spend together at an inn in Gloucester on the following day, on the pretext of visiting the cathedral before returning home, is the pivot on which the action turns. It is not only the moment at which the Prince yields to temptation (for all along it is Charlotte who is doing the seducing); it is also the point from which the Princess at last begins to suspect there is something not quite right or normal about the relationship between her husband and her father's wife. Part Two of the novel begins with Amerigo's somewhat embarrassed late return from Gloucester, as registered by Maggie's troubled, but typically generous and self-critical consciousness. Even when the scales finally fall from her eyes—when she discovers that the golden bowl she has bought for her father was considered years earlier by Charlotte as a wedding gift, but rejected on the advice of the Prince because it was flawed, thus revealing that they were intimate before her marriage—even then Maggie refuses the role of the righteously vengeful betrayed wife. Instead she fights to preserve her marriage, and her father's happiness, by lying. That is the novel's remarkable assertion, which the filmmakers have fully understood: that deception, which is the basis of adultery, can also be used to neutralise its destructive effects. Maggie lies when Charlotte asks her if she has done anything to offend her, and she lies to her father to keep him ignorant of her own unhappiness. But when he proposes to take Charlotte back to American City, to build a museum to house his collection, Maggie realises that he too has been feigning innocence and ignorance, and that he is sacrificing their precious father-daughter relationship to preserve both marriages. When Charlotte then claims that it is *she* who is taking Adam back to America, to remove him from Maggie's dominating presence, Maggie nobly accepts the lie, and the insult. Everybody is lying to everybody else most of the time, out of good motives or bad, and as long as the lies are not exposed the fabric of civilized society is precariously preserved. It is much to the credit of writer, director, and actors that the film manages to dramatise this endemic prevarication without dissolving into confusion or unintentional comedy.

Charlotte's increasingly desperate efforts to discover how much Maggie really knows about her relationship with the Prince is a kind of punishment, as Maggie recognizes, vividly figuring her rival and former friend as a bird in "a suspended cage, the home of eternal unrest, of pacings, beatings, shakings, all so vain, into which the baffled consciousness helplessly resolved itself" (chapter 35). But whereas Maggie emerges very clearly as the triumphant moral heroine of the novel, in the film our interest and sympathy are drawn steadily towards the tormented Charlotte, aghast at the prospect of parting from her lover and banishment to the social and cultural desert of American City. In a moving scene (not in the book), Charlotte relieves her grief and anger in a paroxysm of sobbing, then allows herself to be cradled like a child in the arms of her patient, paternal husband. It is all the more effective because she is lying on her bed in *déshabillé* that recalls the scene (also, needless to say, absent from the novel) of her abandonment to sexual pleasure with Amerigo. In the closing sequence, which deftly splices old newsreel footage with the fictional narrative, we see Charlotte accepting her role as Mrs. Verver in the New World with good grace and a certain regal dignity. If the final emphasis of the novel is on the reconciliation of the Prince and Princess, the film ends by affirming the solidarity of Adam and Charlotte Verver, but James's imaginative vision is not thereby betrayed. The Master would not be displeased by this thoughtful and carefully crafted film.

# chapter eight

# BYE-BYE
# BECH?

When writers decide to write works of fiction about writers and writing they brace themselves, nervously or defiantly, for an adverse response from friends, colleagues, publishers, and, in due course, reviewers. They expect to be told that such a project is incestuous, narcissistic, self-indulgent, and of no interest to anyone but themselves. But when these fears have been overcome, and the work begins, a sense of unwonted ease and enjoyment is apt to ensue. The writer is focused on a subject he really knows intimately, and about which he really cares—more perhaps than he cares about any other: the business of writing, in every sense of the word "business." There is no need tediously to research, or strenuously to imagine, the lives of non-writers—dealers or dentists or down-and-outs. The material is all there in his head, just waiting to be accessed.

Few writers have earned the right to such an occasional easy ride as fully as John Updike, whose oeuvre is remarkable for the scrupulous verisimilitude of its rendering of a variety of occupations, *métiers,* and avocations, in a wide range of social, historical, and geographical settings. For over thirty years—for most, in fact, of his long and prolific literary career—he has also been writing stories about the adventures of a fictitious Jewish American novelist called Henry Bech. The paradox is that the first two collections of Bech stories, *Bech: A Book* (1970) and *Bech Is Back* (1982), slim volumes whose jauntily alliterative titles frankly confess their metafictional jokiness, not to say in-jokiness, have been among the most popular of Updike's productions, more warmly received than some of his "serious" novels. Which is not to imply that the Bech books are not in their own way serious, or that Updike's novels lack wit and humour. But the former are arguably Updike's most overtly comic works, and this no doubt accounts for their popularity. It is all part of the holiday mood in which one intuits they were written: the author's (comparatively) effortless enjoyment of his task communicates itself to the reading experience. The latest installment of Bech's biography, *Bech at Bay* (1998), especially its last two stories, or chapters, suggest an author who is taking a wicked delight in his own invention.

For the benefit of new readers: Henry Bech was born in 1923, and enjoyed a fashionable success in the 1950s with his first novel, *Travel Light,* and a novella, *Brother Pig;* he then produced a long novel called *The Chosen* in 1963 which was intended to be his masterpiece but which was so badly received that Henry succumbed to a chronic writer's block—a condition he relieved by impersonating himself on various American campuses, and in various foreign countries, as a representative of contemporary American fiction. These adventures, which invariably involved Bech in sexual encounters with various female minders, meeters, greeters, and fans, were chronicled in *Bech,* one of the first books to register the fact that writers can now have quite interesting and economically sustainable careers without actually writing anything. It is merely necessary to have written something in the past, on the strength of which one can peddle oneself as a personality, a platform presence, a cultural envoy, or a dissertation subject.

In *Bech Is Back,* after further peregrinations of the same kind, the writer was jolted by a surprising marriage to his mistress's sister into rapidly finishing the work-in-progress he had been ineffectually tinkering with for fifteen years. On the last occasion when Bech submitted a book to his publishers they simply took it, printed it, and paid him a royalty. The finely comic rendering of Bech's bewildered initiation into the world of corporate, market-oriented, and publicity-driven modern publishing was another indication of Updike's sure finger on the pulse of cultural change. Entitled *Think Big,* Bech's new book received ambivalent reviews (for example: "The squalid book we all deserve"—Alfred Kazin; "Not quite as *vieux chapeau* as I had every reason to fear"—Gore Vidal) but became a best-seller on the strength of its saucy sexual content.

Both *Bech* and *Bech Is Back* are classified as short stories on the crowded preliminary page of *Bech at Bay* that tabulates John Updike's prodigious output, but the new book itself is subtitled "A Quasi-Novel," creating an unnecessary puzzle for future bibliographers. The format of all these books (for which Nabokov's *Pnin* is perhaps the model) is the same: a collection of self-contained stories unified by their common protagonist. In *Bech at Bay* there are five. One is the now-it-can-be-told story of a libel case in which Bech was involved back in 1972. The actions of the others date from 1986 to 1999. The book mainly covers, in other words, the hero's old age, to which his self-assessment in *Bech: A Book* still applies: "His reputation had grown while his powers declined." Bech has published nothing significant since *Think Big,* and shows no signs of doing so, but under the benign providence of his creator he ends up, in his seventies, more famous than ever—and still sexually active. So there is hope for us all.

The first story, however, "Bech in Czech," finds the novelist in a sombre mood, his morale at a low ebb. Once again he is on the road as a government-sponsored cultural envoy. He is staying in Prague as the cosseted guest of the American Ambassador, but he feels uneasy in the residence, a palace built by a Jewish banker whose family had to flee Hitler. "For a Jew, to move through post-war Europe is to move through hordes of ghosts, vast animated crowds that, since 1945, are not there, not there at all—up in smoke. The feathery touch of the mysteriously absent is felt on all sides." And nowhere more pervasively than in Prague. It is felt in the old Jewish cemetery where the gravestones of centuries are crowded together at crazy angles like cards being shuffled, and in the newer one on the outskirts of the city where Bech, at the Ambassador's tactful suggestion, makes a pious visit to Kafka's grave. "The vistas seemed endless . . . silent with the held breath of many hundreds of ended lives."

As for the present, it is 1986, and the Velvet Revolution is still three years in the future, unimagined and unimaginable.

Life in Czechoslovakia outside the luxurious precincts of the embassy is drab, depressed, deprived. Bech, uncharacteristically, feels unworthy of the respect accorded to him. All his books are translated and in print, but they "were petty and self-indulgent, it seemed to Bech as he repeatedly signed them, like so many checks that would bounce." A specimen *samizdat* volume shown to him at a gathering of dissident writers gives him, by contrast, "some archetypal sense of what a book was: it was an elemental sheaf, bound together by love and daring, to be passed with excitement from hand to hand." The Ambassador has a theory that the heroic age of Czech intellectual resistance came to an end in 1968, and Bech can see an element of truth in this: the dissident writers he meets have a somewhat weary, middle-aged air, as if resigned to the permanence of their plight. But some of them have suffered terribly for their principles. Imagining himself faced with the threat of torture, Bech "could think of nothing he had ever written that he would not eagerly recant." It is moments of ruthless honesty like this that make him, for all his faults, a rather endearing fellow.

Out of loyalty to the dissident writers, Bech is determined to despise the apparatchiks who run the state publishing network, but this consolation is denied him, for they turn out to be disconcertingly young, hip, and very well acquainted with Bech's work and its place in contemporary American writing. Altogether, Prague is an unhappy place of passage for Bech, equally alienated as he is from its historical past and its political present. Even his sexual appetite seems to be fading. He fancies the Ambassador's wife but lacks the energy or the gumption to make a pass at her until it is too late. Henry Bech, in short, is having a recurrence of the mid-life crisis from which he resurrected himself by marriage and the completion of *Think Big.*

> More fervently than he was a Jew, Bech was a writer, a literary man, and in this dimension, too, he felt cause for unease. He was a creature of the third person, a character. A character suffers from the fear that he will become boring to the author, who will simply let him drop . . . As his sixties settled round him, as heavily as an astronaut's suit, he felt boredom from above dragging at him.

After his lecture, bloated with undeserved praise and embassy white wine, Bech "lay in bed sleepless, beset by panic." The text then segues into passages extracted (a note on the copyright page informs us) from the Czech translation of the story "Panic," in *Bech Is Back,* which set up the final epiphany: "His panic . . . revealed a certain shape. That shape was the fear that, once he left . . . the Ambassador's Residence, he would—up in smoke—cease to exist."

I am not sure about the passages in Czech. They are manifestly inserted by Updike into Bech's consciousness, since Bech doesn't speak or read more than a few words of the language. As a device to express the character's alienation and disorientation it seems less effective and less justifiable than Tom Stoppard's use of Czech dialogue in his BBC television play of 1978, *Professional Foul,* which makes the audience share the English protagonist's helpless incomprehension of a secret police raid on a dissident's home. However, with that reservation, "Bech in Czech" is a very satisfying story. Nothing much happens—but that is in a sense the point; and our attention is held by the delicacy and precision of the prose, always Updike's enviable strength.

Most modern short stories end with either an epiphany or a twist. "Bech Presides" belongs to the latter type, and the fact that you can see the twist coming from miles away doesn't diminish the pleasure of the text, again because of the sentence-to-sentence quality of the writing. The year is 1990 and Bech, back in the Manhattan he loves and loathes, is sixty-nine. He is persuaded by a young editor intriguingly called Martina O'Reilly to contribute a tribute to the seventieth-birthday Festschrift of his old literary acquaintance and rival, Izzy Thornbush. The two writers' reputations have seesawed over the years, but perhaps at this juncture Izzy, the author of great sprawling flawed epics, has a slightly higher profile than Henry, whose most characteristic work aspires to the exquisite condensation of a haiku—or so Izzy's dishy wife Pamela tells Bech, not entirely to his pleasure, while he is looking covetously down the front of her dress.

At a party to launch the Festschrift, Izzy urges Bech to accept the presidency of a privately endowed academy called the Forty to which they both belong, and in his anxiety to leave the party at precisely the same moment as Martina O'Reilly and lure her to his loft apartment in SoHo (a tactic which succeeds), Bech hurriedly agrees to the proposal. Founded to enshrine "the dignity, the integrity, the saintly devotion that had once attached to the concept of the arts in the American republic," and housed in one of the last neoclassical brick-fronted mansions in midtown Manhattan, the Forty has become something of a dodo in the brutal, restless climate of postmodern culture. Its aging members meet at long intervals to consume a dinner, deplore the corruption of modern taste, and elect new members, as old ones die off, to make up the statutory total of forty. But even this task seems increasingly beyond them, so reluctant are they to acknowledge any merit in artists younger than themselves.

Bech rather enjoys the majesty of office, sitting at a desk as big as the deck of an aircraft carrier under the glass dome of the solarium, with a devoted secretariat of civilized, celibate ladies at his command, but he becomes increasingly exasperated at the members' inability to nominate any new members even though the society's continuing existence is in jeopardy. Updike takes liberties with real people, some of them living, in his amusing account of these discussions. "The name of William Gaddis, put forward by Thornbush, was batted aside with the phrase 'high-brow gibberish' . . . and that of Jasper Johns met unenthusiasm in Seidensticker's summation of 'Pop tricks and figurative doodles.'" Toni Morrison may be surprised and not altogether enchanted to read here that her nomination was withdrawn because the proposer forgot she was already a member.

Izzy springs a surprise motion to wind up the organization and distribute its assets among the members, which is passed by a narrow majority. Since the Forty occupies a prime mid-Manhattan site, quickly snapped up by a buyer, the spoils are considerable, but are immediately contested by the family legatees of the founder. It seems that most of the proceeds will probably be swallowed up in legal fees, and the members' greed justly punished thereby; but Izzy proves to have an indirect interest in the deal. Bech belatedly realises that he has been used, but is consoled by the prospect of receiving a cut himself, glimpsed in a final improvised haiku: *"After a life-time / of dwelling among fine shades / a payoff at last."*

*Bech: A Book* carried a mock Foreword in the form of a letter from Henry Bech to John Updike which deftly pre-empted the first interpretative question which is bound to be asked about the whole Bech saga: to what extent is it a serial *roman à clef?* "Dear John," it began, "Well, if you must commit the artistic indecency of writing about a writer, better I suppose about me than about you. Except, reading along in these, I wonder if it *is* me, enough me, purely me." After drawing attention to re-semblances between Updike's portrait of Bech and various well-known Jewish American writers (Mailer's sexuality, Bellow's silver hair, Philip Roth's boyhood, Salinger's writer's block, and so on), Henry Bech perceives also "something Waspish, theological, scared, and insulatingly ironical that derives, my wild surmise is, from you."

By scrambling so many clues drawn from so many sources, Updike has made it impossible for us to identify Bech with any one writer. By making him Jewish, he presumably aimed to establish an ironic distance between his authorial self and material that (as the Foreword concedes) was drawn in part from his own professional life and character. It was a risky strategy: how could a Gentile writer presume to represent the subjectivity of an American Jew in competition with so many brilliant real Jewish writers? Though I can hardly speak with any authority, it seems to me that Updike has risen admirably to the challenge, with the possible exception, oddly enough, of Bech's prose style. Here for instance is an extract from Bech's tribute to Thornbush:

"Here be dragons" was the formula with which the old cartographers would mark a space fearsomely unknown, and my own fear is that, in this age of the pre-masticated soundbite and the King-sized gross-out, the vaulted food court where Thornbush's delicacies are served is too little patronised—the demands that they, pickled in history's brine and spiced with cosmology's hot stardust, would make upon the McDonaldized palate of the reader . . .

And so on, for several more lines before the sentence is wrapped up. Even allowing for the insincerity of the writer in this instance, both syntax and diction strike me as being too precious, too Jamesian, too Nabokovian, too Updikey in fact, to be a plausible pastiche of Jewish American writing. It is just as well, then, that Updike shrewdly abstains from giving us any specimens of the fiction on which Bech's reputation rests—only teasing critical characterizations: "Early Post-Modern . . . Post-Realist . . . Pre-Minimalist." But Bech's speech, especially his wry, laconic one-liners, and his thoughts rendered in free indirect style, would not, it seems to me, look incongruous in the pages of one of Updike's Jewish peers.

In *Bech at Bay* the story that tells us most about Bech's ethnic and social background is perhaps "Bech Pleads Guilty." Back in the early 1970s, it appears, he wrote an article for a new magazine about post-studio Hollywood in which he rashly described an agent called Morris Ohrbach as "an arch-gouger" who for "greedy reasons of his own rake-off" had "widened the prevailing tragic rift between the literary and cinematic arts." This is known to be true by everybody in the business, but it is defamatory, and not easy to prove. The magazine quickly goes out of business. Ohrbach sues Bech for ten million dollars. It is the writer's nightmare that turns out to be waking reality.

Bech's queasy involvement in the legal process, his anxious observation of the court proceedings in Los Angeles, his sense of being a pawn in a kind of game played out by two teams of lawyers with priorities of their own, are acutely and comically observed. But a curious thing happens: when the villainous Ohrbach finally appears in court, Bech begins to feel sorry for him because he reminds him of his father, a salesman in the diamond district of Manhattan who died on the subway in rush hour. Some old Oedipal wound has been opened. Bech wins the case but feels obscurely guilty. Afterwards, in postcoital conversation with a member of his legal team called Rita, he relates:

> "When my father died . . . we found in his bureau drawers these black elastic stockings I had bought him, so his legs wouldn't hurt so much. He had never worn them. They still had the cardboard in them. Pieces of cardboard shaped like feet."
>
> "Sweetheart, O.K. I see it. The cardboard feet. Dying down in the subway. Life is rough. But that other *judío* was trying to eat you. Which would you rather?"
>
> "Baby, I don't know," the defendant responded, touching two fingers to the erectile tip—the color of a sun-darkened, un-sulphur-treated apricot—of her nearer breast. "Neither seems ideal."

As Bech says in another story, "Without guilt, there is no literature." Certainly no Jewish literature.

Like the Woody Allen character in Woody Allen's movies, Henry Bech has been endowed by his creator with an apparently ageless ability to attract young sexual partners. And whereas in the average man, with advancing age, lust is increasingly supplanted by gluttony, Bech enjoys both in the virtual reality of metaphor—*vide* the apricot nipple above, or Martina O'Reilly naked under Bech's bathrobe: "Martina suggested a big blintz—the terry-cloth the enfolding crepe, her flesh the pure soft cheese." As a concession to realism, these consorts have become slightly less ravishing in looks as time goes by, but no older. In "Bech Noir" he is living with a new secretarial assistant, Robin Teagarten, "twenty-six, post-Jewish, frizzy big hair, figure on the short and solid kind . . . He was seventy-four, but they worked with that." The story takes other, more daring gambles with credibility: Bech becomes a serial killer.

As often happens with writers, the older he gets, the more obsessed Bech becomes with his reputation, the more he suffers from a sense of neglected merit, and the more resentful he becomes, retrospectively, about the critical reception of his work. The ministrations of Robin cannot entirely soothe away this persistent discontent. But one day, reading the *Times* over breakfast, Bech comes across the obituary of a critic who had panned *The Chosen*. The gourmet rhetoric takes a new and sinister turn: "A creamy satisfaction—the finest quality, made extra easy to spread by the toasty warmth—thickly covered his heart." More bluntly: "Mishner dead put another inch on his prick."

A week later Bech finds himself on a crowded subway platform three rows back from the edge where he spots, in a vulnerable position, Raymond Featherwaite, the snotty English expat academic and critic who called *Think Big* "prolix and *voulu*" in the "ravingly Anglophile *New York Review of Books*."

He is irresistibly tempted to repeat the satisfaction of Mishner's death. A well-timed push as the train rushes from its tunnel creates a domino effect that sends Featherwaite under the wheels. "It was an instant's event . . . Just one head pleasantly less in the compressed, malodorous mob." Bech slips away, trembling but unobserved, and the death is reported in the next morning's paper as a presumed suicide. Featherwaite's colleagues at CUNY are quick to supply possible motives (and after all, who in the modern world doesn't harbour them?). Having got away with murder once, Bech cannot resist trying again. This time his victim is an elderly lady professor and writer of children's books who long ago wrote dismissive reviews of *Brother Pig* and *Think Big*. He sends her forged juvenile fan letters enclosing stamped addressed envelopes whose gum he spikes with poison.

When Robin figures out what Bech is doing, she is appalled but also fascinated and attracted, to the point of colluding with him. In this way she enacts the response of the reader. We ought to be repelled by Bech's deeds, but in an awful way we enjoy them. We ought to find them incredible, but we suspend our disbelief for the sheer delicious black comedy of the conceit—an old writer's revenge for old insults taking such a literally murderous form. How Updike resolves this tension between morals and aesthetics in narrative terms I will leave the reader to discover, mindful of Bech's resentment of the "cheerfully ham-handed divulgence of all his plot's nicely calculated and hoarded twists" by reviewers of *Travel Light*.

I feel no such constraint about the final story, since its content is given away in the publisher's blurb, and probably by its title, "Bech and the Bounty of Sweden." Yes, Henry Bech wins the Nobel Prize. This is of course even more incredible, given his literary track record, than his murders, and yet again we go along with it for the pleasure of the ride, which has to it an edge of danger, like being on a roller-coaster or a runaway train. There is a kind of exhilarating recklessness about these late stories in the liberties they take with decorum, in the ordinary as well as the literary sense of the word. Updike, unlike Bech, is clearly past caring what reviewers say about him, and indifferent to how his fellow-writers may feel about having their names promiscuously dropped in the Bech chronicles. His account of "the Forty" seems to be a mischievous travesty of the American Academy of Arts and Letters, of which he himself is a member, and whose centennial Festschrift, *A Century of Arts and Letters* (1998), he edited. He is apparently ready to jeopardise his own chances of winning the Nobel Prize (which cannot be negligible) for the sake of having some fictional fun with it. The main narrative question in "Bech and the Bounty of Sweden" is what kind of acceptance speech Bech will give. That I *won't* divulge. Suffice it to say that it is the first Nobel speech given by a recipient holding a baby, and that the last word of the story is "bye-bye." *Bye-Bye Bech* might have been a better title for this book. It is hard to imagine that there could be a sequel—but with Updike you never know.

# chapter nine

# SICK WITH DESIRE: PHILIP ROTH'S LIBERTINE PROFESSOR

Philip Roth's output of fiction in the seventh decade of his life has been astonishing for both quality and quantity. It has been to critics and fellow-novelists a spectacle to marvel at, an awe-inspiring display of energy, like the sustained eruption of a volcano that many observers supposed to be—not extinct, certainly, but perhaps past the peak of its active life. One might indeed have been forgiven for thinking that *Sabbath's Theater* (1995) was the final explosive discharge of the author's imaginative obsessions, sex and death—specifically, the affirmation of sexual experiment and transgression as an existential defiance of death, all the more authentic for being ultimately doomed to failure. Micky Sabbath, who boasts of having fitted in the rest of his life around fucking while most men do the reverse, was a kind of demonic Portnoy—amoral, shameless and gross in his polymorphously perverse appetites, inconsolable at the death of the one woman who was capable of satisfying them, and startlingly explicit in chronicling them. Even Martin Amis admitted to being shocked. Surely, one thought, Roth could go no further. Surely this was the apocalyptic, pyrotechnic finale of his career, after which anything else could only be an anticlimax.

How wrong we were. What followed, with breathtaking rapidity, were three long novels, *American Pastoral* (1997), *I Married a Communist* (1998), and *The Human Stain* (2000), a fictional project more ambitious than anything Roth had attempted before, and a triumphantly successful one. In these books he adopted something like the model of the classic realist novel, in which individual fortunes are traced across a panorama of social change and historical events, the individual and the social illuminating and borrowing significance from each other in the process. Sex is still vitally important to the characters, but not *all*-important. Their lives are also affected by and illustrative of profound convulsions, conflicts, and crises in American social and political life over the past half-century: racial tension, terrorism, the Vietnam War, the collapse of traditional industries, and with them whole communities such as the Newark in which Roth himself grew up, recalled in several places with remarkable vividness and unsentimental affection. The trilogy is a kind of elegy for the death of the American Dream as it seemed to present itself in the innocent and hopeful 1950s, and these novels have been widely and deservedly acclaimed.

Having achieved so much in such a short space of time, Roth might have been expected to take a well-earned rest from literary composition, but only a year after publishing *The*

*Human Stain* he produced yet another novel, *The Dying Animal*. It is a short one, and thematically it reverts to Roth's old preoccupation with the sexual life, especially the sexual lives of men; but in form it is another new departure for this resourceful novelist. If it lacks the broad social vision of the novels that came before, it is nevertheless a tour de force of considerable power, not least the power to challenge (and in some cases probably offend) its readers.

The title comes from Yeats's poem "Sailing to Byzantium":

> Consume my heart away; sick with desire
> And fastened to a dying animal
> It knows not what it is . . .

These lines are quoted by the protagonist and narrator of the novel as he describes resorting to a masturbatory fantasy to assuage his longing for the heroine of the tale, subsequent to the breakup of their relationship. The lines would apply equally well to other aging male characters in Roth's late work, tormented by lust, fearful of impotence, disease, and death. The poem itself, however, proposes an escape from this plight which Roth's narrator passes over in silence. The poet is apostrophising the "sages" of an imaginary and idealised Byzantium: "O sages standing in God's holy fire . . . gather me / Into the artifice of eternity." Neither Roth nor his heroes (or antiheroes) have any time for, or faith in, the artifice of eternity. "Artifice" in Yeats stands for the impersonality of art, the poetics of Symbolism and Formalism, ideas that Roth has frequently attacked and satirised in his fiction, not least in his allusions to academic literary criticism. And "eternity" denotes a religious idea of transcendence that for Roth's characters is so impossible that they don't even bother to challenge it.

Yeats himself, it should be said, was not unequivocally committed to the message of "Sailing to Byzantium." In "News for the Delphic Oracle," for instance, he mocks the desexualised Platonic notion of heaven with a sensual description of the partying that actually goes on there:

> Down the mountain walls
> Intolerable music falls.
> Foul goat-head, brutal arm appear,
> Belly, shoulder, bum,
> Flash fishlike; nymphs and satyrs
> Copulate in the foam.

Crazy Jane is a kindred spirit to Micky Sabbath:

> "Fair and foul are near of kin,
> And fair needs foul," I cried . . .
> "A woman can be proud and stiff
> When on love intent;
> But Love has pitched his mansion in
> The place of excrement . . .

The remarkable energy of Yeats's late poetry is to a large extent fuelled by his resentment and despair at declining sexual power. He would have agreed with an observation in *The Dying Animal*: "as far as I can tell, nothing, *nothing,* is put to rest, however old a man may be."

The narrator and central character of *The Dying Animal* is David Kepesh, who performed the same dual role in two much earlier works by Roth, *The Professor of Desire* (1977) and *The Breast* (1972, revised in 1980). There is a puzzle about the continuity between these books which I shall come to in a moment. The latest one begins like this:

> I knew her eight years ago. She was in my class. I don't teach full-time any more, strictly speaking don't teach literature at all—for years now just the one class, a big senior seminar in critical writing called Practical Criticism.

At first Kepesh's voice seems to be addressed straight to the reader, like that of Roth's favourite narrator and authorial surrogate, Nathan Zuckerman. But it soon becomes clear that there is an audience *inside* the text, a narratee as structuralist critics call it, someone who is listening to Kepesh's discourse and occasionally interjecting comments and questions—which are implied by Kepesh's responses, not rendered directly, until the very last page. The identity of this listener is never revealed, though we might infer from various clues that he is a young or youngish man. In short, the story is a dramatic monologue, a form well suited to the presentation of eloquently persuasive but morally subversive individuals, like the speaker of Dostoevsky's *Notes from Underground* or any number of Browning's characters.

The story, then, is being told on a single occasion, which we eventually discover is late one night towards the end of January in the year 2000, in Kepesh's apartment. He is seventy years old at this time, so he was sixty-two, and already feeling his age, when Consuela Castillo enrolled in his class, a beautiful young woman of twenty-four, the beloved and loving daughter of rich Cuban exiles. He was immediately in thrall to her beauty ("I'm very vulnerable to female beauty, as you know"), and his story is essentially about his infatuation with her, their passionate affair, which lasts about a year and a half, his three years of depression and frustration after she breaks it off, and her dramatic re-entry into his life on New Year's Eve, 1999. But the time-scheme of the book is very complex, for it operates on two planes simultaneously, which converge only on the penultimate page. There is the time of the main story, which is not unrolled in a straightforward linear fashion, but cut up and rearranged according to the prompting of memories and associations in Kepesh's consciousness, and frequently interrupted and suspended by digressions about his personal history, other women he has known, and his views on life and death in general. Then there is the "real time" of the narration itself, Kepesh's long speech act that constitutes the text, interrupted only when he has to leave the room twice to answer the telephone. This plane is communicated in the present tense, but Kepesh sometimes uses the rhetorical device of the "historic present" on the other plane to give special immediacy to some evocation of the past, such as Consuela's first apparition in his classroom:

> She has black, black hair, glossy but ever so slightly coarse. And she's big. She's a big woman. The silk blouse is unbuttoned to the third button, and so you see she has powerful, beautiful breasts. You see the cleavage immediately. And you see she knows it.

Because, as well as being a professor, David Kepesh enjoys a certain modest celebrity as a cultural critic on public TV and radio, his course attracts a generous quota of nubile young women, but in the era of Political Correctness, and specifically since the Sexual Harassment Hotline number was posted outside his office door by an anonymous hand in the mid-1980s, Kepesh has learned to be cautious. He never makes a pass until the course is over, grades have been awarded, and he is no longer *in loco parentis;* then he invites the students to a party at his apartment, where by the end of the evening one of them is sure to share his bed, curiosity and the glamour of his status overcoming any queasiness they might feel about his sagging flesh. After all, "many of these girls have been having sex since they were fourteen" and it is no big deal to them. Consuela is sexually experienced, but she is more old-fashioned than the other girls, more mature and more serious, so it takes Kepesh a little longer to get her into bed. Just as she genuinely seeks to learn from him the secret of how to really appreciate high culture, so he makes her conscious of her own beauty by the strength of his desire; he makes her into a work of art for her own enjoyment. Nevertheless the cultural initiation has to precede and legitimise the sexual, as Kepesh cynically notes. She won't sleep with him until he has shown her his Velázquez reproductions and let her hold his precious Kafka manuscript and taken her to the theatre and played classical music to her.

> All this talk! I show her Kafka, Velázquez . . . why does one do this? Well, you have to do something. These are the veils of the dance. Don't confuse it with seduction. This is not seduction. What you're disguising is the thing that got you there, the pure lust . . . You know you want it and you know you're going to do it and nothing is going to stop you. Nothing is going to be said here that's going to change anything . . . I want to fuck this girl and yes, I'll have to put up with some sort of veiling, but it's a means to an end.

In spite of this disclaimer, Kepesh's account of himself often reminds one of arch seducers in earlier literature, like Johannes, the callous but eloquent author of "The Seducer's

Diary" in Kierkegaard's *Either/Or*, who represents the "aes-thetic" attitude to life as against the "ethical," and the libertine anti-heroes of eighteenth-century fiction, such as Richardson's Lovelace and Laclos's Valmont, for whom seduction was a form of resistance to, and critique of, the foundations of orthodox morality. Historically the word "libertine" meant a free-thinker as well as a man of loose sexual conduct, and Kepesh expounds a philosophy of life that insistently identifies sexual freedom with personal freedom. "The problem is," he says, "that emancipated manhood never has had a social spokesman or an educational system." Kepesh's heroes are the great mythical and historical philanderers, the lords of mis-rule: Don Juan, Casanova, Thomas Morton (who presided over the pagan orgies of Merrymount that scandalised the Puritans of New England and excited the imagination of Hawthorne), and, in modern times, Henry Miller.

"Pleasure is our subject," he declares, like one of Browning's expansive monologists. "How to be serious over a lifetime about one's modest, private pleasures." He describes the sexual starva-tion of his adolescence and early adulthood in the 1940s and 1950s, when "sex had to be struggled for, against the values, if not the will of the girl." All that changed in the sixties, and Kepesh honours the memory of the promiscuous coeds in his classes who helped create the permissive society and welcomed him into it, "a generation drawing their conclusions from their cunts about the nature of experience and the delights of the world." His wife (he married in his twenties, "marrying and hav-ing a child seemed, in '56, the natural thing even for me to do") threw him out when she discovered what he was up to with these self-styled Gutter Girls, but he is quite unrepentant about that, because marriage too is the enemy of pleasure: "the nature of ordinary marriage is no less suffocating to the virile hetero-sexual . . . than it is to the gay or the lesbian." (Though now even gays and lesbians want to marry, a form of erotic suicide that Kepesh shakes his head over.) He has a son, Kenny, now forty-two, who has never forgiven his father for walking out on the nuclear family, and upbraids him for his selfish, immature behaviour: "Seducing defenseless students, pursuing one's sex-ual interests at the expense of everyone else—that's so very nec-essary, is it? No, necessity is staying in a difficult marriage and meeting the responsibilities of an adult." Kepesh can shrug off the criticism because Kenny is tired of his own marriage and is having an affair with another woman. He bores Kepesh with his scruples about deserting his children, and excites his derision by planning to divorce and remarry into an even more suffocating family scene. "Oh boy, the little prison that is his current mar-riage he is about to hand in for a maximum-security facility. Headed once again straight for the slammer."

There is a puzzle about Kenny's appearance in the story. Kepesh never names his wife in this book, but says that he had just "the one marriage," so Kenny's mother must be Helen, whom Kepesh marries in *The Professor of Desire*. But they don't have a child in that novel, though they talk about having one and wonder whether it would have saved their marriage. And Helen does not "throw out" Kepesh because of his philander-ing—*she* walks out on *him*, runs off to the Far East where she had lovers in the past, and gets into trouble from which he has to rescue her. He brings her back to America but soon after-wards they divorce, after some three years of marriage. Some years later, when he has been rescued from a long period of depression and loss of libido by a rather saintly woman called Claire, Helen remarries.

It is hard to know what to make of these anomalies. Roth must be aware of them, and know that many of his readers will notice them. One can see why he wanted to use the "professor of desire" as the mouthpiece for an eloquent, disturbing apologia for the libertine life. David Kepesh, it will be remembered, in that earlier novel dreads the prison-house of marriage, or any monogamous faithful relationship. He silently apostrophises the good, comely, loving Claire, thus: "Oh, innocent beloved, you fail to understand and I can't tell you. I can't say it, not tonight, but within a year my passion will be dead. Already it is dying and there is nothing I can do to save it . . . Toward the flesh upon which I have been grafted and nurtured back toward something like mastery over my life, I will be without desire." He starts to write a lecture, imitating Kafka's "Report to an Academy," to introduce a course on erotic literature and to "disclose the undisclosable—the story of the professor's desire." It is a private exercise; he never gives the course or the lecture. One might say that *The Dying Animal* is the belated completion of that project. But the discontinuity between the two novels remains a puzzle, on which that amusing *hommage* to Gogol and Kafka, *The Breast,* throws no light. Read independently, each novel is written in the code of realistic fiction, creating a consistent illusion of life, with no metafictional frame-breaking. Put together, they generate distracting aporias. Perhaps Roth thought that was a small price to pay for effects that were more important. The character of Kenny was created, one presumes, to offer some resistance to the libertine philosophy of life—though he is made to seem such a weak and ineffectual figure that his criticisms don't carry much weight. Even the unnamed interlocutor dismisses him. "He doesn't get anything? He must. He is by no means stupid . . . He is? Well, perhaps so. You're probably right." The real challenge to Kepesh's libertinism (and the source of real tension in the book) is revealed by Kepesh himself as he unfolds the story of his relationship with Consuela.

That challenge is simply a heightened awareness of his own mortality. It is David Kepesh's fate, rather than his good fortune, to possess a supremely beautiful young woman when himself on the threshold of old age, so that his enjoyment of her is always troubled by anxiety. It is not an ordinary anxiety about sexual potency, which for the time being he can rely on, but a more existential dread about his ability to continue to possess the object of his desire, and it afflicts him from the very first sexual encounter between them. "The jealousy. The uncertainty. The fear of losing her, even while on top of her. Obsessions that in all my varied experience I had never known before. With Consuela as with no one else, the siphoning off of confidence was almost instantaneous." Consuela's vitality and beauty make him feel his own age on his pulses. "You feel excruciatingly how old you are, but in a new way." He can imagine all too easily how some cocksure young man is going to steal her away from him because he was once such a young man himself.

Part of Consuela's fascination for Kepesh is that she is socially and culturally a foreigner to him: bourgeois, Latin, Catholic, devoted to her family, and intending to make a conventional marriage herself one day. The old-fashioned respectability of her social self contrasts excitingly with her limitless capacity for sensuality, just as her conservative tailored outfits cover "nearly pornographic" underwear. There is a comical moment when, on first agreeing to go to bed with this ageing roué, she tells him solemnly "I can never be your wife," and he says "Agreed" but silently reflects, "Who was asking her to be my wife? Who raised the question? . . . I merely touch her ass and she tells me she can't be my wife? I didn't know such girls continued to exist."

Their relationship has no ordinary social dimension because they belong to different social worlds. It exists only in the erotic space of his apartment, where she visits him from time to time. She does not like to be seen in public with him for fear of appearing in gossip columns, and he shrinks from confrontation with the virile young Cubans in her circle whom he imagines as her suitors. Indeed, their affair is abruptly terminated by an angry Consuela when, for that very reason, he fails to turn up at her graduation party. To Consuela this signifies an arrogant indifference to her happiness, but really it is a failure of nerve. He is even jealous of her past lovers. When she tells him of the adolescent admirer whose odd and only desire was to watch her menstruating, and how she satisfied it, nothing will satisfy Kepesh but that she grants him the same privilege, and then he out-transgresses his phantom rival by licking the blood from her flesh.

It is rather shocking to be told that, while this affair was going on, Kepesh was having another sexual relationship of a more comfortable and less intense kind with Carolyn, one of the original Gutter Girls whom he met again by chance—now a successful professional woman, twice divorced, somewhat heavier around the hips but still attractive, and always up for some recreational sex when she flies in from one of her business trips. This convenient arrangement is jeopardised when Carolyn finds Consuela's bloody tampon in Kepesh's bathroom trash can. Without guessing exactly what it signifies, she suspects he has been cheating, and furiously upbraids him:

> "You have everything as you want as you want it—fucking like ours outside of domesticity and outside of romance— and then you do this. There aren't many like me, David. I have an interest in what you're interested in . . . Harmonious hedonism. I am one in a million, idiot. So how could you possibly do this?"

The message is clear: Kepesh is betraying his own libertine philosophy by the obsessive nature of his infatuation with Consuela. He does not deny it, but lies his way coolly out of the crisis. Carolyn is appeased. "Fortunately she did not leave me when I most needed her. She left only later, and at my request," he chillingly comments. Kepesh remarks that his son's conduct is governed by his fear of being called selfish; he himself has no such qualms.

Roth illustrates Kepesh's view of human sexuality with two remarkable descriptions of modern paintings. His contention that marriage, or any exclusive lasting sexual relationship, is incompatible with erotic satisfaction, because passion is by its nature ephemeral, is epitomised for him by Stanley Spencer's celebrated double nude portrait of himself and his wife, which he saw in London's Tate Gallery:

> It is the quintessence of directness about cohabitation, about the sexes living together over time . . . Spencer is seated, squatting, beside the recumbent wife. He is looking ruminatively down at her from close range through his wire-rimmed glasses . . . Neither is happy. There is a heavy

> past clinging to the present . . . At the edge of a table, in the
> immediate foreground of the picture, are two pieces of
> meat, a large leg of lamb and a single small chop. The raw
> meat is rendered with the same uncharitable candor as the
> sagging breasts and the pendant, unaroused prick displayed
> only inches back from the uncooked food. You could be
> looking through the butcher's window, not just at the meat
> but at the sexual anatomy of the married couple.

Kepesh is right about the unhappiness but, as it happens,
wrong about its cause. The woman in the painting is Spencer's
second wife, Patricia Preece, and it was painted two months
before their marriage in 1937, after Spencer had split with
his first wife, Hilda, whom he married in 1925. Preece cast a
strange and sinister spell over Spencer. She was a lesbian who
was in a long-term relationship with another woman when
she met him, and remained in it. She refused to have sex with
Spencer both before and after their marriage, in spite of taking
both money and property from the infatuated artist. The
uncooked joint is usually interpreted as a symbol of non-
consummation. It certainly doesn't signify the stale familiarity
of marital sex. As there is no textual hint to the contrary, we
must assume that it is not only David Kepesh but also his creator who has jumped to the wrong conclusion. The mistake
doesn't really matter in terms of the fictional story, but it is a
reminder that there are more ways than one of making oneself
sexually miserable.

The other painting is Modigliani's *Reclining Nude (Le Grand
Nu)* of 1919, a postcard reproduction of which Consuela sends
to Kepesh some time after the end of their affair. It took him
three years to get over that separation, three years overshadowed by depression and a raging jealousy that only music and

pornographic fantasising could temporarily assuage. Even so the postcard—the picture rather than the banal message scrawled on its back—tempts him to reply,

> which I believed I was being invited to do by the cylindrical stalk of a waist, the wide pelvic span, and the gently curving thighs, by that patch of flame that is the hair that marks the spot where she is forked . . . A nude whose breasts, full and canting a bit to the side, might well have been modelled on [Consuela's] own . . . A golden-skinned nude inexplicably asleep over a velvety black abyss that, in my mood, I associated with the grave. One long, undulating line, she lies there awaiting you, still as death.

The painting is reproduced on the dust jacket of *The Dying Animal,* so readers may appreciate the exactness of Kepesh's description, especially the brilliantly observed "velvety black abyss" under the model's hips that reminds him of death.

Here we come to the heart of the matter. According to Kepesh's libertine credo:

> "Only when you fuck . . . are you most cleanly alive and most cleanly yourself . . . Sex isn't just friction and shallow fun. Sex is also the revenge on death. Don't forget death. Don't ever forget it. Yes, sex too is limited in its power. I know very well how limited. But tell me, what power is greater?"

The anonymous narratee evidently can't think of one, for no reply from him is implied. The question remains rhetorical. But one possible answer is of course love, the love of which Paul wrote to the Corinthians:

> Love is always patient and kind; it is never jealous; love is never boastful or conceited; it is never rude or selfish; it does

not take offense, and is not resentful. Love takes no pleasure in other people's sins but delights in the truth; it is always ready to excuse, to trust, to hope, and to endure whatever comes. Love does not come to an end.

It does not come to an end because, the hope of personal immortality aside, if you give your self to another, unconditionally, in love, then death cannot absolutely take it away. Regarding the carved figures of husband and wife on a medieval tomb, the man's hand withdrawn from his gauntlet to grasp his wife's, Philip Larkin, most agnostic of poets, reflects:

> The stone fidelity
> They hardly meant has come to be
> Their final blazon, and to prove
> Our almost-instinct almost true:
> What will survive of us is love.
>                 ("An Arundel Tomb")

Love in this large sense is *agape* rather than *eros,* but the two are not incompatible in romantic love, or even in the kind of obsessive, transgressive fixation Kepesh has on the person of Consuela. His friend George O'Hearn perceives this danger and counsels him not to respond to the postcard. George himself is a libertine, though he has contrived to combine a life of sexual adventure with marriage, thanks to a tolerant or perhaps merely indifferent wife. He acts as Kepesh's worldly confessor, listens to the latter's account of his affair with Consuela, and urges him not to renew it. Otherwise, he says, it will destroy him. "'Look,' he told me, 'see it as a critic, see it from a professional point of view. You violated the law of aesthetic distance. You sentimentalised the aesthetic experience with this girl.'" George tells Kepesh he crossed a dangerous threshold when he licked the girl's blood: "'I'm not against it because it's disgusting. I'm against it because it's falling in love . . . People think that in falling in love they make themselves whole . . . I think otherwise. I think you're whole before you begin. And the love fractures you.'" Kepesh takes his advice, and does not respond to the postcard.

Some years later, a few months in fact before the time of the story's telling, George has a stroke and dies. Kepesh watches his last hours of life. Diapered against incontinence, unable to speak, George draws on unsuspected reserves of energy to signify his desire to embrace the people gathered around the hospital bed. He kisses his children on the mouth, and likewise the astonished Kepesh. He kisses his wife, and then begins to fumble with her clothing in a grotesque, yet to Kepesh oddly touching, attempt to undress her. "Yes, that was something, wasn't it?" his wife comments drily to Kepesh afterwards. "I wonder who it is he thought I was." Whether George's deathbed tableau is sublime or ridiculous, a vindication of or a judgement on his life, remains ambiguous.

And so the story moves towards its climax (and at this point I would recommend that any readers who have not yet read *The Dying Animal* put this essay aside until they have done so). On New Year's Eve, 1999, the last day of the millennium, Kepesh receives a phone message from an evidently distressed Consuela, to say that she wants to tell him something face to face. After some hesitation, fearing the disruption of his hard-won peace of mind, he agrees. She shows up at his apartment, as beautiful as ever, but ominously wearing a fez. She quickly reveals that she has breast cancer and has been having chemotherapy to shrink the tumors. Now she faces surgery for partial removal of one of the breasts that Kepesh once told her were the most beautiful he had ever seen. She wants him to "say goodbye to them": to touch them, and to photograph them, but not to take this intimacy any further. Kepesh realises he wouldn't be able to anyway, once he has felt the lumps under her armpit. "At that moment I knew hers was no longer a sexual life. What was at stake was something else."

Consuela's life-threatening illness also threatens Kepesh's libertine philosophy. To succumb to inevitable death after a lifetime of licentious pleasure, as George O'Hearn did, is one thing. To do so when one is only thirty-two is quite another. In fact Consuela has been told she has a 60 percent chance of cure, but her intuition tells her otherwise. "Time for the young is always made up of what is past, but for Consuela time is now how much further she has left, and she doesn't believe there is any." She is experiencing her own mortality prematurely, out of the natural order of things. Kepesh's maxim, "Sex is the revenge on death," would be of no use or consolation to her. All he can do is hold her and comfort her, as they distract themselves by watching the television coverage of the millennium celebrations sweeping around the globe, their vacuous cheeriness and vulgar spectacle suiting the medium perfectly: "TV doing what it does best: the triumph of trivialization over tragedy."

That happened three weeks ago, he tells his companion. She left his apartment at one-thirty in the morning of New Year's Day, saying she would get back in touch after her surgery. He has been waiting for her call ever since, wondering uneasily what kind of claim on him she might have if she survives the operation. He fears that she might decide to try out sex again "first with someone familiar and someone old." He knows from a previous experience that he couldn't make it with a woman mutilated by even a partial mastectomy. He associates the lump of raw meat in the Stanley Spencer painting with Consuela's threatened breast and the failure of sex. He recalls the pathos of her ravaged head when she took off her fez, covered by a thin, meaningless fuzz that was worse than perfect baldness. He kissed the head again and again.

> What else was there for me to do? . . . She's thirty-two, and she thinks she's now exiled from everything, experiencing each experience for the very last time. Only what if she isn't? What—
>
> There! The phone! That could be—! At what time? It's two A.M. Excuse me!

The time of the story has finally caught up with the time of its telling. Kepesh returns to report that the call was indeed from Consuela. She is having a panic attack. Her surgery is due in two weeks' time, and the doctors now tell her they have to remove the whole breast. She wants him to go to her, to sleep in her bed, to look after her, feed her. He has to go immediately. The story ends in a staccato exchange of dialogue, with the narratee's words quoted in direct speech for the first time:

> "Don't."
> What?
> "Don't go."
> But I must. Someone has to be with her.
> "She'll find someone."
> She's in terror. I'm going.
> "Think about it. Think. Because if you go, you're finished."

The narratee is probably right that if Kepesh answers Consuela's call for help he is going to be sucked into a maelstrom of appalling emotional stress, but of course he won't be "finished" in the sense that Consuela will be finished if she dies. But what if she recovers and lives on, wounded, traumatised, burdening Kepesh with her pain and fear and sexual insecurity? Possibly that would "finish" him psychologically. Kepesh himself has already feared as much. The narratee, speaking like a reincarnation of George O'Hearn, urges him not to take the risk. Should he go or not?

If 1 Corinthians 13 is invoked, there is no question—of course he must go. He must give a helping hand to Consuela in her hour of need, without weighing up the possible long-term consequences. And that gesture of kissing her unappealing, fuzz-covered head suggests that he is capable of such a selfless act. But by ending the story where he does, Roth leaves the reader free to suppose that Kepesh doesn't go, perhaps shouldn't go. Certainly, if he goes, he will be repudiating everything he has asserted in the previous one hundred and fifty pages. What the implied author himself thinks is inscrutable, because of the chosen form. Like many works of modern literature, *The Dying Animal* ends on a note of radical ambiguity and indeterminacy. What is unusual about it is the way it challenges the reader at every point to define and defend his own ethical stance towards the issues raised by the story. It is a small, disturbing masterpiece.

# chapter ten

# KIERKEGAARD FOR SPECIAL PURPOSES

*In 1996 I was invited to address an international conference of Kierkegaard scholars, gathered in Copenhagen to discuss "Kierkegaard and the Meaning of Meaning It." What follows is a shortened version of what I said on that occasion. I never discovered the meaning of the conference's title.*

This is not an academic paper, but if there were a branch of Kierkegaard studies called (by analogy with linguistics) "Kierkegaard for Special Purposes," that is where it might belong. In my novel *Therapy* there is a good deal of reference to Kierkegaard, to his writings and to his life story, and I will try to explain how and why I used him in this way, and what special fictional purposes he served for me.[1]

Readers of novels often assume that the knowledge of a particular subject displayed in their pages must be the visible tip of a submerged iceberg of information, when in fact there is often no iceberg—the tip is all there is. Some years ago I wrote a novel called *Nice Work*. Much of the story concerns an engineering factory and the professional life of its Managing Director. This was based on a few weeks' research on my part, visiting factories and "shadowing" a friend who was MD of an engineering company. After the novel was published I received several invitations to address seminars and conferences on business management and industrial relations. In declining these invitations, I had to explain that *Nice Work* contained everything I knew about business management and industrial relations. Of *Therapy* I might say that it contains *more* about Kierkegaard than I know, because it contains several passages quoted from his writings, the full meaning of which has certainly eluded me.

If I admit that until I started to work on this novel, in the winter of 1992–93, I had never read anything by or about Kierkegaard except Walter Lowrie's short biography,[2] and that in the process of writing it I read only a few of his works, and skimmed through some others, you will not expect any profound or original insights from me into Kierkegaard's philosophy. But it may be of interest to learn how a novelist could be stimulated and enlightened by even such a hurried and selective encounter with Kierkegaard's life and work, and how the distinctive fictional and ludic strains in his philosophical writings made them especially suggestive and inspiring to me. If I have any light to shed, it will be on the nature of the creative process, rather than on the "Meaning of Meaning It."

*Therapy* did not start with my discovery of Kierkegaard, but with a number of loosely linked ideas, situations, and themes, mostly arising out of my own experience. The most important of these elements was depression, and it was the theme of depression which led me to Kierkegaard. As I have grown older I have become more and more vulnerable to bouts of anxiety and depression, though the material circumstances of my life have become steadily more comfortable and secure. This seems to be a fairly common experience. To judge by newspaper reports and magazine articles, there is something of an epidemic of depression in contemporary British society, and in the world generally. Here is a revealing journalistic comment on the phenomenon (published after I had finished my novel) written by Helen Fielding, before she became famous as the creator of Bridget Jones:

> Next Sunday the Defeat Depression Campaign will be hold-
> ing a "Fun Run" in Battersea park. Last Tuesday the Samari-
> tans launched a new advertising campaign to encourage
> despairing people to call them more readily, before they
> reach the brink. "Ringing the Samaritans should be as com-
> monplace as going to the Post Office," enthused their com-
> munications manager. The Depression Alliance, a self-help
> group for depressed people, launched two weeks ago, is
> receiving 250 enquiries every day. This week's *Melody Maker*
> includes a special feature on the extraordinary number of
> depressive letters the magazine is receiving from young
> people, and how depressing grunge lyrics are . . . Sometimes
> it seems that the whole world has just got really fed up . . .
> that the globe is being swept by an end-of-millennium fug of
> existential *angst,* gloominess and ennui.[3]

The scale of this spiritual and psychological malaise has provoked a corresponding growth of therapies to cope with it:
psychotherapy in all its various forms, pharmaceutical therapy,
and numerous alternative and holistic therapies like acu-
puncture, aromatherapy, yoga, reflexology, and so on. Even
shopping is called "retail therapy" these days. If the 1960s

were about politics, the seventies about sex, and the eighties about money, then (it seemed to me) the nineties were about therapy. I decided to write a novel about this general subject—depression, anxiety, loss of self-esteem, and the diverse therapies we use to cope with these things, using one or two narrative ideas I had been turning over in my mind for some time.

I began to develop a character called Lawrence Passmore, known familiarly as "Tubby" because of his portly build, the writer of a successful TV situation comedy called *The People Next Door*. He is in his late fifties. Some of the circumstances of his life correspond to mine; in other respects he is very different from me. He is, for instance, a largely self-educated man, whose formal education ended at sixteen, apart from a spell at drama school.

Tubby is professionally successful, affluent, and in a long-lasting stable marriage to Sally. He has all the material possessions he desires. Yet he suffers from depression, anxiety, insomnia, panic attacks. His only concrete cause for complaint is an intermittent pain in the knee, a mysterious injury which does not respond to surgical treatment. He seeks relief or cure for these afflictions in a variety of therapies:

> I have a lot of therapy. On Mondays I see Roland for Physiotherapy, on Tuesdays I see Alexandra for Cognitive Behaviour Therapy, and on Fridays I have either aromatherapy or acupuncture. On Wednesdays and Thursdays I'm usually in London, but then I see Amy, which is a kind of therapy too I suppose.

Amy is a female friend in the television business with whom Tubby has a secret but platonic relationship.

What happens to Tubby Passmore in the course of the story is that both his professional and private lives go into a state of crisis soon after the beginning of the novel. First, the producers of his sitcom threaten to hire someone else to write the scripts; then Tubby's wife stuns him by announcing that she cannot stand living with him any longer and asks for a divorce. These twin disasters jolt Tubby from a state of low-pulsed, nonspecific anxiety and depression into something like a full-blown nervous breakdown. One symptom of his derangement is a series of absurd and unsuccessful attempts to make up for a lifetime's marital fidelity by getting into bed with any woman who has shown the slightest interest in him in the past.

I had two other ideas for this novel at an early stage in its genesis. One was the notion that Tubby would somehow resolve his personal crisis by seeking out his first sweetheart, after an interval of nearly forty years. And I had long wanted to write a novel in the first-person colloquial style which the Russian Formalist critics called *skaz*—a type of narrative discourse which is modelled on casual speech rather than writing. I decided that Tubby would tell his story through keeping a journal, but, as he says himself: "I can only write as if I'm speaking to someone . . ."

So where and how did Kierkegaard come in? As I prepared to start writing, it seemed to me there was some danger that, if the whole novel were contained within Tubby's limited perspective and limited language, it might be rather monotonous and ultimately unsatisfying. I felt the need of another discourse, another perspective, another (parallel) story. This is a feature of several of my novels, and is something I learned, as did many other writers, from James Joyce's use of Homer's *Odyssey* in *Ulysses,* and T. S. Eliot's allusions to the Grail legend in *The Waste Land. Small World,* for example, is based on a structural equivalence between the lives of modern academics jetting around the world attending conferences, competing for glory and sometimes love, and the adventures of the knights of chivalric romance. The story of *Nice Work* recycles, echoes, and inverts the plots of the Victorian industrial novels on which its heroine is an academic expert. For me, conceiving this "structural idea" is usually the most important stage of a novel's genesis.

When I am preparing to write a novel, I keep a notebook dedicated to that project, in which I write down ideas, observations, character-sketches, provisional synopses, and memos to myself. I wrote in the *Therapy* notebook, one day, regarding the restrictiveness of Tubby's perspective: "Perhaps Tubby should read Kierkegaard." As noted earlier, all I knew about Kierkegaard at this point was Lowrie's short biography, which I had read some years before in connection with *Paradise News,* a novel that deals in part with modern theology (there is just one fleeting reference to Kierkegaard in it). What I chiefly remembered from Lowrie's book was that Kierkegaard had been sorely afflicted by depression—or, as he called it, "melancholy"—and that his philosophy and somewhat eccentric lifestyle were in part driven and shaped by his unceasing struggle with this affliction. I also recalled that he had had a strange, poignant, unhappy, obsessive relationship with a young girl, Regine Olsen, to whom he was engaged for a time. I had a hunch that in Kierkegaard's depression and lifelong obsession with Regine I would find what I wanted: an intertextual strand for *Therapy,* a parallel story to Tubby's, which would yield a different perspective on his plight and a different language for talking about it. The fact that I had already decided to write the novel in the form of Tubby's journal, and that Kierkegaard was one of the great journal writers of literary history, was further encouragement to pursue this notion.

Of course, the idea of a self-educated television comedy scriptwriter reading Kierkegaard—and not only reading him, but becoming obsessed with him to the point of identifying with him, seeing himself as a kind of reincarnation of Kierkegaard—is inherently risible, "absurd" in the ordinary, not the existentialist sense. But that was very much to my purpose. I was determined from the outset to write a novel about depression that would not be depressing, and comedy was the best way to ensure that result. There would be nothing amusing in a novel about an *intellectual*—a professional philosopher, say—who became obsessed with Kierkegaard. Such structural ideas are like metaphors: there must be difference as well as similarity between the two things compared. There was the additional advantage to me, a complete novice in the work of this difficult writer, that, since the whole novel is narrated by Tubby, it wouldn't matter if he misunderstood Kierkegaard, as long as he did so in an interesting and instructive way.

Tubby begins his reading in Kierkegaard by choosing, at random, *The Concept of Dread,* and is put off by its abstract and heavily religious language. But a few days later, he dips into *Either/Or,* and is hooked. He is particularly struck by the chapter entitled "The Unhappiest Man":

Kierkegaard explains that the unhappy man is never present to himself because he's always living in the past or the future. He's always either hoping or remembering. Either he thinks things were better in the past or he hopes they'll be better in the future, but they're always bad *now*. That's ordinary common-or-garden-unhappiness. But the unhappy man "in a stricter sense" isn't even present to himself in his remembering or his hoping. Kierkegaard gives the example of a man who looks back wistfully to the joys of childhood which in fact he himself never experienced (perhaps he was thinking of his own case). Likewise the "unhappy hoper" is never present to himself in his hoping, for reasons which were obscure to me until I came to this passage: "Unhappy individuals who hope never have the same pain as those who remember. Hoping individuals always have a more gratifying disappointment."

I know exactly what he means by "gratifying disappointment." I worry about making decisions because I'm trying to guard against things turning out badly. I *hope* they'll turn out well, but if they do turn out well I hardly notice it because I've made myself miserable imagining how they could turn out badly; and if they turn out badly in some unforeseen way (like clause fourteen in the Heartland contract) that only confirms my underlying belief that the worst misfortunes are unexpected. If you're an unhappy hoper you don't really believe things will get better in the future (because if you did you wouldn't be unhappy). Which means that when they *don't* get better it proves you were right all along. That's why your disappointment is gratifying. Neat, eh?

Tubby's fumbling attempts to understand Kierkegaard reflect my own reading experience, and the things which interest and excite him in Kierkegaard's writings are those which interested and excited me: the early works rather than the later ones, the secular works rather than the religious ones, the pseudonymous books rather than the ones Kierkegaard published under his own name. In particular I was impressed by Kierkegaard's insights into the subjectivity of happiness and unhappiness, into the perverse habits of unhappy hoping and unhappy remembering by which we rob ourselves of contentment and fail to enjoy each moment of life for what it is; and I was struck by the paradox that this man could see so clearly into these matters, and yet be so incapable of putting their lessons into practice in his own case.

The most important act of Kierkegaard's life was, arguably, the breaking off of his engagement to Regine, by which he deprived himself of the chance to discover whether he was capable of "ordinary" human happiness in marriage, and was tormented forever afterwards by the awareness of an opportunity foregone. Many of his books, perhaps most of them, can be traced back to this decisive act of indecision, this perverse and self-punishing reversal of a choice (the choice of a spouse) by a philosopher who insisted on the necessity of commitment. What makes Kierkegaard appealing to many nonspecialist readers who have great difficulty in understanding his quarrel with Hegelianism, and find his version of Christianity forbiddingly austere and exclusive, is the man's own vulnerability, inconsistency, even folly. As Tubby says, contemplating Kierkegaard's relationship with Regine: "What a fool. But what an endearing, entirely human fool." Kierkegaard does not lecture us from some pulpit of assumed impartiality, objectivity, and omniscience. He speaks to us out of the flux and the fray of human existence. He grounded the perennial problems of philosophy in man's self-consciousness, which reason alone can never satisfy.

---

In the course of writing *Therapy* I discovered many more parallels, or equivalences, between Kierkegaard and Tubby Passmore than I had anticipated when I first decided that my hero should become interested in the philosopher's work. This is a common experience in creative writing, and is perhaps the most exciting and satisfying aspect of what is for the most part an anxious and labour-intensive vocation. What happens with novels that are structured on some kind of equivalence and contrast between two stories, one original and one received, is that the precursor story begins to influence the composition of one's own story in unpredictable ways. It is as if the two stories, or texts, that have been brought together by the writer begin to talk to each other, generating ideas and narrative material which would not otherwise have come into existence. The writer happily accepts this unexpected bonus of meaning.

An example: in the latter part of *Therapy*, Tubby is by chance reminded of his first sweetheart, Maureen Kavanagh, a transparently innocent Catholic girl whom he knew as a teenager in South London in the early 1950s, whose love and devotion he enjoyed for about two years until he pressured her into breaking off the relationship. In the course of writing a memoir of Maureen, Tubby convinces himself that this long-suppressed act of bad faith is the source of his lack of peace of mind and lack of self-esteem. Obviously I intended to draw a parallel between Tubby's treatment of Maureen and Kierkegaard's of Regine—and Kierkegaard's reworking of this experience in the *Diary of a Seducer* and *Repetition*. Tubby himself is aware of some of the parallels, and remarks on the resemblance between the two girls' names: Maureen/Regine. But in the process of composition, a further parallel developed. In the biographies of Kierkegaard I was reading I came across references to Regine's husband, Johan Frederik Schlegel, who had been attracted to her before Kierkegaard won her heart, who successfully urged his suit about a year after Kierkegaard broke off his engagement, and who (rather priggishly, it seemed to me) refused to allow Kierkegaard to meet Regine socially or correspond with her in later life. These glimpses of this minor figure in Kierkegaard's life story suggested to me the character of Bede Harrington, the stiff, pompous rival of Tubby for Maureen's affections in the Catholic youth club to which they all belonged in the 1950s, who eventually marries Maureen and is surprised and not a little suspicious when Tubby turns up forty years later in search of her.

I introduced Kierkegaard into my novel because I felt the need for some other, quite different frame of reference for the investigation of my theme than the character of Tubby Passmore. But merely having Tubby read Kierkegaard, and draw out the parallels between himself and the philosopher, did not seem to expand the horizons of the novel sufficiently. I felt the need for other points of view and other voices. I consequently decided to present Tubby's manic behaviour after his wife leaves him through the eyes of several other characters, who narrate their stories in the form of dramatic monologues, addressing interlocutors whose responses are implied, not quoted. Tubby's friend Amy describes to her psychoanalyst his belated attempt to turn their platonic relationship into a carnal one, with farcically catastrophic results. Then a female Hollywood film producer, Louise, tells a friend in a telephone conversation how Tubby, whom she met four years previously and tried unsuccessfully to seduce, suddenly reappeared in Los Angeles to invite her out to dinner. His behaviour puzzles Louise until, halfway through the meal,

> I suddenly realised what this date was all *about*. I realised that it was in this very restaurant that I had tried to seduce him . . . Yeah! . . . This whole date was like a reprise of the one all those years ago. The Venice restaurant, the table outside, the Napa Valley Chardonnay . . . That was why he was so upset that I'd changed my car and the fish restaurant had turned into a Thai restaurant . . . He was trying to recreate the exact circumstances of that evening four years ago as far as possible in every detail. Every detail except one . . . Exactly! Now that his wife had walked out on him he wanted to take me up on my offer to fuck him. He'd flown all the way from England specifically for that purpose. It didn't seem to have occurred to him that my circumstances might have changed, not to mention my mood.

Tubby is seeking a kind of impossible, inauthentic Repetition, like Constantine Constantius in Kierkegaard's novella of that name, who on his second visit to Berlin tries to repeat exactly the experiences of his first visit, and finds that "the only thing repeated was the impossibility of repetition."[4] When Louise explains that she has a partner and is pregnant, Tubby is devastated, and quotes Kierkegaard to her: "The most dreadful thing that can happen to a man is to become ridiculous in his own eyes in a matter of essential importance." This remark in the *Journals* is thought to refer to Kierkegaard's feelings on discovering that Regine, with whom he still secretly hoped to be reconciled, was engaged to Schlegel.

In another monologue, the producer of Tubby's sitcom, Ollie Silvers, describes to a drinking companion how the distraught and deranged Tubby proposed in all seriousness to write a television mini-series based on the life of Kierkegaard. Samantha, an ambitious young script editor, relates how Tubby invited her to accompany him to Copenhagen, ostensibly to do research for his Kierkegaard film project, but really, she assumed, to have a sexual fling with her. This was indeed Tubby's intention, but he is so affected by the poignancy of the relics in the Kierkegaard Room at the Bymuseum, and by the pathos of Kierkegaard's modest grave in the Assistens cemetery, that he is unable to exploit Samantha's eagerness to be seduced. As Tubby himself puts it later, in his journal:

> Something held me back, and it wasn't the fear of impotence, or of aggravating my knee injury. Call it conscience. Call it Kierkegaard. They have become one and the same thing. I think Kierkegaard is the thin man inside me who has been struggling to get out, and in Copenhagen he finally did.

Shortly after I began writing Part Two of the novel, in which the monologues are presented under the names of their respective speakers—"Amy," "Louise," "Ollie," and so on—I decided that they would in fact be written by Tubby himself, though this fact would be concealed from the reader until Tubby reveals in Part Three that he wrote them as a kind of therapeutic exercise prescribed by his psychotherapist. What happens therefore is that the reader of the novel assumes the monologues are objective, independent reports of Tubby's deranged behaviour, but then has to re-evaluate them as evidence that he is able to recognize his own weakness and folly, and is therefore on the way to recovery.

I was surprised that some British reviewers objected strongly to this twist in the novel's narrative method, as being either incredible in itself, or as retrospectively depriving the monologues of their significance. This seemed to me an illogical response. If I, as author, could create convincing monologues for these fictitious characters, it is surely possible that Tubby, a professional scriptwriter, could do the same for people he knows personally, and plausible that he should develop the exercise suggested by his psychotherapist in this way. I concluded that my reviewers were annoyed at having been "tricked" into thinking the monologues were testimonies independent of Tubby, as if I had broken some fundamental contract between writer and reader. Kierkegaard, of course, irritated and exasperated many of his contemporary readers by the multiplicity and complexity of pseudonymous narrators and embedded narratives in his writings. It occurred to me that I had perhaps written a more Kierkegaardian novel (in a purely generic sense) than I had myself been aware of. Intertextuality is often as much an unconscious as a conscious element of the creative process.

One of the epigraphs to *Therapy* is taken from Graham Greene's autobiographical volume, *Ways of Escape:* "Writing is a form of therapy." In the original text, the passage continues: "sometimes I wonder how all those who do not write, compose or paint can manage to escape the madness, the melancholia, the panic fear which is inherent in the human condition."[5] Writing was certainly therapy for Kierkegaard. "Only when I write do I feel well. Then I forget all of life's vexations, all its sufferings, then I am wrapped in thought and am happy," he wrote in his journal in 1847—a passage quoted by Tubby in his own journal. Tubby's journal originates in his psychotherapy—he begins it after his therapist asks him to write a description of himself—but it turns into more than an exercise or private confession. As a professional scriptwriter, he has relied upon actors and pictures to flesh out his lines of dialogue. Writing his journal, writing the dramatic monologues, above all writing his memoir of Maureen, Tubby becomes a more self-conscious and literary writer—what he calls, in his homely idiom, a "book-writer." In the process he turns negative, subjective experience into something positive and shareable. That is what literature does, and it is the great consolation and reward of being a book-writer. Kierkegaard knew it was so; Tubby Passmore discovers it is so; I have certainly found it so.

# chapter eleven

# A
# CONVERSATION
# ABOUT
# *THINKS . . .*

*The tri-quarterly magazine* Areté *published an interview with me in its spring-summer issue of 2001, divided into two parts. The first part, conducted by a Polish journalist, ranged over a variety of topics. The second part was a conversation with Craig Raine, the editor of* Areté, *about my novel* Thinks . . . *I have used it as the concluding piece of this book because it touches on several topics discussed in the first essay and elsewhere, though in a more informal way. I have lightly edited the transcript in the interests of clarity and readability, but have not altered the sense of any statement, although there are some that I would probably not have made, or would have qualified, in a written discourse. Readers who have not read* Thinks . . . *and intend to do so are warned that this discussion reveals much of the plot.*

C.R. In *Thinks* . . . there are some sharp parodies of Rushdie, Amis, Gertrude Stein, Henry James. And a take-off of Irvine Welsh which completely cracked me up. The premise of parody is that there's something distinctive there to parody. Do you think it's essential that a writer should have a distinctive style, or not? And how would you describe your own style?

D.L.  That's a very good question. It has occurred to me to wonder whether you could parody me and how you'd set about it. In a way, it may be impossible for writers themselves to identify what is parodiable in their own work. It may be dangerous even to contemplate it. I've just been reading Edith Wharton's memoirs. She says that Henry James really hated to even *hear* that anybody had parodied him. Yet you'd have thought that he must have been aware that, as a mannered stylist, he *could* be parodied.*

One would suppose that any writer who's any good has a distinctive voice—distinctive features of syntax or vocabulary or something—which could be seized on by the parodist. But what they are in my case, I don't actually know. I think I'm rather a ventriloqual kind of novelist. I imitate a lot of different voices rather than having an obvious distinctive one of my own.

C.R.  In your last novel, *Therapy,* you were frankly engaged with polyphony. It seems to me in *Thinks . . .* you're still in pursuit of polyphony—a prose carnival. Not only the parodies we've mentioned but also the truncated prose of e-mail and Messenger dictating into his recording machine. What specially interests you about polyphony? What engages you when you "do the police in different voices"?

D.L.  In some ways, it's been a feature of my work from the very beginning. My first novel, *The Picturegoers,* has a huge number of characters. I tried to evoke the way they think—the

---

*Henry James knew and enjoyed Max Beerbohm's famous parody of him, "The Mote in the Middle Distance," in *A Christmas Garland* (1912), but that was more of an *hommage* than a satire.

language they would use to think in. Looking back, I think Dylan Thomas's *Under Milk Wood* had a terrific influence on me. I heard it on the radio in early adolescence. What fascinated me about it was the polyphony. A number of my novels have got quite a lot of characters. Some, like *Out of the Shelter* and *Ginger, You're Barmy,* are limited to one character's voice, but more and more in later works I've wanted to introduce a lot of different voices into the texture. Long before I'd ever heard of Bakhtin. I think I got it partly from Dylan Thomas and then later from Joyce. *Ulysses* had an enormous influence on me. I read for the first time as an undergraduate and I taught it later. I do think a novel should do more than one thing—it should have more than one level and tell more than one story, and should have more than one style, in fact many styles. So the parodies in *Thinks* . . . came in—it wasn't planned—partly as a result of thinking that the alternation of Ralph's monologue with Helen's diary was going to become a little predictable. I needed extra variety. I needed more than information about cognitive science flooding one way from Ralph to Helen. There had to be some reversal of that flow: a literary imagination playing with the ideas of the scientist in an unpredictable way and throwing them back at him. And that's how the parodies came about really. In narrative terms they're hardly necessary—cut them out, you wouldn't notice.

C.R. No, it's true—they don't advance the story.

D.L. No, not at all.

C.R. But the parodies do a great deal for the dynamic of the book—lend it orchestral colour, as it were. Which brings me to my third question. It's relatively easy to parody the distinctive—the Irvine Welsh, the Henry James—but I think it's difficult to pastiche the undistinguished, the stylistically inert. Isn't a great coup of *Thinks* . . . the prose used by Helen in her journal? Without any coarse signposting, you let us know that she's nice, intelligent—but a writer poised somewhere between the mediocre and the passable.

D.L.  Is there such a space between those two?

C.R.  As a person she's obviously fine. She has her limitations. She's not as interesting as Ralph Messenger. But I was thinking in terms of her prose. Everything depends on the reader picking up the quality of her prose. Which is ratcheted down a couple of categories: "a distant rattle of tumbrils over the intellectual cobblestones of Paris"; "razor-sharp minds"— that's not exactly razor-sharp; "the psychological point of no return"; "I slipped into the building like a thief"; "an African gentleman" for a black man.

D.L.  Mhm—slightly prim.

C.R.  You feel here is a novelist who is intelligent and so on. But actually what you're parodying is her kind of stylistic neutrality.

D.L.  I didn't want her to be flashy. It would have been quite wrong if her journal appeared to have been written to impress posterity. It's a relief to her own feelings, and a way of keeping the muscles of writing exercised. It's therapeutic really, this diary she's keeping. I think it's more finished and polished than Ralph's obviously. She is a writer who can't write an ill-formed sentence. She can't even write e-mail in a slapdash way.

C.R.  But she has a slightly overwrought style—she talks about "repasts," not about meals. When you read "it was dark outside . . ."; "sought to mitigate," you think, "here is a woman who is still under the influence of Henry James."

You're actually creating a prose style for her that isn't neutral, it's tinged with the second-rate. That seems to me an extraordinary thing to do—because you have absolutely to rely on the reader to pick this up. Though there are two verdicts passed on her work in the book. One of them is Ralph's. He says he's speed-read *The Eye of the Storm,* "it's a rather tedious story." And we kind of believe him. Then Sandra Pickering—who's had the affair with her husband—suggests Helen's literary limitations too. She says that "men wearing odd socks" is a bit of a cliché. And Helen is rather wounded by this. We get a sense that we're not meant to admire her as a writer.

D.L.  *The Spectator* says that she's one of the most brilliant contemporary novelists.*

C.R.  Yeah, but we don't believe this. Because what you're offering is somebody who isn't brilliant. All the brilliant bits in *Thinks . . .* come from you in the third-person omniscient narration—where you talk about the windsurfers with "shards of sails." That's something completely beyond her.

D.L.  Yeah, interesting.

C.R.  Do we need these two verdicts by Ralph and Sandra Pickering?—slightly pushing us in one direction. Or do you feel that polyphony means neither comment should be read as authoritative and the reader has to decide?

D.L.  I think that's true. I wasn't foolish enough to give any example of Helen's fiction.

C.R.  Except the seduction.

D.L.  Er, yes—though that's sort of autobiography.

---

*I misquoted my own text. The wording of this fictitious source is actually "one of England's finest contemporary novelists" (p. 250).

C.R.  But she can't tell it head-on. She does it as fiction.*

D.L.  What did you think of that? Is that second-rate?

C.R.  Well, I thought it would have been more interesting if it had been unfiltered. The central formal idea of the novel seems to me to be a reversal of sympathy. At the beginning, Ralph looks predatory and coarse. Helen looks sensitive and thoughtful. But in fact he's much more interesting than she is. He's much less conventional than she is. He's much more prepared to say what he thinks. So in the course of the book, you change your opinion of the characters completely. You see her limitations, and you see his strengths. One of his strengths is that he's prepared to tell the truth more often than she is. For her, fiction is a slight refuge from the truth.

D.L.  I wouldn't dispute anything you've said, but some of it slightly surprises me. I certainly didn't set out with the intention of making Helen second-rate. I had an idea of a certain kind of literary lady novelist that I was trying to evoke. And I certainly meant to suggest that some people found her a good novelist. She's obviously not a great novelist, but I meant her to be a good novelist. The kind who wins small literary prizes. In writing the novel the way I did, without any authorial judgement and interpretation, I deliberately left it open to readers to make their own assessments. So I don't think there's anything in what you've said that's incompatible with the book—but it's not the only way to read it. Some people read in a very different way. I accept what you say, but lots of people would draw different moral conclusions.

C.R.  Well, I think she's presented as a respectable novelist.

*Not exactly "as fiction," because she refers to herself by her own name, but in the style of fiction.

The kind of novelist who'd be asked to teach a creative writing course at a university. As you say, she'd win some prizes. But neither of us would actually cross the street to buy one of her books.

D.L.  OK, fair enough.

C.R.  Let's move on. I wanted to ask you about the role intuition plays in this book. Intuition seems to me to be absolutely central.

D.L.  Intuition? You're saying the role of intuition in human life—the place of it, is one of the things thrown up by the book?

C.R.  Yes. Where do you think intuition fits into consciousness? Let me give you an example. Ralph's potency fails him as soon as he's threatened—before he *knows* he's threatened. It's intuitive. Carrie sees the surgeon Henderson, and knows he's an incompetent shit, by intuition.

D.L.  That's true. Again it's a theme which I can't say I consciously formulated. But I think it comes out of the literature that I read. For instance, one of these neurobiologists said that it's almost impossible to use the facial muscles to fake a smile. You can always tell a social smile from a real one. And that, if you like, is exercising the intuitive judgement of people. We seem to have some way of interpreting that kind of data which you could describe as intuition.

C.R.  But in fact it's rational. It's based on evidence. It's not mystical.

D.L.  Yeah. I suppose we're all always rather haunted by the idea that there *is* some totally immaterial form of intuition. Telepathy is the extreme example of this. Have you ever experienced that? Do you think it exists? Even Ralph is tempted by this—when Douglass commits suicide at the very moment that Ralph hears he's reprieved. Ralph's tempted by the idea that it's not a complete coincidence, that there must be some kind of system behind this. Is that the sort of thing you mean?

C.R.  Yes: I think everyone is tempted by that. I've just been rereading Milan Kundera's *The Joke*. A brilliant book. In it Ludwig asks the question, "What is life trying to tell me all the time?" We all feel that life is trying to tell us something. Of course, it's not, it's pure subjectivity. What I meant by intuition was this: you give examples of very accurate intuitions. OK, they're based on covert evidence. But don't they effectively destroy the validity of Ralph's models of consciousness? He thinks the body is a machine. So he thinks that sex can be just recreational. But the very first example—him fucking Isabel Hodgkiss—shows that it isn't recreational. She needs him to say that he loves her. And he needs her to say something incredibly filthy back. And then they can do it. It's not recreation, it's not two machines at work. Doesn't this undermine the scientific paradigms on offer?

D.L.  Yes—except that Ralph would use the word "machine" in a rather different way from you. He's not saying merely that the *body*'s a machine, but that consciousness is like software being run on the hardware of the brain's machine. That consciousness is a virtual machine. So anything that processes information is a machine—that doesn't mean it's made of metal and wires and things. It can be just a binary system. He would say that it doesn't in any way undermine his position— that concepts like "love," or pretending to love in order to get more enjoyment out of sex, can be incorporated within his theory of the mind. It's a part of the cultural construction of consciousness. And it can all be simulated, in his view, in a computer program. *My* position would be that there's something about the interface between the virtual machine and the real physical flesh-and-blood machine of the body—it's very different from whatever you do with a purely material, inorganic machine. That's really what I'm exploring. The existence of the flesh and the mortality of the flesh make such a difference to consciousness, that I can't imagine it ever being simulated in a program.

C.R. Presumably emotion is the great thing. You can't have virtual emotion.

D.L. Well, they reckon that they're going to do it one day. I don't know how.

C.R. There is an interesting strand in your novel about lack of affect. Oliver, the autistic son of the Richmonds, has certain limitations and certain gifts. He can't distinguish between truth and falsehood. He can't distinguish between the fictional and the real. And he has a deficit of affect. He doesn't have the right emotions. Just as a computer doesn't have emotions either. What's interesting about this is the play between Oliver and Ralph. When Carrie's father is ill, Carrie accuses Ralph of a lack of affect—not feeling the right things. How do Oliver and Ralph go together? I think he's just being honest. That's his great thing. He doesn't pretend to more emotion than he actually has.

D.L. I think that's true. The crucial scene is the little girl, Ralph's daughter, asking about death. And I think you can read that scene in two ways. Some people would find Ralph's behaviour absolutely unacceptable. Other people would see it rather more sympathetically. From your point of view, he's being honest, he's not pretending. He's being consistent with what he believes, and other people are not being honest. Normally, we pretend to feel emotions we never actually feel—in order not to hurt people's feelings.

C.R. Well, Ralph too is capable of doing that. When Douglass hangs himself, Messenger says, in effect: "I go round saying how shocked I am, because people would be shocked if I said I wasn't shocked—they'd think I was callous." So he's aware of the need for tact—but also he's honest. What do you feel about the conversation with the daughter? Which side do you take?

D.L. The fact that I put the two sides means that I don't really want to say. But in real life I think I would not sympathise with Ralph. I would take his wife Carrie's view: why destroy this kid's sentimental myth about heaven, why not let it just drop away like milk teeth? Personally, I think that's the right thing to do.

C.R. Is *Thinks* . . . ultimately a novel about intimacy? About being inside another person's consciousness? Messenger proposes an exchange of journals. But Helen's reaction to Messenger's violation of her journal—he hacks into her laptop, calls up her journal, and effectively ends their relationship—this suggests that we also have a need for privacy. In other words, we have two conflicting needs—the need for privacy and the need for intimacy. Is this what the novel's about?

D.L. I wouldn't say that. That would be making it too central and too explicit. It's one of the things that emerges out of the novel. The novel is about consciousness in all its aspects and implications. The way you interpret my book—in a very professional literary-critical way—interests me, pleases me, and slightly surprises me. It's the only way you can do it, of course. You articulate very clear thematic oppositions, pairings, and so on. But for me these things are all rather intuitive—following my characters, trying to imagine how they would react to each other, in particular circumstances. I'm not saying your reading's illegitimate, but it's not the way I created the book.

C.R. The qualia of the book are different.

D.L. They are. But yes, it's true. There is a sort of innate contradiction. Certainly Helen is torn between the desire for privacy and the desire for intimacy. I think it applies to her rather more than it does to Ralph—partly because of her bereavement she's very lonely, and she craves intimacy. But it's partly the nature of her own temperament. (And I think, to some extent, it's an occupational thing. She's a novelist. And novelists don't want to give away too much of their own thought processes, because that may invalidate or make too personal the general truths they try to articulate in their work. Lots of novelists are rather cagey about answering questions like these, for instance.) What you propose is a good take on Helen. I'm not sure it applies to Ralph. I'm not sure he wants intimacy in quite that way actually. He's very independent and rather egotistical—and he's quite confident that he can defend his own privacy. He's a bit nervous when the police come round to investigate his hard disk.

C.R. But he goes along with it. Whereas Douglass, who has something to hide, doesn't. Let me ask you about Helen's dead husband, Martin. He's worked for the BBC and has been unfaithful serially. She's tremendously wounded by this. I'm not sure what the point of this is. Is it to say that it's absurd to idealise sexual fidelity? Is that one of the things it's saying? And does it also say that we can't ever know people, that there can be no intimacy?

D.L. Central to the novel is the idea that a crucial stage of ordinary human development is the acquisition of a "theory of mind." You discover in infancy that people can have different interpretations of the world. This opens up the possibility of deceiving them. Therefore deception is built into human life very deeply. We do it all the time. It's not necessarily malicious, indeed it may be benevolent. Social life might become impossible if we didn't dissemble, conceal, and suppress a great deal of what we actually feel. It also means, though, that we can betray and cheat. So I wanted a lot of examples in the book of deception and betrayal. I wanted Helen in particular to be confronted with a whole set of deceptions—partly to motivate her decision to have an affair with Ralph. She has a kind of moral resistance, an innately prim and proper character. So I needed something to precipitate her, make her ripe for having an affair. One thing is the discovery that her husband wasn't faithful. Second, her discovery that Carrie is unfaithful to Ralph. And there are other examples.

C.R. What you're doing is complicating her life for her. She's not a great novelist because she doesn't live with enough complication. She's ready to sort things and simplify things, but you complicate her life and make her more interesting than she would have been.

D.L. I think it's what novelists do all the time.

C.R. I was going to ask you about Annabel Riverdale. She spills the beans when she's drunk. In other words, she gives us access to her inner life, intimacy, unwillingly. This is the exception that proves the rule. Normally we don't have access.

D.L. Yeah, I suppose so. I mean I was a little disappointed with her. She had possibilities I wasn't able to follow through. I thought she might be a more interesting character. It's partly the constraints of the form I'd set myself . . .

C.R. You have Ralph and you have Helen. You have third-person omniscience. You have parodies, e-mails. Julian

Barnes's *Love, etc.* has quite small bits of interior monologues by characters who are minor cogs in the machine. You didn't think of trying that?

D.L.  No, I didn't. Because in terms of the rules of the game that I'd set myself, I would observe the constraints Ralph establishes for the truthful representation of consciousness. It's got to be a first-person account. Description of people has to be a behaviourist account if it's in the third person. So there are two first-person accounts and a third-person narration which is objective, on the surface. All the other little parodies, the e-mail, etc., count as third person. They don't go into the consciousness of our characters. They are documents. So, until the very last chapter, where I'm writing as a conventional omniscient author, everything else observes that rule. And Helen in a way alludes to it, when she says the only way to write fiction and satisfy Ralph would be to stay on the out-side—not to invent anybody's consciousness at all. So in a more conventional novel possibly, I could have spread myself, followed up more of the characters. But I'm not sure that would have been a good idea.

C.R.  So you mean Annabel Riverdale was there as a possi-bility for development rather than representing an idea?

D.L.  To tell you the truth, she was one of those characters I put in early on, thinking, "I may do something with this woman later." And it never happened that I needed to.

C.R.  It's interesting that you say Helen has a commentary on the method. One of the real pleasures of your book is what a sly writer you are. In *Nice Work,* for instance, you invoked and then used the narrative conventions of the Victorian novel end-ing. Though half of *Thinks* . . . is stream of consciousness, you make Helen say: "The stream of consciousness novel is rather out of fashion." Which seemed to me a rather wonderful joke. And at the beginning of chapter 13 you have Helen advising Carrie about her novel, and saying she should separate the family from the historical material: "Having Alice think so much about local politics and the architecture of the city, and so on, seems rather unnatural"—this in a novel where the two main characters exchange information about science and consciousness all the time. You see the criticism and you preempt it.

D.L. I'm a metafictional novelist, I suppose, because I was a teacher of fiction and therefore a very self-conscious novelist. I think this is generally true of the present literary period. We're all very conscious of what we're doing. So if you want to write a realistic novel, you have to signal to the audience that you're operating a convention. But, basically, it's because I was involved in teaching and analysing fiction formally for so long. That's why my work is riddled with this sort of allusion and joke.

C.R. When you're reading *Thinks* . . . you're just fascinated by the information. The sheer interest of it stops you raising an objection.

D.L. That has to be the case, I think. I couldn't bear to read a novel with just tricks. You have to believe in the characters and care what happens to them.* These little jerks of the strings—which show you it's actually a device—can give you an extra frisson, but then you go back into the flow of the real. Did you notice the little joke when Helen's trying to choose a passage to analyse in her lecture to the Cognitive Science Insti-

---

*I misunderstood the question. By "information" C. R. obviously meant the information about consciousness, artifical intelligence, and so forth.

tute at the end? She wonders about doing Henry James's scene with Strether on the river. And then decides it's been done already.

C.R. The scene at the end of *The Ambassadors,* where Strether knows intuitively that Chad and Marie de Vionnet must be lovers?

D.L. Helen thinks of taking that example and then rejects it "because it's been done." The joke is that I did it. In *Language of Fiction.*

C.R. All novelists now seem to be committed to science. Are you? Or was consciousness just another interesting idea like Kierkegaard in *Therapy?* Have you been changed permanently by the reading you did for this novel?

D.L. I think it's made it even more difficult for me to subscribe to any transcendental religious faith. I think it's been a great education. I'm not quite sure if it's changed me *permanently:* it's just opened out the world in an interesting way. I know exactly where I got the idea for *Thinks . . .* In 1994 I read this review of two books by Daniel Dennett (then unknown to me) and Francis Crick, the DNA man. While I was doing the research and writing the novel—which wasn't immediately—a number of other novelists started to show that they too had tuned into science. It's partly because there's been so much good popular science writing recently and partly because of the "end of ideology." And partly too because literary criticism is up the creek. So the neo-Darwinists have moved in to occupy those areas and have suddenly become a stimulus for thinking about human nature, the world, what it's all about. It's the zeitgeist.

C.R. Talking about "what it's all about," what about Messenger's name? He brings the news? What is the news? Is it that

Eros and Thanatos are linked? *Thinks* . . . begins with Isabel Hodgkiss and sex, but it turns out she died of breast cancer. So sex and death are there at the beginning. And the novel almost ends with the same combination. Ralph has a potentially fatal disease. Moreover, his disease—the virus he's suffering from—which isn't terminal cancer—is picked up at the time of his first sexual experience with Martha.

D.L. I don't know if I want to tell you all this really—take you into the workshop . . . Basically, I'd decided early on that Messenger should experience some real shock—to do with his mortality. Something that would really challenge his self-confidence and his rather arrogant materialist ideology. We would see what he's made of. I hadn't really decided how he was going to react. But I wanted him to fear that he had a terminal disease. So I asked my G.P. To find some disease confronting you with the possibility of death, without your having suffered a lot of pain or obvious distress up to that point. A disease that would fulfill certain realistic criteria. And my G.P. suggested this condition—that you can pick up from sheepdogs, that people who work with dogs or cattle can pick up. (It's common in Wales, apparently.) I read up a lot about sheep. And I invented this episode which I think fits into this pattern of Ralph's mind. He always goes to his sexual life whenever he starts to free-associate. So you think, as a reader, that the episode on the sheep farm is just one in a sequence of erotic memoirs. Then it turns out to have another function in the story. I always feel that's a satisfying combination. That's why it was there.

C.R. You wanted to shock his materialism, his confidence in Eros.

D.L. Yeah.

C.R.  Do you think the value of Eros is increased by the idea of Thanatos? That sex is some kind of talisman against death? In Peter Nichols's *Passion Play* the hero says: "fucking is all there is against death."

D.L.  I think that's very much Ralph's philosophy. I don't entirely endorse it. It depends on your being rather healthy to start with, and not hideously ugly, or confined to a wheelchair. So it's not an answer for everybody. But many people, perhaps men most of all, feel that. In *Small World* Phillip Swallow thinks he's going to get killed in an air crash and when he escapes he has this erotic experience with the British Council wife. Telling the story to Morris Zapp, he says he was "fucking his way out of the grave."

C.R.  Two last questions. One is a tiny thing—on p. 135 Douglass is flexing his glove after the party. On p. 156 the doctor flexes the fingers of his gloves. Is there a reason for this repetition?

D.L.  No, just a mistake. Any repetition that's not motivated is a mistake.

C.R.  It's odd. Because, as a reader, you think, "ah, that's interesting . . ."

D.L.  You're an *incredibly* attentive reader. Not many people would notice. They're separated by about twenty pages.

C.R.  Well, it's very effective. It's a very Joycean moment, a piece of observed ordinary behaviour which is brought home to you. You register it very powerfully so it's not surprising you remember it, and ask why.

D.L.  I can't say it was intended.

C.R.  What is the point of Ludmila Lisk—the bit on the side. She blackmails Messenger. Do you intend to say that all intimacy carries risk?

D.L. The reason for the whole episode in Prague was Ralph's image as a media don, a guy always flying here and there, having adventures abroad. We have to see him doing it. That's his image. That's one reason. The other is that I wanted to prepare for the revelation that he has this dangerous liver condition. But I wanted something with good cover—preparatory, but you wouldn't guess it at once. So in Prague he overindulges in rich food and comes back with what he thinks is merely chronic indigestion. And if he went abroad he had to have some kind of sexual adventure. But the adventure is merely going through the motions. His heart's not in it. He's the Don Juan type, trapped in his own philandering mould. And I wanted him to feel "I'm really getting too old for this." To pile up circumstances against him, to put him to the test, because he'd been so arrogant and confident in himself, I would put him in jeopardy on several different fronts at once at the end of the book. He is really cornered, like a lion at bay, threatened with a mortal illness, the possibility that his wife would discover his affair with Helen, and finally that this groupie would turn up from Prague and cause a lot of additional trouble. I tend to do this. I like to accelerate a narrative as it gets towards the end, to turn up the tempo of increased complication. So most of my novels open rather leisurely and then things get more complicated and tense towards the end. Which is the right way round, I think.

---

## 1 CONSCIOUSNESS AND THE NOVEL

1. Daniel Dennett, *Consciousness Explained* (Penguin, 1993), p. 210.

2. Francis Crick, *The Astonishing Hypothesis* (Touchstone, 1995), p. 3.

3. *The Tablet*, 25 June 1994.

4. Anne Michaels, *Fugitive Pieces* (1997), pp. 176–177.

5. David Lodge, *Thinks . . .* (2001), p. 42.

6. Francis Crick and Cristof Koch, "Towards a Neurobiological Theory of Consciousness," *Seminars in the Neurosciences 2* (1990): 263–275.

7. Anthony Smith, "Brain Size," in *The Faber Book of Science*, ed. John Carey (1996), p. 442.

8. David J. Chalmers, *The Conscious Mind* (1996), p. xi.

9. James Trefil, *Are We Unique?* (1997), p. 181.

10. V. S. Ramachandran and Sandra Blakeslee, *Phantoms in the Brain: Human Nature and the Architecture of the Mind* (1998), pp. 231–232.

11. Steven Pinker, *How the Mind Works* (1997), p. 92.

12. Quoted in John Horgan, *The Undiscovered Mind* (1999), p. 47.

13. Gerald Edelman, *Bright Air, Brilliant Fire; On the Matter of the Mind* (1992), p. xiii.

14. Ibid., pp. 114–115.

15. Joseph Conrad, 1914 Preface to *The Nigger of the Narcissus* (1897).

16. Edelman, *Bright Air, Brilliant Fire*, pp. 162–163.

17. Antonio Demasio, *The Feeling of What Happens: Body, Emotion, and the Making of Consciousness* (1999), p. 168.

18. Ibid., p. 188.

19. Ibid., p. 189.

20. Ibid., p. 217.

21. Dennett, *Consciousness Explained*, p. 418.

22. Demasio, *The Feeling of What Happens*, pp. 190–191.

23. Ibid., p. 226.

24. Patricia Waugh, "Revising the Two Cultures Debate: Science, Literature, and Value," in *The Arts and Sciences of Criticism*, ed. David Fuller and Patricia Waugh (Oxford University Press, 1999).

25. Nicholas Maxwell, "The Mind-Body Problem and Explanatory Dualism," *Philosophy* 75 (2000): 57–60.

26. C. P. Snow, *The New Men* (Penguin edition, 1959), p. 184. Page numbers for subsequent quotations are given in the text.

27. Page references in the text are to the HarperPerennial edition (New York, 1996).

28. Ramachandran and Blakeslee, *Phantoms in the Brain*, p. 229.

29. Milan Kundera, *Testaments Betrayed* (1995). Quoted by Thomas J. Scheff, in "Multipersonal Dialogue in Consciousness," *Journal of Consciousness Studies* 6 (2000): 3–19.

30. Henry James, *The Wings of the Dove* (Penguin edition, 1986), p. 55.

31. Demasio, *The Feeling of What Happens*, p. 231.

32. Ian Watt, *The Rise of the Novel* (Penguin edition, 1963), p. 32.

33. Susan Greenfield, *The Human Brain: A Guided Tour* (1999), p. 149.

34. Quoted in obituary by Claire Messud, *The Guardian*, 25 July 2001.

35. *The Guardian*, 13 September 2001.

36. Unfortunately I have mislaid the reference for this quotation.

37. *Henry James: A Life in Letters*, ed. Philip Horne (2000), p. 360.

38. Reprinted in *20th Century Literary Criticism*, ed. David Lodge (1972), pp. 86–91.

39. I have demonstrated this in *The Modes of Modern Writing* (1977), pp. 140–144.

40. Erich Auerbach, *Mimesis: The Representation of Reality in Western Literature* (Princeton University Press, 1953), p. 534.

41. Hermione Lee, *Virginia Woolf* (1996), p. 197. "Freudian Fiction" was a review of *An Imperfect Mother*, a novel by J. D. Beresford, published in the *Times Literary Supplement*, 25 March 1920, p. 199. Rather deviously, Virginia Woolf used the anonymity of the *T.L.S.* in those days to pretend that she was writing purely as a critic, and not as a novelist, in asserting that psychoanalytical theory, especially concerning the effects of traumatic experience in childhood on adult life, is a key that "simplifies rather than complicates, detracts rather than enriches."

42. See Michael Shepherd, *Sherlock Holmes and the Case of Dr. Freud* (1985).

43. Quoted in Horgan, *The Undiscovered Mind*, p. 223.

44. Rodney Cotterill, *No Ghost in the Machine: Modern Science and the Brain, the Mind, and the Soul* (1989), pp. 217–218.

45. Ramachandran and Blakeslee, *Phantoms in the Brain*, p. 152.

46. Edelman, *Bright Air, Brilliant Fire*, p. 145.

47. *The Letters of D. H. Lawrence*, ed. James T. Boulton (1981), p. 183.

48. Dennett, *Consciousness Explained*, p. 119.

49. Quentin Bell, *Virginia Woolf: A Biography*, vol. 2 (1972), p. 107.

50. Evelyn Waugh, *Vile Bodies* (Uniform edition, 1947), pp. 176–177.

51. Anthony Powell, *Afternoon Men* (Fontana paperback edition, 1973), p. 49.

52. *The Essays, Articles, and Reviews of Evelyn Waugh,* ed. Donat Gallagher (1983), pp. 57, 59.

53. Carlos Baker, *Ernest Hemingway* (Penguin edition, 1972), p. 165.

54. Ernest Hemingway, *The Snows of Kilimanjaro and Other Stories* (New York, 1955), pp. 72–73.

55. Reprinted in Evelyn Waugh, *The Complete Short Stories,* ed. Ann Pasternak Slater (1998).

56. *The Essays, Articles, and Reviews of Evelyn Waugh,* ed. Gallagher, p. 58.

57. Jeremy Treglown, *Romancing: The Life and Work of Henry Green* (2000), p. 72.

58. Ibid., p. 51.

59. Christopher Isherwood, *Lions and Shadows* (Signet edition, 1968), pp. 52–53.

60. Henry James, *The Portrait of a Lady* (World's Classics edition, 1947), p. xxvii.

61. Graham Greene, *Collected Essays* (1969), p. 116.

62. Graham Greene, *Brighton Rock* (Penguin edition, 1943), p. 242.

63. Alain Robbe-Grillet, "A Future for the Novel," reprinted in *20th Century Literary Criticism,* ed. Lodge, pp. 467–472. All quotations in the text are from this source.

64. Henry Green, *Concluding* (1978 edition), p. 55.

65. Samuel Beckett, *The Unnamable,* in *Three Novels* (New York, 1965), p. 398.

66. Nicholson Baker, *The Mezzanine* (Penguin edition, 1990), p. 14. Page numbers for subsequent quotations are given in the text.

67. A. S. Byatt, *On Histories and Stories* (2001), p. 102.

68. Clifford Geertz, "The Nature of Anthropological Understanding," in *American Scientist* 63 (1975): 48.

69. Dennett, *Consciousness Explained,* p. 410.

70. *Nice Work* (1988), pp. 21–22.

71. See Alan Sokal's spoof article "Transgressing the Boundaries: Toward a Transformative Hermeneutics of Quantum Gravity," published as a serious contribution in *Social Text* 46/47 (1996): 217–252. For a full account of the affair see Alan Sokal and Jean Bricmont, *Intellectual Impostures: Postmodern Philosophers' Abuse of Science* (1998).

## 2 LITERARY CRITICISM AND LITERARY CREATION

1. T. S. Eliot, "Tradition and the Individual Talent," *Selected Essays* (1961), p. 13.

2. Matthew Arnold, "The Function of Criticism at the Present Time," *Essays in Criticism: First Series* (1911), p. 6.

3. Ibid., p. 38.

4. Eliot, *Selected Essays*, p. 24.

5. Ibid., p. 32.

6. Ibid.

7. W. K. Wimsatt and Monroe C. Beardsley, "The Intentional Fallacy," reprinted in *20th Century Literary Criticism,* ed. David Lodge (1972), p. 335.

8. Ibid.

9. Ibid.

10. Eliot, *Selected Essays,* pp. 17–18.

11. Graham Greene, *Ways of Escape* (1980), p. 134. There may be an allusion to a short story by Henry James, "The Figure in the Carpet."

12. D. H. Lawrence, "John Galsworthy," in *Selected Literary Criticism,* ed. Anthony Beale (1961), p. 118.

13. Virginia Woolf, *A Writer's Diary,* ed. Leonard Woolf (1978), p. 51.

14. Ibid., p. 24.

15. Eliot, *Selected Essays,* p. 24.

16. *The Works of Oscar Wilde,* ed. G. F. Maine (1948), p. 966.

17. Ibid., p. 967.

18. See Jacques Derrida, "Structure, Sign, and Play in the Human Sciences," reprinted in *Modern Criticism and Theory,* ed. David Lodge (1988), pp. 108–123.

19. Harold Bloom, *The Western Canon* (1994), p. 16.

20. See "Milton I" in T. S. Eliot, *Selected Prose,* ed. John Hayward (1953), pp. 123–131; originally published as "A Note on the Verse of John Milton" in 1936.

21. Reprinted in *20th Century Literary Criticism,* ed. Lodge, p. 650.

22. *The Works of Oscar Wilde,* ed. Maine, p. 959.

23. Graham Greene, *Reflections,* ed. Judith Adamson (1990), p. xii.

24. Eliot, *Selected Essays,* p. 30.

25. "Adam's Curse," in W. B. Yeats, *Collected Poems* (1936), p. 88.

26. Quoted in Daniel C. Dennett, *Consciousness Explained* (1991), p. 245.

27. Wimsatt and Beardsley, "The Intentional Fallacy," p. 335.

28. Dennett, *Consciousness Explained,* p. 236.

29. Ibid., p. 241.

30. Ibid., p. 418.

31. Gerald Edelman, *Bright Air, Brilliant Fire* (1992), p. 114.

32. Ibid., p. 146.

33. Ibid., p. 176.

## 3  DICKENS OUR CONTEMPORARY

1. Jane Smiley, *Charles Dickens* (Lipper/Viking, 2002). The Penguin Lives series consists of short critical biographies of major literary, intellectual, and political figures by authors who are distinguished in their own right, usually for work of a different kind. Jane Smiley is the author of several highly

acclaimed novels, including *A Thousand Acres,* which won the Pulitzer Prize, and *Moo.*

2. Philip Horne, ed., *Henry James: A Life in Letters* (1999), p. 38n.

## 4 FORSTER'S FLAWED MASTERPIECE

1. Daniel Born, "Private Gardens, Public Swamps: Forster and the Psychology of Edwardian Culture. *Howards End* and the Re-valuation of Liberal Guilt," in *Novel: A Forum on Fiction,* vol. 25, no. 2, pp. 141–159. Born makes some particularly interesting connections between *Howards End* and the arguments of the contemporary American pragmatist philosopher, Richard Rorty.

2. Matthew Arnold, *Culture and Anarchy* (Bobbs-Merrill, 1971), pp. 7–8. First published in 1869.

3. E. M. Forster, *Howards End,* ed. Oliver Stallybrass (Penguin, 1989), p. 72. Subsequent page references in the text are to this edition.

4. P. N. Furbank, *E. M. Forster: A Life* (Oxford University Press, 1979), vol. I, p. 28.

5. Ibid., p. 142.

6. Ibid., p. 165.

7. Born, "Private Gardens, Public Swamps," p. 149.

8. Kay Dick, ed., *Writers at Work: The Paris Review Interviews* (Penguin, 1979), p. 10.

9. Thomas Carlyle, *Past and Present* (Dent Everyman edition, 1912), p. 1.

10. Benjamin Disraeli, *Coningsby* (Longmans, Green, 1882), p. 69.

11. C. F. G. Masterman, *The Condition of England,* ed. J. T. Boulton (Methuen, 1909), pp. 162, 164–165.

12. *Abinger Harvest* (Edward Arnold, 1936), p. 100.

13. Frederick C. Crews, *E. M. Forster: The Perils of Humanism* (Oxford University Press, 1962), pp. 7, 14.

14. Masterman, *The Condition of England*, p. 76.

15. *Journal of Katherine Mansfield*, ed. J. Middleton Murray (Constable, 1954), pp. 120–121.

16. F. R. Leavis, *The Common Pursuit* (Penguin, 1962), p. 269.

17. Lionel Trilling, "Forster and the Liberal Imagination," in *Forster: A Collection of Critical Essays*, ed. Malcolm Bradbury (Prentice-Hall, 1966), p. 72.

18. *Aspects of the Novel, and Related Writings* (Edward Arnold, 1974), pp. 102–116.

19. Joseph Frank, "Spatial Form in Modern Literature," *Sewanee Review* (Spring, Summer, and Autumn, 1945).

20. Dick, ed., *Writers at Work*, p. 15.

21. *Aspects of the Novel*, p. 55.

22. Quoted by Furbank, *E. M. Forster*, vol. I, p. 188.

23. *Times Literary Supplement*, 27 October 1910. This anonymous review was in fact written by Percy Lubbock. See Derwent May, *Critical Times: The History of the Times Literary Supplement* (2002), p. 75.

24. *The Daily News*, 7 November 1910.

25. *The Westminster Gazette*, 19 November 1910.

26. *Nation*, 12 November 1910.

27. Furbank, *E. M. Forster*, vol. I, p. 131.

28. Ibid., vol. I, p. 190.

## 5 WAUGH'S COMIC WASTELAND

1. *The Essays, Articles, and Reviews of Evelyn Waugh*, ed. Donat Gallagher (1983), p. 567.

2. Ibid., p. 304.

3. Ibid., pp. 57–58.

4. D. H. Lawrence, "Morality and the Novel," reprinted in *20th Century Literary Criticism*, ed. David Lodge (1972), p. 128.

5. *Essays, Articles, and Reviews*, ed. Gallagher, p. 304.

## 6 LIVES IN LETTERS: KINGSLEY AND MARTIN AMIS

1. *The Letters of Kingsley Amis,* ed. Zachary Leader (HarperCollins, 2000).
2. Martin Amis, *Experience* (Cape, 2000).

## 7 HENRY JAMES AND THE MOVIES

1. Laura Jones, *The Portrait of a Lady: The Screenplay Based on the Novel by Henry James* (Penguin, 1996). All quotations in the text are from this edition.
2. See my essay "Hardy as a Cinematic Novelist," in *Working with Structuralism* (1981), pp. 95–105.
3. Hossein Amini, *Henry James's The Wings of the Dove: A Screenplay* (Methuen, 1998), p. vi. All quotations in the text are from this edition.

## 10 KIERKEGAARD FOR SPECIAL PURPOSES

1. *Therapy* (Secker and Warburg, 1995).
2. Walter Lowrie, *A Short Life of Kierkegaard* (Princeton University Press, 1970).
3. Helen Fielding, "Why Are We So Depressed?" *The Independent on Sunday,* 2 April 1995. The Samaritans is a voluntary organization in Britain that offers confidential telephone counselling 24 hours a day to people in despair.
4. *Repetition: An Essay in Experimental Psychology,* trans. Walter Lowrie (1942), p. 70.
5. Graham Greene, *Ways of Escape* (1980), p. 9.

Adaptations of literary fiction for film, television, or stage are indexed under title.

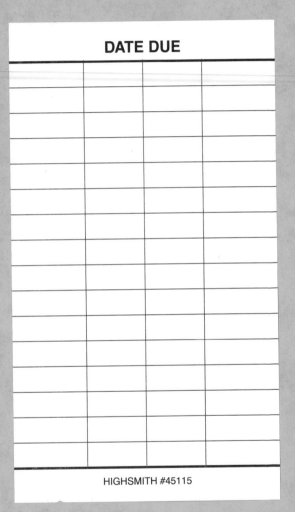

## DATE DUE

HIGHSMITH #45115